ANNA RICHARDS

PADDLING
FRANCE

40 BEST PLACES TO EXPLORE BY SUP, KAYAK & CANOE

T0332285

Bradt Guides Ltd, UK
Globe Pequot Press Inc, USA

First edition published March 2024
Bradt Guides Ltd
31a High Street, Chesham, Buckinghamshire, HP5 1BW, England
www.bradtguides.com
Print edition published in the USA by The Globe Pequot Press Inc,
PO Box 480, Guilford, Connecticut 06437-0480

Project Managers: Emma Gibbs & Anna Moores
Cover research: Pepi Bluck, Perfect Picture

ISBN: 9781804691069

British Library Cataloguing in Publication Data
A catalogue record for this book is available from the British Library

Photographs © individual photographers credited beside images & also those
from picture libraries credited as follows: Alamy.com (A); Dreamstime.com (DT);
Shutterstock.com (S); Superstock.com (SS)

Front cover Top: Paddleboarding at Mont Saint-Michel (Hemis/A); below: The
calanques at Cassis (proslgn/S)
Back cover Paddleboarding through the Tarn gorges (Sarah_Dias/S)
Title page Kayaking at Cap d'Antibes (Anna Richards)

Maps David McCutcheon FBCart.S. FRGS & Daniella Levin

Typeset and designed by Ian Spick, Bradt Guides Ltd
Production managed by Zenith Media; printed in the UK
Digital conversion by www.dataworks.co.in

AUTHOR

Anna Richards is a travel and outdoor writer based in Lyon. She specialises in France, promoting Slow, flight-free travel. Her work has been featured in the *Independent*, *National Geographic*, the *Daily Telegraph* and many other publications, and she's contributed to guidebooks for other major publishers. This is her first book.

AUTHOR'S STORY

I grew up by the water, in Falmouth, Cornwall. Some of my earliest memories are of going sailing, returning home sun-drenched with salt-encrusted skin. My dad taught me to row aged just six, as soon as I'd mastered swimming.

My love affair with paddleboarding, I believe, comes from my love of a journey. In 2019, I took a career break to backpack around South America. I'd worked in Argentina during my studies, and ever since had been itching to get back, drawn by remote mountain trails and glaciers, and the dream of night after night under canvas.

In March 2020, when the Covid-19 pandemic broke out and spread like wildfire across the world, I found myself back in Cornwall, living on the charity of friends, out of work, and the seemingly limitless freedom I'd been experiencing now confined to the back garden.

But two things that shaped my future came out of this time. I began to write for an audience, sending my (half-baked) articles to travel magazines. Amazingly, a few notable publications took a chance on me, and I began to get bylines under my belt. Then, as restrictions in Cornwall eased, the local paddleboard club resumed business and I signed up. I realised that by water I could access remote camping spots, and set off for days at a time, just as I had done while hiking. A passion for SUP-packing was born, and I began to see Cornwall through fresh eyes.

My move to France came from tragic events and a monumental life crisis. In June 2021, when I was 28 years old, we lost my dad. I quit my job and ran away to France with no home to go to and a vague plan of 'making it as a travel writer', setting up base in Lyon. A long way from the sea, I'd mistakenly believed that my paddleboarding days were behind me.

When Claire Strange, Bradt's commissioning editor, asked if I'd be interested in writing a paddleboarding and kayaking guide to France, it felt as though all the loose threads of my life had come together. After 14 months of researching, thousands of kilometres, one car accident and many an aching muscle later, here it is. Tried and tested, the best places to paddle in France.

ACKNOWLEDGEMENTS

Without the support, companionship and enthusiasm of my friends, writing a guidebook would have been a very lonely job. Thank you to everyone who joined my floating office – in no particular order, Johan Calleja, Rhona Kappler, Polly Waters, Clea Gibson, Layla Claridge, Victor Thivillier and Michelle Tucci (who also took the most wonderful photos). Special thanks go to Amy Hughes and Charlotte Westlake, who came along for the ride twice. To Adèle Thivillier, who lent me her car for my travels in southern France, and didn't bat an eyelid when I crashed it in a snowstorm in Corsica. I bet she's happy I now have my own wheels, though. To Valentin Allard, for tireless emotional support, but most of all for feeding me and taking care of me when I was swamped by guidebook work. To Mark and Sue, for letting me use their home near Sète as a base and allowing me to do copious amounts of laundry. Thank you to all the watersports clubs that advised me, the hotels that hosted me, and the local tourism boards that provided logistical support in my wild zigzags across l'Hexagone. Thank you to Claire Strange, my commissioning editor, for your hard work and for signing me for my first book; my childhood self is still turning backflips in joy. Thank you to Emma Gibbs and Anna Moores for the most thorough edits and 'nagging' any writer could wish for; I value your help so much. A final thanks to my wonderful family and, in particular, my mother, who is at once my harshest critic and my most unwavering supporter.

DEDICATION

To my dear Pa, who loved the water, and this country. I wish we could have paddled these together.

FEEDBACK REQUEST

At Bradt Guides we're aware that guidebooks start to go out of date on the day they're published – and that you, our readers, are out there in the field doing research of your own. So why not tell us about your experiences? Contact us on ☏ 01753 893444 or e info@bradtguides.com. We will forward emails to the author who may post updates on the Bradt website at ⌂ bradtguides.com/updates. Alternatively, you can add a review of the book to Amazon, or share your adventures with us on Facebook, Twitter or Instagram (@BradtGuides).

↑ Der-Chantecoq Lake is a great spot for families, page 64 (Virginie THIBAULT)

→ Two aboard the paddle near the Pont Vieux in Béziers, page 120 (Anna Richards)

CONTENTS

INTRODUCTION
WITH *LIZZIE CARR, AUTHOR OF BRADT'S* PADDLING BRITAIN

There's so much variety in France, from the storm-battered granite cliffs of Brittany and rivers like the Loire that snake past châteaux for hundreds of kilometres, to alpine lakes that shine as bright as sapphires, giving perfect paddling conditions amid mountain peaks. My selection of routes is intentionally varied to reflect the country as a whole. Some routes are rural and some are urban; some I've chosen because you can access fantastic restaurants by water (after all, France is famed for its gastronomy!). There are routes for all abilities, from complete novices to expert paddlers.

You can approach the routes suggested in this book on a stand-up paddleboard (usually known by the acronym SUP), canoe or kayak. I'm a paddleboarder at heart, mostly because it's much easier to travel with an inflatable paddleboard than a canoe or kayak (even the inflatable kind), but some of the routes in this book are better adapted to kayaks or canoes than SUP. This is generally owing to shallow water which can scrape a paddle fin, rapids, or even simply where there's a lot of seaweed that wraps around fins and creates a nuisance. Much of my advice is common to all three pursuits – but there are also specific differences worth noting.

The rise of affordable and easily transportable entry-level equipment – notably boards, including inflatable ones, and paddles – has democratised waterborne activities such as paddling. Many watersport enthusiasts are skilled and knowledgeable, and understand full well the importance of carrying the relevant safety equipment and checking conditions. The following words are a reminder

↑ Sunrise paddlers at Mont Saint-Michel, page 28 (Anna Richards)

of what they already know. For people trying the activity for the first time or with little prior experience or appreciation of how conditions affect paddling, reading the following sections is a must – although, for the avoidance of doubt, not a substitute for a proper lesson from a qualified instructor.

Paddling isn't the fastest way to travel, which for me is part of its charm – the perspective you get travelling by water is so very different to travelling by road. Slow down and take time to appreciate the landscapes and wildlife around you via the waterways of France. The risk is that, like me, you'll fall under its spell so much that you'll never want to leave.

GETTING THERE & AROUND

Visiting France from the UK is, generally, very straightforward – even with the complexities added by Brexit – and with great ferry and rail connections it's the ideal destination for Slow travel. Of course, in addition to the transport detailed in this section, there are also many international airports and domestic flights available (though note that the French government has banned internal flights less than 2½ hours in length). However, I'd urge you to take an alternative form of transport if you can. Thankfully, getting around the country by train is a particular pleasure.

BY CAR If you want to take your car into France, the quickest option is the Eurotunnel (⊘ eurotunnel.com) from Folkestone to Calais, which takes just 35 minutes. Ferries are operated by Brittany Ferries (⊘ brittany-ferries.co.uk), P&O Ferries (⊘ poferries), Irish Ferries (⊘ irishferries.com) and DFDS (⊘ dfds.com) from ports on the UK's south coast to northern France. Journey times range from 90 minutes (Dover to Calais) to six hours (Plymouth to Roscoff), with ferries also leaving from Portsmouth, Southampton, Newhaven and Poole.

Driving in France does require some preparation: you'll need to carry a reflective jacket, a warning triangle in case of a breakdown, and breathalysers in your car. You'll also need to display a UK/GB bumper sticker and buy stickers to put on the headlights that deflect the beam and stop you from dazzling other drivers.

The French drive on the right. Motorways (any road starting with 'A' for autoroute) aren't free so take cash and cards for the tolls if you're planning to use them. Charges can mount up quickly, though: if you're on a budget, and/ or have the time, it's worth taking dual carriageways or smaller roads, rather than the motorway. The standard speed limit is 130km/hr on the motorway but doesn't exceed 110km/hr on dual carriageways, and speed limits in towns are often as low as 30km/hr.

If driving in cities, be aware that new measures to control pollution mean that you need to display a Crit'Air sticker, which is an evaluation of how polluting

your car is. Depending on your type of vehicle you may not be allowed to drive in certain areas or on certain days. To get a Crit'Air for your vehicle and check restrictions, visit ⊘ certificat-air.gouv.fr.

Anyone over the age of 18 can drive in France provided they have a valid driving licence, regardless of where that licence was obtained. Note that you cannot bring a foreign vehicle into France for more than a year continuously and most insurance companies will only cover a UK vehicle in France for up to 90 days. You must have valid insurance, and I'd recommend getting breakdown cover too.

There are car-hire outlets at all French airports, and most of the major train stations too. Most common are Europcar (⊘ europcar.fr), Hertz (⊘ hertz.fr) and Avis (⊘ avis.com). A cheaper alternative is to rent a privately owned car through Getaround (⊘ getaround.com). It works a little like Airbnb for car rentals and its use is widespread in France.

Corsica Ferries (⊘ corsica-ferries.fr) runs regular crossings between Marseille, Toulon and Nice in the south of France, and Ajaccio, Île Rousse, Bastia and Port-Vecchio in Corsica, with journey times typically taking upwards of 12 hours.

BY TRAIN & BUS Eurostar (⊘ Eurostar.com) runs multiple daily services to Paris (2 hours 20 minutes) and Lille Europe (1½ hours) from London St Pancras. Inflatable paddleboards and kayaks will largely fall into the excess luggage bracket, which means you'll need to book them in and pay extra in advance (at the time of writing, this was a supplement of £48 for sports equipment booked more than 48 hours in advance of your trip).

↑ The cliffs of Étretat inspired many of Monet's works, page 36 (Marti Bug Catcher/S)

Once ridiculed for continually being late, cancelled or on strike, France's train system is fantastic (although strikes still happen!). There are two main types of train: TGV and TER. TGV trains are high-speed trains, connecting major cities extremely quickly (eg: Paris to Lyon in 2 hours and Paris to Marseille in just 3 hours). You need to buy an advance ticket to travel on these services, and doors often shut 5 minutes before departure. Many of the TGV lines are also subject to luggage restrictions, so if you're travelling with your own paddleboard or kayak make sure you check to avoid on-board charges. TER services are the standard trains linking the rest of the country. You can often buy your ticket just before you board, and these trains are usually more convenient if you're travelling with heavy luggage, like an inflatable paddleboard or kayak.

To book trains in France and check timetables, visit the SNCF website (⊘ sncf-connect.com), or Trainline (⊘ trainline.com). If you're aged between 30 and 65 and planning on taking multiple trains in France, a *carte avantage* is a really good investment (buy through SNCF Voyageurs ⊘ sncf-voyageurs.com). A one-off payment of €49 gets you a year-long pass that takes an average of a third off your rail fare, which quickly counterbalances the cost of the advantage card.

In really rural areas (particularly in mountainous places like the Auvergne, Jura, the Alps and the Pyrenees), buses are your only option. Blablabus (⊘ blablabus. fr) and Flixbus (⊘ flixbus.fr) cover long-distance – including international – journeys, and are usually really good value. For short journeys, check local bus lines – information is generally available through the local town council website.

CARPOOLING & HITCHHIKING Sharing rides is extremely common in France, and even in the remotest parts of the country it's worth checking Blablacar (⊘ blablacar.fr) to see if other people are going your way. If you're driving and have spare seats, I'd encourage you to offer your ride on Blablacar, particularly if you're taking the motorway. Tolls and fuel are expensive and it can save you a lot of money.

Hitchhiking is much more widely tolerated in France than it is in the UK, but it's not without its risks. Use your common sense and always tell someone where you're going. Hitchhiking in urban areas is tricky, but in places where public transport is sparse (for example the Auvergne and Brittany) you'll often see people with their thumbs out.

PADDLEBOARDING: THE BASICS

One of the many fantastic things about paddleboarding (SUP) is how accessible it is. Anyone can learn to paddleboard and it can be as physical or relaxing as you like. Plus, with so many inflatable paddleboards on the market, you have the flexibility to go on your own adventures anywhere where there's a body of water.

HOW TO PADDLE Ideally, the best way to learn to paddleboard is to take a lesson or two, either in France or in the UK before you go, though be aware that in France not all watersports guides will speak English. The following advice is very much the basics, and if you haven't paddled before I strongly recommend that you practise in shallow, sheltered water before testing any of the routes in this book.

- Adjust your paddle. I make sure my paddle is the right length by putting the blade on the ground, holding the paddle vertically by my side, and extending my hand above my head with a slight bend in my elbow. Your wrist should be able to rest on what is called the T-grip (the 'T'-shaped handle at the top of the paddle), with your hand dropping over the other side. If you are straining to reach the T-grip, the paddle is too long for you.
- Face your paddle the right way. Having your paddle backwards is one of the most common mistakes that I see among new paddleboarders. The part of the blade that is scooped, like a spade, should face behind you.
- Kneel on the board, with your knees roughly hip distance apart, and practise paddling on your knees. If you feel comfortable, rise to a standing position.
- Stand up tall – posture is important, both for efficient paddling and to minimise the stress on your body. Stand tall with your feet shoulder-width apart. Place one hand on the T-grip at the top of the paddle and the other on the shaft at a point marginally wider than the distance between your feet. Look straight ahead and bend your knees slightly – the flex will help you stay stable on the board. One tip for standing is to get some momentum by paddling, as the forward movement helps keep the board stable.
- The key to good stroke skills is to 'stack' your arms along the paddle. This means keeping your top hand (which is on the T-grip) and bottom hand (which holds the shaft) perpendicular to one another as you enter the water. Then draw back alongside the board. Finish the stroke at your ankles; resist the temptation to draw back further as this creates drag that will accelerate fatigue. To move forwards, plant the paddle in the water in front of the board, and drag the water backwards. To move backwards, plant the paddle in the water behind you and draw the water in front of you. Use your core to propel yourself; your arms hold the paddle but the majority of the power should be coming from your glutes and abdominal muscles.
- It's important to master board control before taking on more challenging paddles. There are some simple core techniques to practise to get you started. First, place the paddle in the water and push water towards the tail of the board on one side and the nose on the other – making a wider circular motion around the board. Turning the face of the blade away will help you turn more swiftly. Second, get to grips with a stroke called the 'Big C'.

Push the paddle into the water at the front and arc a wide 'C' around the board until you bring the paddle in behind you. This is another stroke that enables you to turn the board quickly if you need to alter direction.

HOW TO CHOOSE & MAINTAIN A PADDLEBOARD *The following advice is from Andy McConks, CEO of McConks SUP (& mcconks.com), the company that made the board that I used to research the majority of this book.*

Choosing a paddleboard A paddleboard between 11 to 12ft in length, around 30 to 40 inches wide and six inches thick is good. Shorter paddlers can use a narrower board; if you're tall and heavy you should opt for a wider board. If you're planning on paddle surfing, go for a shorter board. Inflatable boards are much more transportable and, if you get a good quality one, they're pretty much indestructible. Hard boards are good if you want to surf or race.

Change the fin that you use according to your environment. A long, rigid fin will help you to track much more easily, so if you're in deep water or on the sea it's a good choice. If you're in shallow water, a short, flexible fin is best so that it doesn't catch or damage if you hit rocks. This is also where side fins come in. If you're using a shallow, three-inch flexible fin you might struggle to cut a straight line, but having flexible side fins will help you to mark a straighter course.

↑ Start on your knees until you feel comfortable enough to paddle upright (Jean-Luc PFIFFERLING)

Maintaining your board If leaving your board inflated, don't leave it for prolonged amounts of time in direct sunlight or outside in cold conditions. To clean your board, use fresh water and a mild detergent. This is more to avoid cross-contaminating water bodies if you're paddling in lots of different places rather than because your board needs to be cleaned.

KAYAKING & CANOEING: THE BASICS

HOW TO PADDLE *Richard Hounslow (double Olympic silver medallist in the Canoe Slalom)*

This advice is very much the basics. I strongly recommend that you visit the British Canoeing website, Go Paddling (⌗ gopaddling.info), to find out more about getting started and to brief yourself on aspects ranging from equipment to types of paddling.

For kayaking, you use a double-ended paddle that is suitable whether you are right- or left-handed. Posture is important. Sit up straight, with a slight bend forward at the hips. As you paddle, reach forward with a slightly bent elbow. Pull the blade towards your hips and rotate for maximum power and efficiency. Repeat this motion on the opposite side, building up into an efficient paddling rhythm.

For canoeing, it is best to use a single-bladed paddle with a 'T-grip'. This is similar to the paddle used for stand-up paddleboarding, but shorter. Again,

↑ The key to good stroke skills is to 'stack' your arms along the paddle (Véronique MONTANE)

posture is key. Sit up straight, reach forward with a slightly bent elbow and flex forward at the hips. Pull the blade towards your hips and then sit up straight again. Repeat to gain momentum. Steering involves switching the side that you paddle or using a 'cross bow stroke', where you reach across the bow (front) of the canoe.

There are several basic turning strokes that are useful for both kayaking and canoeing. Here are three:

- **Sweep** Reach forward with your stroke and 'sweep' towards the stern (back of the boat) in a wide arc. This moves the boat away from the stroke.
- **Bow rudder** Slice the blade forward, opening out its face as you do so. This draws the boat towards the stroke.
- **Reverse** Place the blade in the water then, using the back of the blade, move it towards the bow (front) of the boat in a wide arc. This also moves the boat towards the stroke.

HOW TO CHOOSE & MAINTAIN A KAYAK *The following advice was given by Ian Wood, a kayaking guide licensed by the Fédération Française Canoë Kayak and owner of Kayak La Baie, Mont Saint-Michel (⊘ kayaklabaie.com).*

Choosing a kayak Sit-on-top kayaks are great for beginners but you can get lost choosing from the huge range of models. The type you choose should depend on what kind of environment you paddle in, and it's important to make sure that the back support is adequate. If you want to use a sit-in kayak with a spray deck you need a certain amount of experience and training so that you don't get stuck in the kayak if you capsize. Choosing your paddle depends on your environment (flat water, white water or sea water, for example) and the type of activity (long-distance touring, slalom, surf, etc). For an average-height adult a length of around 210cm is good.

PADDLEBOARD & KAYAK HIRE IN FRANCE

In each chapter, I've included a recommendation of where to hire a kayak or paddleboard. Note that in France the vast majority of hire centres open from April to October, with some only opening between June and August. It's always a good idea to call in advance to check.

If you're paddling off season and don't have your own gear, I recommend checking for the closest Decathlon (⊘ decathlon.fr), of which there are numerous branches in France. Most of the larger stores hire paddles and boards, and inflatable kayaks (store pick-up or home delivery within mainland France).

Maintaining your kayak Rinse your kayak using fresh water and store out of direct sunlight when possible.

WHAT TO TAKE

There are some basics I feel should be on every kit list: a leash (for paddleboarders; see opposite); a buoyancy aid (page xx); refillable water bottle with purification filter (but only use with fresh water); maps; suncream; spare clothes; and a waterproof phone case (or a waterproof phone). If you are travelling beyond sheltered waters then I also suggest taking four waterproof items: compass; watch; GPS; and torch (plus working batteries).

There's an abundance of gear on the market and much of it will be down to personal preference, but these were my choices for the routes in this guide. See also *Safety*, opposite.

PADDLEBOARD OR KAYAK I used a McConks 12'6" inflatable

paddleboard for many of these routes, except some that were better adapted to kayaks, for which I borrowed a mixture of sit-on and sit-in kayaks from clubs. My paddleboard is longer than the average board because I also use it for touring (going off for several days with my camping gear strapped to the board), so I appreciate having the extra space. Whichever board you go for, make sure the paddle floats! Many cheap paddleboards have dense paddles that sink to the bottom very quickly, so if you drop it, you're really in trouble. It's easy to hire paddleboards in France, either from the local watersports' clubs listed in each chapter or from Decathlon (page xvii). I tried out several of these routes by

↑ The turquoise waters in the Verdon gorges are caused by sunlight reflecting off the limestone sediment in the water, page194 (Konmac/S)

kayak, generally with the assistance of local clubs that kindly loaned me rigid, sit-on kayaks or sea kayaks. However, inflatable kayaks for one to two people are in abundant supply from Decathlon (if purchasing within France it's possible to have them delivered to a store or a pick-up point). Itiwit, Decathlon's own watersports brand, also allows you to rent inflatable kayaks and paddleboards and all the gear that goes with them (buoyancy aid, pump, etc), starting from just €37 per month.

DRY BAGS An essential piece of kit, even if you're only paddling with a picnic (no-one wants a soggy sandwich). I use McConks dry bags; they've got detachable rucksack straps so you can choose whether to wear them on your back or strap them to the board.

SWIMSUIT, WETSUIT, BOOTS & GLOVES I used a wetsuit for many of these routes, even the summer ones where I was on the water for a long time. A wetsuit that is 3–4mm thick is good for most paddlers, but if you're paddling in extreme conditions, go for a thicker one or consider a drysuit. I largely wore a swimsuit from Tri-Fit, which was streamlined and comfortable, and didn't stretch even after repeated uses in salt water. I also took wetsuit gloves and boots (with a rigid sole) on my winter paddles. See also *What to wear*, page xxi.

PUMP I used a manual hand pump, and it's probably my biggest regret of the project. If you paddle regularly, and regularly inflate and deflate your board, learn from my mistakes and buy an electric car inflator.

SAFETY

All watersports come with inherent risks, so follow the advice below to stay safe while using this guide.

CHOOSE THE RIGHT BOARD Many of the routes included can be tackled by kayak or paddleboard, but some (particularly river itineraries with rapids or shallow water) are better undertaken on a flat-bottomed kayak. Where a route is better adapted to one or the other, I've included icons to indicate this (page xxiv). Much of it boils down to personal preference, however, and whether you're more comfortable on a kayak or a paddleboard.

WEAR YOUR LEASH If you fall in the water, your board can quickly get swept away from you. As your most buoyant piece of equipment, this isn't a situation you want to be in, so always wear a leash, whether you're a beginner or an experienced paddler.

WEAR A BUOYANCY AID A Personal Flotation Device (PFD) not only keeps you safe but also warm. There are various types of buoyancy aids available – from life jackets like those found on tourist boats to waistbands that you pull a cord to inflate. For adults engaging in paddling pursuits, a standard type-III foam PFD is the default best option. These allow adequate arm movement and provide buoyancy. Ensure you have the correct size for your weight. Personally, I like ones with pockets, as these are helpful for safeguarding phone, keys, energy bars etc. Ensure that your PFD fits correctly and that all straps are securely fastened. If crotch straps are fitted, use these too.

KNOW THE WEATHER & TIDE TIMES Check the weather before you set off on any of these routes. Magic Seaweed (🖑 magicseaweed.com) is a great site for looking up the surf and swell on ocean paddles. For wind speeds and directions (often much more important than ordinary weather reports for paddlers), I recommend downloading the application Windy (🖑 windy.app) or checking Windfinder (🖑 windfinder.fr). For general weather reports in France, look at Meteo France (🖑 meteofrance.com).

TELL A FRIEND If setting out paddling alone, tell someone where you're going and what time you expect to be back. If you're travelling solo, tell staff at your accommodation. You should also carry a suitable means of calling for help. In most cases, this will be an adequately charged mobile phone, ideally

↑ A calm day on Serre Ponçon is perfect for SUP yoga, page 200 (Bertrand Bodin)

carried in a waterproof case or dry bag. In an area of little reception, take a VHF radio as well.

AVOIDING WATERBORNE ILLNESSES Be aware of waterborne diseases when paddling on channels and inland waterways. Current widespread problems include cyanobacteria and Weil's disease. Before you eat, either wash your hands in clean water or use hand sanitiser. Wash your kit thoroughly after use.

WHAT TO WEAR In warmer months, loose, breathable clothing (not jeans!) is fine, but cooler or windier weather (and thus damper conditions) will likely make a wetsuit preferable. It's best not to paddle barefoot (because of the risk of puncture wounds). Suitable footwear includes neoprene boots, sports sandals or old trainers. A hat is important, whether a cap (summer) or warm, woolly hat (winter). If you are paddling on white water, wearing a helmet is always recommended.

EMERGENCIES The emergency number for the French coastguard is 196. This line is manned 24/7.

TAKE SUPPLIES Always pack water and a snack, and make sure you stay hydrated when paddling. Paddleboarding can burn up to 400 calories an hour,

so it's important to refuel, and although it's a low-impact sport, if you're out for several hours you can easily work up a sweat. It's a good idea to have suncream and a sunhat, and a warm layer to put on post paddle.

RESPONSIBLE PADDLING

If you're reading this book, the chances are that you're a water lover and want to keep France's waterways healthy and looking gorgeous. Here are some simple ways you can paddle responsibly.

RESPECT AQUATIC WILDLIFE Paddling responsibly means being aware of seasons and what this means for aquatic wildlife. There are some routes that paddle past protected areas or islands, to which access is forbidden at various times of the year (eg: the breeding season for birds). Please ensure that you check and adhere to these restrictions. Additionally, please respect individual animals: allow seals and the like to approach you rather than chasing after them.

WILD CAMPING There's something very special about a multiday paddling adventure, and camping by the bank of a river or lake – or within earshot of the sea – is a wonderful experience. In France, the rules are less strict than in the UK. It is forbidden to wild camp (pitching a tent, stringing up a hammock or positioning a tarp to sleep under in a place of your choice, outside of a commercial

↑ Never chase after wildlife – allow seals and the like to approach you (Philippe PATERNOLLI/S)

campsite) in nature reserves and other protected spaces, within 500m of a national monument, 200m of a drinking water source, public roads and on the seashore. The following tips cover the basics for paddlers, but for more information – consult *Wilderness Weekends* by Phoebe Smith.

- Camp well above the high-tide line, and secure your boat/board soundly.
- Stay clear of houses and settlements. Camp for one night, and leave fairly early.
- Leave no trace. Take all rubbish with you. Aim to leave a wild place – bankside camping spot, cave or beach – better than how you found it.
- Avoid lighting fires – it draws attention and can damage fragile ecosystems.
- Perform toilet functions at least 50m from any waterway; bury your waste and pack out all paper and sanitary products.
- Be respectful. If asked to move on, do so (otherwise you may receive a fine).

LEAVE NO TRACE On and off the water, practise the principle of 'leave no trace'. Never throw rubbish in the water, and if you see rubbish floating past you, fish it out and dispose of it properly so that it doesn't damage local wildlife.

Author of Bradt's *Paddling Britain*, Lizzie Carr, is the founder of **Planet Patrol** (∂ planetpatrol.co), an organisation that aims to rid the world's waterways of rubbish. The aim is not only to restore rivers and canals back to their original beauty, but to intercept the 80% of plastic that emantes from inland locations yet ends up in our oceans. You can join organised clean ups or log any rubbish you collect on your paddles on the Planet Patrol app.

MINIMISE THREATS FROM NON-NATIVE WILDLIFE

Another important issue affecting France's rivers and lakes is the spread of non-native species of plants and animals. 'Invasive alien species' (as they are often known) are having a detrimental impact on indigenous French species and ecosystems. Sometimes their presence can be so disruptive that they can alter the entire ecology of a waterbody. Paddlers can unwittingly transfer animals, eggs, larvae and plant fragments between waterbodies via their clothing and equipment. Accordingly, please follow the Check–Clean–Dry biosecurity procedure (∂ nonnativespecies.org/checkcleandry/) to help prevent such movement.

If facilities allow, hose down all equipment and clothing, ideally avoiding any watercourses or drainage system. Clothing and equipment should be allowed to dry for 48 hours before being used elsewhere.

CHECK IF YOU NEED A PERMIT There are a couple of routes in nature reserves included in this guide which require you to purchase a permit.

Where this is the case, I've included details in the chapter introduction. Please note that it is generally forbidden to canoe, kayak or SUP on canals, particularly if they're used for commercial boat traffic.

USING THIS GUIDE

In this book, I suggest 40 incredible itineraries on France's lakes, rivers and seas. I've used a mix of French and English names for the locales covered, opting for English where that might be more recognisable to an English-speaking reader; for example: Brittany rather than Bretagne. Where it has made sense to do so, I have also included the current name for the administrative region in France (for example: The Lot, Occitanie) to cover all bases. You may be wondering why I haven't included any routes in Paris. Sorry to disappoint, folks, but Paris isn't paddle friendly – it's actually illegal to paddleboard or kayak on the Seine in Paris.

Most of the routes I have included you can paddleboard, kayak or canoe, but if a route is unsuitable for paddleboarding (eg: tricky rapids to navigate) I've drawn attention to this in the introduction. I've also included ⚓ (kayak/canoe) and/or 🏄 (paddleboarding) icons in the information panels at the start of each route to give you an at-a-glance indication of which pursuit might be best (see also page xxvi).

Each chapter starts with the launch point complete with a What3Words reference (///; see opposite) and whether it's a one-way, return or round-trip paddle. I've also included the distance of each in kilometres, the standard unit of measurement in France, and given a difficulty rating (page xxvi) based on tackling the route on a paddleboard.

After the vital statistics, I describe what makes this route special (you could fill a whole bookshelf with paddling routes in France, so selecting just 40 was a tough order!). The detailed description of how to follow each route comes next, entitled *Paddle this way*. Use this in conjunction with a smartphone GPS app, the What3Words app, and if you prefer, a physical map too, and you shouldn't get lost.

At the end of each chapter is a list of practicalities. *Getting there* tells you how to travel to that part of France and get to the launch point. I've largely steered away from recommending flights, partly because I prefer to promote lower emission forms of travel, and partly because if you're travelling with your own paddleboard or kayak, it's difficult to take this on the plane. The *Hire & lessons* section lists local watersports centres. For the most part, these centres are seasonal, open from April to October, but I've mentioned opening months for those places not open year-round. Generally speaking, between April and October is the best time to paddle weather-wise in France, but I've also given destination-specific advice in the *When to go* section of each chapter. When visiting popular tourist

hotspots, particularly in the south of France, be aware of the French school holidays, particularly the long summer holidays that run through July and August; the French are big domestic travellers, and southern beach towns in particular can get extremely crowded.

Where to stay & eat includes a selection of hotel, campsite and restaurant recommendations, generally very close to the itinerary start or end point. I've included recommendations for a variety of budgets. Booking accommodation in advance is strongly recommended. Finally, I've also included a section called *Titbits,* which has ideas of what to do off the water, such as local hiking trails, museums or châteaux. France is an endless source of fascination to me, and it was impossible to put all of the ideas I wanted to into a small box, so take time to explore the area you're visiting, and visit my website (annahrichards.com) to find mini guides to many different areas of the country, for more inspiration.

USING WHAT3WORDS
What3Words (what3words.com) is an application that uses a unique combination of three words to identify every 3m^2 in the world. For paddling routes, where there are often no street names or even landmarks, this allowed me to plot my routes so that you can recreate them exactly. What3Words is not a navigational app but rather a way of giving map coordinates without having to use a set of 18 digits for a map reference.

↑ Anna paddling the Dordogne River, page 108 (Michelle Tucci Studio/michelletuccistudio.com)

If your GPS signal is poor and not showing your location accurately, pull up the satellite image – this helps the GPS locate more accurately. What3Words is available in 50 different languages, and you can display two languages at the same time. Note that the grid references are completely different in each language, not translations. This guide uses What3Words references in English.

VISITING FRANCE: THE BASICS

Most visits to France are problem-free, but I recommend having good **travel insurance** in place before your trip. British **SIM cards** generally work fine in France, but check costs with your network provider before you go, and be aware of roaming charges.

It's a good idea to carry some **cash** in euros. While most places will accept card (and contactless is widespread in larger cities), as you go further into the countryside it's not uncommon for bars and restaurants to refuse card payments, especially for bills under €15.

At the time of writing, British citizens didn't need a **visa** to enter France, but as of 2025 all British citizens will need to apply for an **ETIA** (electronic travel authorisation) via ⌀ etiasvisa.com, which costs €7.

HOW HARD IS THE ROUTE? *Lizzie Carr*

Each route in this book has been allocated two grades based on the following system, which apply to SUP 🏄) and then kayak/canoe (🛶). Where routes are better adapted for kayaks than SUPs I've put an advisory in the chapter; see also page xxiv.

① Easily paddled by beginners. It consists of non-tidal and largely sheltered routes.
② Good for amateurs looking to improve their skills on the water. Some consideration around tides and weather conditions is needed.
③ Suitable routes for experienced paddlers, plus novices wanting more of a challenge. These routes require some knowledge and understanding of tides and weather conditions.
④ For intermediate to more advanced paddlers who are competent and experienced in tidal waters.
⑤ Not for the faint-hearted. Only attempt these challenging routes if you have significant skills, knowledge and experience. Examples include long coastal paddles with little chance to 'escape' once you have committed, to fast-flowing white waters that demand considerable strength, agility and skill.

Reproduced with permission from Bradt's Paddling Britain.

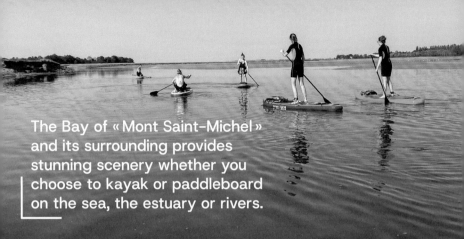

The Bay of « Mont Saint-Michel » and its surrounding provides stunning scenery whether you choose to kayak or paddleboard on the sea, the estuary or rivers.

KAYAKLABAIE

Qualified guide, Ian Wood, offers excursions for all levels as well as barefoot walks across the bay.

A cosy gîte can be availaible for 4 to 6 people close to the bay!

+33 6 08 77 04 37
www.kayaklabaie.com
kayalabaie@orange.fr

1 THE CELTIC COASTLINE

THE 'THOUSAND LAYERS' OF THE CROZON PENINSULA'S STRIPED CLIFFS ARE ALL THE MORE IMPRESSIVE SEEN FROM THE WATER, PARTICULARLY FROM THE MULTICOLOURED CAVES WITHIN THE ROCK FACES THEMSELVES.

WHERE	Morgat, Brittany
STATS	11km return ⛵ 🏄 ③
START/FINISH	Centre Nautique de Crozon Morgat, Port de Morgat, 29160 Crozon /// dollies.mapmaker.configure

Whenever I go to Brittany, I feel as though I'm returning home – in part due to the landscape. This part of Brittany, the wild and rugged Crozon Peninsula, reminds me of Zennor and Pendeen in Cornwall, characterised as it is by rocks that look like they've been battling with the elements and outsiders alike for generations. While much of Brittany is 50 shades of blue, Crozon is kaleidoscopic. The vertiginous cliffs seem harsh and imposing, but heather and gorse make the clifftops burst with colour when spring arrives, and the rocks you'll paddle around have more colourful stripes than a retro coach seat.

Then there's the weather, of course. As in Cornwall, you pack for all seasons here: an idyllic summer's day suddenly becomes a tempest or torrential downpour, before brightening up so beautifully you wonder if you imagined the whole thing.

But the real charm in Brittany is its sense of otherness, a fierce pride that this region is first and foremost Celtic and Breton, with its Frenchness secondary. The black and white Breton flag is everywhere and I commonly saw more flags of other Celtic nations being celebrated than the tricolore. On one flag in Camaret-sur-Mer, on the Crozon Peninsula, I saw Galicia, Scotland, Ireland, Brittany, and my own dear Cornwall, all harmoniously together; the blue, white and red stripes were nowhere in sight.

The Crozon Peninsula is known for spectacular and often wild views, but the place that gets people travelling (or paddling) from miles around is Île Vierge Beach. It's striking: a crescent of white sand framed by sandstone cliffs topped with Scots pines. The real showstopper is the sea arch that protects the little cove from the elements.

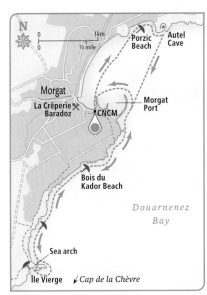

Considered one of the most beautiful beaches in Europe, Île Vierge has become a victim of its success. The number of visitors means that the fragile, sandstone rocks of the arch and cliff path have begun to erode, and it's now forbidden to alight on the beach (note that you'll risk a hefty fine if you do so). The cliff path down to the beach has been closed off, so the best (and only) way to see the beach is from the water.

← The Crozon Peninsula has some of the wildest, most untouched coastline in the country (Ekaterina Pokrovsky/S)

Against the white sand, the water glows turquoise, and on a clear day the seabed is easily visible. It's not hard to see why the beach became so popular, but the whole paddling route is a pleasure, following sandstone cliffs and little sandy coves; take your time, and don't miss the smaller beaches where it's still permitted to alight.

This paddling route is mimicked on land with a famous hiking trail that forms part of the GR34, a 1,700km route which covers the entire Breton coastline. This particular section is a popular day hike between Morgat and Cap de la Chèvre, the headland south of the paddle's start/finish point.

Although you can paddle this itinerary in either direction, if there's much wind I strongly recommend following the itinerary the way I've laid it out. The bay is the most exposed part of the paddle, so it's easier to tackle when you've still got wind in your sails. Be sure to stock up on litres of water before you head off as there's nowhere to refill en route.

Brittany holds a very special place in my heart – we used to holiday here every year when I was small, braving the rain and consuming our body weight in crêpes – but it is entirely without bias when I say that it offers some of the finest kayaking, paddleboarding and canoeing in the country, if not the world. Just don't forget to pack suncream, a raincoat and plenty of good humour.

PADDLE THIS WAY

Launch from the slipway at the Centre Nautique de Crozon Morgat (CNCM /// dollies.mapmaker.configure). Paddle out into the bay, keeping the yacht-filled harbour to your right-hand side. Make a straight line for the sandy beach directly opposite your launch point. Between tides, little sandbank islands form in the shallows – if paddling at low tide, stay further out to sea to avoid running aground.

Crossing the bay is a distance of around 2km. Porzic Beach (/// wavelets.taster. blasts), with its clear, turquoise waters, is quieter than the beach at Morgat and a lovely place to stop for a dip, though bear in mind you've still got a long way to paddle. Hidden in the headland to the left of Porzic Beach (when facing out to sea) are numerous caves, many deceptively deep. Leaving Porzic behind you, paddle a couple of hundred metres to your left, hugging the headland, to find a series of caves. They're difficult to spot from the water until you're very close to them, and not visible from the beach; use the What3Words reference to find the largest of them, Autel Cave (/// atoning.episodes.unleash), over 80m long and accessed through the largest crevasse in the rock that you'll see on this headland.

The cave is mesmerising. The rocks inside are striped; they start off mauve where the rocks meet the water, then a blood-like, crimson layer, before going kind of yellowy green higher up and on the roof. On the outside of this cliff, the rocks look like they've been scored diagonally with a scalpel – the lines are so straight that it's hard to believe they've been created by nature. The red stripes in the rock come from iron and magnesium oxide; much of the rest is layered

↑ Former sardine port Morgat is now a popular seaside town (Pascale Gueret/S)

→ Exploring Autel Cave (Emmanuel LATTES/A)

Armorican sandstone. This sedimentary rock is often described in French as *millefeuille* which, although synonymous with the famous layered pastry dessert, literally means 'a thousand layers'. It's not hard to see why the rock is described like this when you're in the cave. Play around with the echoes while you're in here – your voice carries a long way. From Autel Cave, numerous other caves and passageways branch out in all directions. The darkness is almost suffocating, and you'll need a strong headlamp if you want to explore further (it's also beneficial for the other, smaller caves, too).

Leave the caves and paddle straight across the bay again, this time keeping the CNCM, harbour and dyke to your right. If you prefer to stay sheltered (or if winds dictate the necessity), hug the coastline. After the harbour, there's a little calm

↑ The approach to Île Vierge's sea arch (Anna Richards)

area blocked off by yellow buoys, and straight after you'll start rounding granite rock pillars. There are plenty more caves to explore (too many to count), and you can explore them, particularly at high tide, but none of them are as large and impressive as Autel. There are also some sandy beaches, inaccessible or almost inaccessible by foot, so, if you choose to alight (and you're allowed to here), it will only be you and other kayakers and paddleboarders. The cliffs are steep, and there are numerous little sea arches and rocks eroded into stubby, semi-submerged columns like well-worn molars. Don't miss paddling around these in your haste to get to cover girl Île Vierge, because a lot of these sea arches are arguably even prettier. The first major sandy beach is Bois du Kador (/// frets.bakery.suave), 2km after the dyke, which has some little rocky outcrops just offshore, shaped a little bit like soft shark fins.

Continue following the coast southwest and 2km after Bois du Kador Beach is another sandy beach without a name (/// symmetrical.island.they). This is the final beach before Île Vierge, which is now under a kilometre away. You'll know you're almost at Île Vierge by the peninsula of rocks jutting out that cuts across your path if you're still hugging the coast. Here, still heading southwest, sandy coves have been replaced by cliffs and vegetation. The rocky outcrop juts into the sea in ridges like the spine of a Stegosaurus, with a narrow channel cutting through the middle of it. You can go through the channel that slices through the middle of the rocky peninsula, but take care and don't attempt this in rough seas as there are lots of rocks under the water and it's very shallow at times. Take particular care if you're using a long sea fin, as it could catch on the rocks. If seas are rough, you should round the peninsula instead, which only adds a hundred or so metres to your paddle.

As you come through the channel, Île Vierge (/// faithless.betrayer.dismiss) is on your right. Despite its name, it's not an island, but the beach and famous, much-photographed, sea arch are extremely pretty, in part due to the backdrop of pine-crested cliffs and aquamarine waters. The pines on the cliff above have, despite their aesthetic appeal, actually been as damaging to the rock as the influx of tourists. They were planted in 1910, but as the soil is too fragile for this sort of tree they have contributed to coastal erosion here, particularly exacerbated after large storms. Île Vierge's archway is made from sandstone, a soft, sedimentary rock that erodes easily. As parts of the rock erode, the remaining sand grains on the surface lock together, making it more resistant to erosion, which is why so many interesting shapes like this sea arch have been formed. You can kayak or paddle right through the archway.

After exploring the sea arch and rocks that frame Île Vierge (remembering that it's forbidden to disembark on the beach), turn around and paddle back the way you came, sticking close to the coast and dipping into caves as often as you please.

ESSENTIALS

GETTING THERE The Crozon Peninsula is on Brittany's west coast and is quite isolated and difficult to access using public transport. From the UK, the closest ferry port is Roscoff, from where it's a 2-hour (90km) drive to Morgat. Buses run from Brest to Crozon (1½ hours, 60km), which is just 2km from Morgat, but you'll struggle to explore this area by public transport. Hire a car – **Sixt car rental** (⊘ sixt.fr) has an outlet at Brest SNCF train station – or look for rideshares via Blablacar (⊘ blablacar.fr).

HIRE & LESSONS The **Centre Nautique de Crozon Morgat** (CNCM ⊘ cncm.fr ⊙ Jul–Aug daily, Sep–Jun Mon–Sat with prior reservation and subject to weather conditions) hires paddleboards and kayaks and organises guided tours.

WHEN TO GO The summer holidays are peak season, but this part of Brittany escapes the worst of the crowds owing to its relative inaccessibility. May to June is a particularly lovely time to visit the Crozon Peninsula, when the gorse flowers are in bloom, and September to October is also a good time to come to see the heather turning purple, with fewer crowds. Whatever time of year you come, however, be prepared for changeable weather.

WHERE TO STAY & EAT **Lodg'ing Nature Camp Presqu'île Crozon** (⊘ lodg-ing.com), 11km away at Lanvéoc, has beautiful bell tents that overlook the sea, with views stretching as far as Brest. Breakfast (not included) is a decadent affair and Chloé and Ahmed who run the place are wonderfully friendly with fantastic local intel on the best walks, bars and restaurants in the area.

In Morgat, eat at **La Crêperie Baradoz** (🅕 Baradoz-Morgat), which has a vibrant mural painted on the outside wall. The menu is just long enough to have you deliberating, but not long enough to instil fear.

TITBITS Don't miss hiking sections of the GR34 while in Crozon. Particularly impressive are the fern-covered trails by Cap de la Chèvre (the southwesternmost point of the Crozon Peninsula) and the gorse- and heather-strewn headland west of artist enclave Camaret-sur-Mer (on Crozon's most westerly headland).

↑ The cliffs are so steep that many of the beaches on the Crozon Peninsula are best accessed by kayak or SUP (andre quinou/s)

2 TO THE LIGHTHOUSE

PADDLE OUT ACROSS EUROPE'S LARGEST SEAWEED FIELD TO THE CONTINENT'S TALLEST LIGHTHOUSE, PERCHED ON A GRANITE ISLAND.

WHERE	Plouguerneau, Brittany
STATS	8km round trip 🏊 ③ 🚣 ②
START/FINISH	Glaz Évasion, Kastell Ac'h headland, 29880 Plouguerneau /// kites.that.grapes

There's no place bluer than Brittany, and arguably the bluest place of all is Plouguerneau's bay on a sunny day. I paddled this route on a Monday, with Eiffel 65's *I'm Blue* going round and round in my head, and my eyes almost hurting from the blueness of it all. There are blue houses, their windows reflecting the myriad of blues on the horizon, and blue fishing boats and rowing boats at berth in the harbour. The inner bay is sheltered by granite islands, the often-churning waters where the Atlantic Ocean and English Channel join contrasting with the sheltered sea between the rocky outcrops. Water depth varies, creating splodges so clear they would be the envy of a tropical island, and deep blue pools where the colour is as profound as the depth it masks.

Lighthouses are seemingly everywhere along this coastline and the plethora of islands that splinter from the shore. It's a bit like standing on an Oxford rooftop and counting the dreaming spires, except that here church spires are replaced by beacons. There is one church spire on the horizon, but this too was used as a lighthouse in years gone by,

↑ Île Vierge lighthouse is the tallest in Europe (aurelie le moigne/S)

and the belfry is open to the elements to illuminate the path of voyaging ships. The rocky obstacle course in the bay wouldn't look out of place in a *Crash Bandicoot* remake, but aboard a kayak in good weather it's easy enough to navigate.

Plouguerneau in Finistère is made of three communes (which all get lumped under the name Plouguerneau). This route starts from the seaside village of Lilia, which can be reached by following the D71 northwest from Plouguerneau, the largest of the three villages. I used a sit-in sea kayak for this route. You could use most types of kayak or paddleboard, but if you're using a paddleboard be aware that there's a lot of weed in the water; a long, rigid fin (which is what I typically use for sea paddles) is probably going to have to be de-weeded fairly frequently.

This paddle route takes you out to the highest lighthouse in Europe, Île Vierge, located on the island of the same name and not to be confused with Île Vierge Beach in the previous chapter (it seems the Bretons had a lack of originality with place names). You can alight at several of the islands en route, and it's particularly worth doing at low tide when the retreating water leaves long, golden beaches peppered with rock pools.

Although it's easy enough to do this route independently in good weather, I'd highly recommend a guided trip with Glaz Évasion (based at the route's start point; page 14). Their team's knowledge of the history and geography of the local area really enhances the trip.

PADDLE THIS WAY

Start from Glaz Évasion kayak hire's slipway (/// kites.that.grapes), in Kastell Ac'h on Lilia's headland. You can already see the Île Vierge lighthouse from here, on a rocky island to the north (your right when you're facing out to sea), so it's very difficult to get lost on this route. With the mainland behind you, paddle straight towards the small rocky outcrop directly ahead of you (only 100m or so away); when almost there, turn right to round it to your left. As you circle these first rocks, you'll see Île Stagadon, your first stop, straight ahead (west), 3km away.

Look down at the water as you paddle. This is the largest seaweed field in Europe, and many of the types of seaweed here are edible, including bladderwrack and sea spaghetti. The latter is easy to identify – it looks just like a muddy green spaghetti – and can be eaten raw, although like this it tastes like seawater and can be rather rubbery. Take a bag to forage some sea spaghetti for dinner. Glaz Évasion kayak instructor Jérôme Prieto recommends boiling it in fresh water for ten minutes before frying it with lardons and shallots.

Île Stagadon (/// tonally.refs.spoken) is a fascinating place; it's worth taking the time here to disembark and explore. On the island is a solitary refuge, part of a project set up by l'Association des amis de Jeudi-Dimanche (l'AJD), which helps to get juvenile delinquents and people in difficulty back on their feet. It's now open to travellers for overnight stays (⌀ belespoir.com; €15/night plus a €10 donation to the association), providing panoramic views over the granite islands of northern Finistère's coast, and for much of the day, your own private island and beach (other guests and paddleboarders aside). You'll need to be self-sufficient and take your own bedding, water and food; note too that there's composting toilets, but no shower.

To continue, leave the island behind and paddle northeast towards the largest granite island nearby. There are numerous rocky outcrops to navigate along the way; keep an eye out for common seals, who regularly use the rocks and seaweed fields as a playground. The largest of these rock islands is Île Valan (/// frozen.trappings.coined), 2km after Île Stagadon, but there's no point trying to alight here as it's only a pile of granite.

Instead, push on to Île Vierge (1.5km after Île Valan), continuing in the same, northeasterly direction. There's a slipway (/// hark.every.tumbling) and a rocky beach on the south side of the island where you can alight. The enormous granite

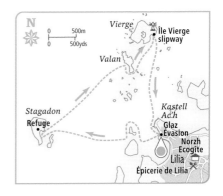

lighthouse here was built between 1897 and 1902, and is the tallest in Europe at a height of 82.5m. It's not the only lighthouse on the island, though, and the (much smaller) lighthouse behind, which was built in 1845, has now been transformed into a luxury *maison d'hôte*.

Monks settled here in the 15th century, arriving with a flock of sheep and staying for 50 years, during which time the sheep decimated everything edible on the island. The monks were forced to return to the mainland where they set up an abbey. Sheep haven't fully left the island though: the opaline inside the newer lighthouse is made from a mixture of sheep's bones and glass. Not content with just being the tallest lighthouse in Europe, it's also the tallest granite lighthouse in the world (and was amazingly built without scaffolding, a risky strategy that – surprisingly – resulted in no fatalities or even injuries). It's possible to go inside the lighthouse on certain days of the week during the summer, but check the schedule in advance, as opening hours change monthly (⌀ abers-tourisme.com).

Taking to the sea again from Île Vierge, with the mainland in front of you, paddle due south through the tiny islets to round the Kastell Ac'h headland and return to your starting point (you'll usually see a few boats at mooring just before you arrive).

↑ The little islands around Plouguerneau have sand so white it looks tropical (Jérôme Prieto)

ESSENTIALS

GETTING THERE Plouguerneau is a 50-minute drive (49km) from the ferry port in Roscoff. The closest mainline train station is Brest (28km). From Brest you'll need to take two buses to reach Plouguerneau, changing in Lannilis (6km south of Plouguerneau). Having a car will make your travels here much easier; car rental is available from Brest station.

HIRE & LESSONS Glaz Évasion (⟡ glazevasion.com ⊙ year-round, weather permitting) hires paddleboards, sit-on and sit-in kayaks, and organises guided tours. Another of their routes goes down the Aber Wrac'h estuary, the mouth of which is just 2km from the launch point of this paddle route.

WHEN TO GO If the weather is fine, you can go kayaking any time of year in Plouguerneau. That said, the weather tends to be better in the summer months – even in the summer holidays (Jul to Aug) this part of Brittany doesn't usually get too crowded.

WHERE TO STAY & EAT Norzh Ecogîte (⟡ norzh-ecogite.bzh) has fresh-looking rooms made from light wood that accommodate up to four people and is within walking distance of Glaz Évasion. Also in Lilia, **Épicerie de Lilia** (◪ Cocoricco29) sells good-quality local produce for self-catering. A little further down the coast, **Bzzzt Café** (◪ bzzztcafe) has sea views, regular live music events and plenty of local beers.

TITBITS Nearby Fort Cézon is well worth a visit. It's an island fort designed by Vauban, a 17th-century French military architect who designed many of France's most famous forts, including the citadels of Besançon and Briançon. Fort Cézon was built between 1685 and 1694 and has been transformed into an artists' collective and museum. To visit, book a guided tour through **Pays des Abers Tourism Office** (⟡ abers-tourisme.com), a 4km drive from Lilia, in Plouguerneau village.

↑ The original, much smaller lighthouse, built between 1842 and 1845, is now a holiday rental (Anna Richards)

3 THE ROBINSON CRUSOE PADDLE

PADDLE AROUND BRITTANY'S TROPICAL-LOOKING ARCHIPELAGO, WHICH HIDES GLITTERING BEACHES & A WORLD-FAMOUS SAILING SCHOOL.

WHERE	Glénan Islands, Brittany
STATS	11km round trip 🏄 🛶 ③
START/FINISH	Port de Saint-Nicolas de Glénan, 29170 Fouesnant
	/// bathers.weasels.seemingly

I watched the skies with some trepidation in advance of my trip to the Glénan Islands. It seemed as though the Atlantic Ocean was being drained and emptied on my head. I caught the boat from Bénodet, southern Finistère, one of the main embarkation points for reaching the islands. The rain was so dense I couldn't see the village on the opposite bank of the river, just a few hundred metres away.

The following day, rain was replaced by wind. Fortunately, in the shelter of the islands, the seas were (just about) calm enough to paddle, although I still got much more of a workout than I'd bargained for. These islands are Brittany's little slice of paradise: the whiter than white sand is sprinkled with fine pieces of quartz that give the impression

↑ The lagoon in the middle of the Glénan archipelago is renowned for its clear water (Solo Ditwood/S)

that it's sparkling under the sun. And the water, on a calm day at least, is impossibly clear, and ideal for snorkelling.

The Glénan Islands are an archipelago of nine islands, some 10 nautical miles off the Fouesnant Peninsula in southern Brittany. There's just one holiday house, two restaurants, a dive centre and a sailing school on the islands, all of which are only open during the summer season. The restaurants and holiday house are all on Île Saint-Nicolas, the largest island in the archipelago, which is where boats from the mainland arrive and depart. The Glénan Islands are best known for their sailing school, which originated here but now has four outposts in Brittany, in addition to one in Marseille and one in Corsica. The archipelago is also home to a rare flower that only grows on Île Saint-Nicolas. The Glénan narcissus is a white, odourless flower that grows to between 15 and 40cm tall. To preserve it, the walkways around the island are bordered by fences, but most visitors will still be able to spot the flowers. Most magical of all, though, are the white-sand beaches, which have led to the Glénan Islands being described as 'French

Tahiti', and make a paddling trip here feel as remote as Robinson Crusoe must have felt on his desert island.

Considering that all food and booze needs to be shipped over from the mainland, prices on the Glénans aren't quite as extortionate as you might expect (count on €7 for a pint). The exception is bottled water, which is eye-wateringly expensive (there are no freshwater sources on the islands). There are two bar-restaurants by the main arrival dock on Île Saint-Nicolas but no shops, so you'll need to be largely self sufficient on the islands. I'd recommend bringing a picnic and plenty of water with you – the beaches are lovely for picnicking.

Check the wind direction in advance to decide which way round to do your paddling circuit (it's always nicer to finish paddling *with* the wind, right?). I went anti-clockwise, hence the route outlined here, but it can easily be reversed. If it's blowing a hoolie (as it often can; the Glénans are very exposed) and still safe enough to paddle, I recommend cutting this route down to a triangular itinerary between Îles Saint-Nicolas, Drénec and Loc'h, which are more sheltered.

PADDLE THIS WAY

Begin your adventure where the ferry disembarks, on the main slipway on Île Saint-Nicolas (/// bathers.weasels.seemingly). From here, paddle the 1km southwest across to Île de Drénec (/// mongrel.unspent.radar), the island directly across the bay from your start point. The little building on the island is an old farm, and now belongs to the Glénans Sailing School. There are a few scattered trees and a gorgeous little beach here.

It's a further kilometre or so from Île de Drénec to Île du Loc'h, depending on how far along the beach you go. The easternmost tip of Drénac is splintered into

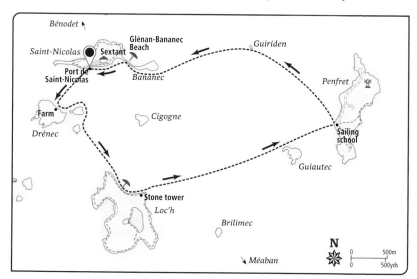

several rocky islets, but since the water isn't deep enough to paddle through the middle of them, you'll need to skirt around the outside. Keeping the easternmost headland of Île de Drénec on your right, round it, paddling southeast. Head squarely for the middle of the long strip of white sand now a little to the left in front of you. There's stiff competition for the prettiest beach in the Glénans, but Île du Loc'h's north-facing sandy bay (/// aided.beginning.blends) is a high contender. The island is owned by the children of Gwenn-Aël Bolloré, who was a World War II resistance fighter, businessman, writer and oceanographer. The island itself is fenced off, but that doesn't pose a problem because the beach is public (hooray for France, where you're not allowed to privatise the coast!). The beach curves around to form a really sheltered bay, and there's a mysterious little stone tower at the far end.

From Île du Loc'h, paddle to Île de Penfret (/// dazed.guzzled.disobeying), approximately 3.5km due northwest. You'll be able to see the long strip of white sand, and the stubby little Penfret Lighthouse, on the northernmost end of the island, from Île du Loc'h. En route and to your right, there are a couple of small, rocky islands, home only to seabirds. Île de Brilimec is the first one, followed by two which are little more than rock piles: Les Méaban, and Guiautec. The only defining feature of the latter is a ship's navigational marker.

Île de Penfret is the base for the world-famous Glénans sailing school. Les Glénans (page 21) teaches sailing and watersports to pupils of all levels – from dinghy and catamaran sailing to windsurfing. Founded in 1947 by Hélène de Chauvelin and Philippe Viannay, it's grown to be one of the most prestigious sailing schools in Europe.

Land on the long stretch of white sand that runs the length of Penfret's west coast. You'll be able to see the little red light tower of Penfret's lighthouse to your left. Built in 1838, it was still manned during most of the 20th century and was

↑ Anna approaching Penfret by SUP (Anna Richards)

only automated in 1993. During World War I and in the years that followed, a lighthouse keeper lived here with his wife and four children – by the time the family left there were 11 kids (hey, there's not much to do on a lighthouse). The lighthouse is only open to the public on Journées du Patrimoine (third weekend of September).

Launching again from Île de Penfret, it's time to complete your loop back to Île Saint-Nicholas. Ahead, just to your right (northwest), is Île de Guiriden, a tiny island little more than a sandbank with a few rocks and sparse vegetation at either end, roughly 2.5km after leaving Île de Penfret. It's enormously popular with kite- and windsurfers, and the lack of buildings and trees means that the wind whistles past the island at great speeds. On a calm day, it's the most idyllic place to picnic, and you may well end up with your own private sandbank. To the north, the sea stretches on seemingly endlessly, interrupted only by passing boats and seabirds. From the top of the sandbank you can take in views of the entire Glénan archipelago. It's the kind of view visitors to the Maldives would pay thousands for to enjoy a private dining experience, but paddle up here with a sandwich and you've got it all for free. To your southwest (your left), in line with Île Saint-Nicolas but in the middle of the circle formed by the Glénans, is the military fort on Île Cigogne, which is also only open during the Journées du Patrimoine. It was built on the rocky island in 1717 by the Maréchal de Montesquiou to ward off corsairs.

From Île de Guiriden, paddle the final 3km due west back to Île Saint-Nicolas, which is clearly visible in front of you. En route, you may want to stop at the adjoining Île Bananec, linked thanks to a narrow strip of beach, Glénan-Bananec (/// onlookers.abdomens.cove). It's another contender for prettiest beach in the Glénans, though it gets much busier than Île du Loc'h because it's accessible by foot from the port. Note also that the skinny strip of sand is often completely submerged at high tide. Île Bananec and the eastern end of Saint-Nicolas are peppered with semi-submerged rocks that you can paddle in and out of to admire fish darting through the seaweed in the crystalline water.

↑ The Glénan Islands are often described as the 'Breton Tahiti' (Jef Wodniack/S)

ESSENTIALS

GETTING THERE The closest airport to the ferry ports with boats to the Glénan Islands is Rennes in Brittany, which has seasonal direct flights to London. It's best to rent a car from here rather than relying on public transport although you can catch a train to Quimper and take a bus to either Bénodet, Concarneau or Loctudy.

Vedettes de l'Odet (⊘ vedettes-odet.com ⊙ Apr–early Oct) run boats between Bénodet, Concarneau, Beg-Meil, Port-la-Forêt and Loctudy on the mainland and the Glénan Islands. Boats between Bénodet and Concarneau are the most frequent, ranging between two crossings a day outside of the school holidays and four crossings a day during July and August. Book in advance.

HIRE & LESSONS One- or two-person kayaks are available to rent in advance through **Vedettes de l'Odet** (see above), or upon arrival on Île Saint-Nicolas, booked through the rental agency also run by Vedettes de l'Odet. You can also book kayak hire as a package with your boat fare (advisable if visiting in the summer holidays as kayak numbers are limited).

WHEN TO GO You can only visit the Glénan Islands between April and early October, as outside of this period there are no passenger boats running between the archipelago and the mainland.

WHERE TO STAY & EAT There are just 30 beds in Île Saint-Nicolas's sole refuge, **Sextant** (⊘ sextant-glenan.org); book early to avoid disappointment. Most people choose to stay on the mainland and visit for the day – a good choice is Bénodet, a beautiful little town with a sheltered beach at the mouth of the River Odet. Here, **Bateau Libre** (⊘ bateaulibre.com) has modern, minimalistic rooms and a great bistro.

There are only two restaurants on the islands, both on Île Saint-Nicolas. **La Boucane** (no website) serves reasonably cheap beer and bar snacks, and **Les Viviers** (⊘ lesviviersdesglenan.fr) has a menu almost entirely comprised of seafood, which is expensive for what you get. Book in advance as it fills up quickly. I recommend bringing a packed lunch for your visit and plenty of water.

TITBITS The archipelago's world-famous sailing school (Les Glénans) runs an English-language sailing course as well as courses in French. They take roughly 15,000 trainees each year and it was started as a charitable association set up by the Resistance. Courses are available for all abilities – from complete novices to experienced sailors – and typically last a week minimum. For dates, prices and more details visit ⊘ glenans.asso.fr.

4 THE LITTLE SEA

TEMPESTUOUS & WILD, THE GULF OF MORBIHAN IS ONE OF THE MOST REWARDING & CHALLENGING PLACES TO KAYAK IN THE COUNTRY.

WHERE	Gulf of Morbihan, Brittany
STATS	Route 1: 7km round trip 🛶③ 🛶②; Route 2: 23km round trip 🛶⑤ 🛶④
START/FINISH	Route 1: At the corner of Le Berly and Route du Berly, 56400 Le Bono /// baroque.mailbag.spends; Route 2: Embarcadère, Île-aux-Moines /// reforms.competitions.rotations

There are islands everywhere in the Gulf of Morbihan, of all shapes and sizes, reminding me of photos I've seen of Vietnam's Ha Long Bay. Most of the islands have pretty dense tree cover, resembling bunches of broccoli in the waters of this immense bay that can be as still as soup one moment and as violent as boiling water the next.

The Gulf of Morbihan is one of the most dangerous spots in the country for paddling or kayaking, so don't be deceived if you visit on a calm day and the water looks like a millpond. The tide is everything here, and the estuaries that feed into the bay can empty and refill with a speed that beggars belief. The bay is also extremely exposed, protected by just a few narrow headlands and islands from winds and waves that charge all the way across the Atlantic, gathering momentum as they go.

This is one place where I strongly recommend booking a guided tour, unless you're an extremely experienced sea kayaker. Paddleboarders should take extra care – with the wind, tide and currents, you risk finding yourself dragged out into the open sea.

There are roughly 40 islands in the gulf, although this number depends on the tide – some are submerged at high tide and during the particularly strong spring tides. Local legends say that the gulf has as many islands as there are days of the year. The largest islands are Île-aux-Moines and Île-d'Arz, both of which it's possible to kayak around (but, at the risk of sounding like a broken record, do be sure to check the tides and the weather in advance).

I was not fortunate with the timing of my visit to the Gulf of Morbihan. Weather warnings crackled through the speaker every time I turned on the radio. The wind was gusting at 100km/hr, the rain lashing down, the sea giving the appearance of the scene building up to the big wave in George Clooney's *The Perfect Storm*. My intention had been to kayak the 23km loop around Île-aux-Moines, but it was clear this would be pure folly, so instead I walked the coastal path around the circumference of the island, hair blowing into a bird's nest, and then kayaked the only route feasible in such inclement conditions, up the Auray River (again, in driving rain, but at least without the risk of ending up in the Americas).

It ended up being a bonus, and the wealth, breadth and variety of Morbihan merits having two possible routes anyway. That way, if the weather's bad (as it often is), if you're happier on a paddleboard, or if you're an intermediate kayaker who prefers to explore in autonomy rather than with a guide, I recommend the first route. If you're looking for a longer challenge, the weather's fine, you're going with a guide or you've got decent sea-kayaking experience, tackle the perimeter of Île-aux-Moines, and you won't regret it.

← 'Morbihan' means 'little sea' in Breton (Hemis/A)

PADDLE THIS WAY
ROUTE 1: THE AURAY
RIVER This is one of the few routes in the Gulf of Morbihan that is accessible for paddleboarders, although it can of course be undertaken by kayak, too. Start from the slipway on Le Berly, a little road that runs along the banks of the Auray River, to the south of the fishing town of Le Bono (/// baroque.mailbag. spends), on the headland that juts out into the Bay of Kerdréan. From here, cross the river to the other bank and paddle upstream, keeping close to the riverbank to stay out of the way of any passing boats. Under a kilometre later,

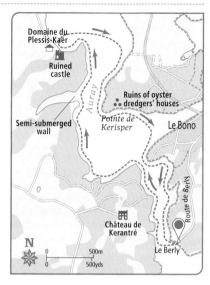

you'll reach the Château de Kerantré (/// rivers.liabilities.pebbled). The castle itself is hidden in dense foliage, but easily visible is a statue of the Virgin Mary, looking out from the greenery. The castle dates back to the 18th century and was built on the site of an old manor house that itself dates from much earlier.

Take your time along here: the birdlife is exceptional and thanks to conservation efforts, much of the foliage has been left to grow naturally (the coastal path doesn't manage to come right down to the river on this side). There are many types of gull (common, herring, brown and great black-backed), fish eagles, cormorants, herons, oystercatchers, curlews and egrets, among others.

Keep paddling 3km upstream along the same bank, past lush vegetation and thick woodland. You'll arrive at the Domaine du Plessis-Kaër (/// gobbled. guidebook.lushly), with an eerie-looking ruined château just before it. Halfway between Domaine du Plessis-Kaër and Château de Kerantré a small tributary of the Auray branches off to your left, blocked off by a semi-submerged dyke, which – with a shallow or flexible fin – you can easily paddle past. Paddling down this channel as far as the wall at the far end is just 400m in either direction if you'd like to make the detour. The foliage on either bank is dense, so you won't get any different views but, if you're a keen birder, then this is one of the quietest spots on the river for birdlife. A 57ha estate with extremely upmarket hotel rooms, Domaine du Plessis-Kaër is lined with tall, Beverly Hills-style palms that meet the water and is often rented out for functions. The old château next to it dates from the 12th century and is in a state of disrepair. In its heyday it had stables, an orangery, a dovecote and farm buildings in the grounds.

From the hotel, cross over to the other bank and head back south to round the small headland (Pointe de Kerisper), a short paddle of just 1.5km. You'll see ruined old buildings with roof tiles strewn over the ground (/// basked.turbulence. moisten) – this is what remains of a once-thriving oyster trade on the Auray River, until the oyster beds were over dredged. Keep paddling south, across the Bono River which empties in the Auray here. A final 1.5km paddle will take you back to your starting point.

ROUTE 2: ÎLE-AUX-MOINES From Port Blanc (/// vipers. collaboration.humbles) on the mainland, catch the ferry that runs between Port Blanc and Île-aux-Moines (approximately 10 minutes), a short crossing of 500m. You'll arrive at the island's jetty (/// reforms.competitions.rotations); keeping it on your right, paddle past the main town, with its little restaurants and a sheltered harbour and sandy bay. Keep hugging the coast and follow the long headland that juts out to the north of the island. The northernmost point is a 2.5km paddle from the jetty where you began. Pointe du Trec'h (/// diviner. defers.petites), marked on land by a large stone cross, has fantastic views over the mainland.

Stay as close to the shore as you can and watch out for passing ferries as you round the headland – this is the crossing point for several ferry lines. Leaving Pointe du Trec'h behind you, keep the coast to your right as you make for the next headland. It's 3km south, hugging the coastline to your right-hand side, to a long bay called Anse du Guéric (/// cashless.doorbell.luncheon) – if you're hungry, stop before the bay at the waterside oyster shack, Ets Martin. Anse du Guéric to Pointe de Brouel (/// aired.generating.piecing), the next headland, jutting out to the east, is only 1.5km. There are more magnificent views from Pointe de Brouel, this time looking out over the second-largest island in the gulf, Île d'Arz. It's quite exposed, so this is a place to take extra care in case the wind picks up. Keeping the coast on your right-hand side at all times, round Pointe de Brouel. Paddle west, continuing with the land to your right, and 2km further along you'll arrive at Port Miquel Beach

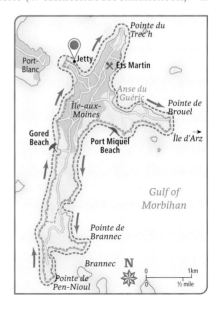

(/// passage.photograph.dive). A stone wall and pretty little slate-roofed cottages line the waterfront. Île-aux-Moines sticks out at all angles like static hair and so it's 5km before you reach the next headland, Pointe de Brannec (/// flirts. heartfelt.jammers), which is significantly smaller than the two you've already

ESSENTIALS

GETTING THERE The Gulf of Morbihan is easiest to explore by car with rental outlets at the airport in Rennes, Brittany (seasonal direct flights to London) and from the train station in Rennes (high speed services to Paris). Both the airport and train station are just over 100km from the Gulf of Morbihan. By public transport, catch the train to Vannes, on the northeastern side of the bay and its largest town. Boats depart directly from the port here to Île-aux-Moines (45 minutes), so this is the best place to base yourself to take trips out to explore the islands if you don't have your own wheels.

HIRE & LESSONS Gîte & Contre Gîte (⊘ gitecontregite.com) runs immersive, professional tours using sit-in kayaks around the islands of the Gulf of Morbihan and up the Auray River. They also run sea kayaking skills lessons, and their knowledge of local flora and fauna is unparalleled.

WHEN TO GO April to October is the best time to visit the Gulf of Morbihan, but this is a part of France where the weather can change at the drop of a hat at any time of year. Don't set out paddling alone unless you've thoroughly studied the weather forecast, told someone where you're going and are confident that you can navigate the tides and currents.

↑ Île-aux-Moines is the largest island in the Gulf of Morbihan (Cavan Images/A)

passed. It's thought that 'Brannec' means 'group of crows', coming from the Breton 'bran' for 'crow' and 'bek' for group.

After Brannec, the headland dips sharply back in on itself west in an 'L' shape, past a short pier used for launching boats, which is easily identifiable by its red marker. The island then juts down to its most southerly point, Pointe de Nioul (/// aspiring.volley.backers), 2km further on. As you're paddling to Pointe de Nioul you'll have a clear view of smaller neighbouring islands Brannec and Govihan to the southeast. When you arrive at the headland, the mainland looks almost close enough to touch.

Round the peninsula again to start paddling north, up the western side of the island. Tide depending, this section is much quicker, and the west side of the island is comparatively straight compared to the myriad of prongs on the eastern side. Two thirds of the way up, some 3km later, stop at Gored Beach (/// vaguest.temp.blackouts), one of the prettiest on the island, in a curve so perfect it looks as though it was scooped out by a digger. After Gored, you'll pass many more buildings and stone walls than on the rest of your journey. When the headland starts to jut out west in front of you, keep close to shore and round it again. No sooner have you rounded the headland than you'll see the port where ferries arrive from Port Blanc on the mainland (3km from Gored), the same port at which you arrived and began your paddle.

WHERE TO STAY & EAT Vannes has the widest range of accommodation in the area, but if you're travelling by car I recommend staying in the countryside as the town tends to get very crowded, and parking is a nightmare. There are several good campsites around the Gulf of Morbihan, including **Camping Lann Brick** (⊘ camping-lannbrick.com), **Camping La Ferme de Lann Hoëdic** (⊘ camping-lannhoedic.fr) and **Camping de Kergo** (⊘ campingkergo.com). Take a good quality tent; it's not uncommon to experience some rain when camping in Brittany.

Le Pie Noir Café (ⓕ PienoirCafe) in Sarzeau (on the southern side of the Gulf of Morbihan) serves home-reared meat and their own cheese from their farm shop and restaurant. **Crêperie Saint-Sauveur** (⊘ creperie-saint-sauveur-auray.fr) in Auray (at the head of the river on the northwestern side of the gulf) faces stiff competition to deliver the best crêpes in the area.

TITBITS Take a boat trip to nearby Île-d'Houat (boats leave from Vannes with **Navix**; ⊘ navix.fr) for some of the best beaches and coastal hikes in Brittany. The sailing club on Houat (**Club Nautique du Rohu** ⊘ voile-en-morbihan.com) hires kayaks and paddleboards if you'd like to tackle a third paddle in the Gulf of Morbihan while you're there.

5 A PADDLE PILGRIMAGE

PADDLING OFFERS AN ALTERNATIVE – & LESS OBVIOUS – WAY TO SEE THE 8TH-CENTURY TIDAL ISLAND OF MONT SAINT-MICHEL.

WHERE	Mont Saint-Michel, Normandy
STATS	10km one-way 🛶④ 🛶③; Bonus route: 5km return 🛶 🛶⑤ (both routes)
START/FINISH	Picnic tables, 11 rue de la Grève, 50220 Pontaubault /// certain.juiced.front; Bonus route: Mont Saint-Michel car park, Le Bas Pays, 50170 Beauvoir /// fastens.accents.tirades.

Welcome to the cover girl of paddling routes. It's somewhat strange to admit that, despite living in France and working as a travel writer, I'd never been to Mont Saint-Michel before working on this guidebook. My first sighting of it was with a massive paddleboard strapped to my back as I walked over the causeway in the half-light of dawn.

Mont Saint-Michel is a place I'd fully expected to give me Paris syndrome (that feeling of disappointment when you've heard so much about a place, and seen so many photos, only for it to be smaller, duller and generally less impressive than you'd anticipated). I was sceptical – how could the island live up to all the photos I'd seen of it? Reader, it lives up to it and more, and especially so when experienced from the tranquillity of the water.

Mont Saint-Michel looks a little like a Gothic version of the Disney castle, often shrouded by sea mist, its spire piercing brooding clouds. It's almost perfectly triangular, the fortified walls and abundance of medieval buildings creating an island that has so many levels it could be made out of stone-coloured Lego. You can see as many photos as you like of Mont Saint-Michel before you visit, but it will still blow your mind.

As one of the most famous sites in France, I felt this place deserves two paddle routes. The first is one you can do independently if you're a competent paddler, although – as a one-way paddle in a fairly remote location – it's difficult to organise unless you've got someone prepared to drop you off and pick you up at the end. It starts upriver from Mont Saint-Michel, the monastery spires slowly coming into view before opening out to a panorama over the tidal island at the end. You've also got to be aware that there's plenty of quicksand here. While this isn't generally much of an issue if you need to wade through shallow water, dragging your paddleboard, you should avoid standing still for too long. If you do feel yourself start to sink, rotate your legs in slow, gradually widening circles to free them, rather than trying to jerk them free. Look for the darker patches of water to stay afloat; the lighter patches are where the sand is closer to the surface.

The second, bonus paddle is one I really, strongly advise that you do with a guide. Not just because it requires excellent knowledge of tide times, but because you've got to cope with an often violent tidal bore and, um, more quicksand, which tends to be stronger than the quicksand on route one.

The tide dictates every water-based activity here, so be sure to check in advance no matter which route you do, and don't attempt either of the routes in spring tides. For both, I recommend booking through Kayak La Baie (⌀ kayaklabaie.com).

← Some 2.5 million tourists and pilgrims visit Mont Saint-Michel each year (Andia/A)

The first paddle route goes down a section of the Sélune, an 85km-long river that empties into the English Channel to the east of Mont Saint-Michel. Since this part of the River Sélune is a tidal estuary, you'll travel much faster if the tide is going out. Avoid doing this paddle at or just before high tide, as a tidal bore often forms an hour or so before high tide. At low tide, you risk having very little water and wading for much of the paddle. The difficulty rating for this paddle is based on the conditions rather than the level of physical activity, and most paddlers of reasonable fitness should be able to tackle it. Views over Mont Saint-Michel are fantastic, but you don't alight on the island. The bonus route skirts around Mont Saint-Michel, launching from the island itself, but requires a considerable amount of technical ability and prior paddling experience.

PADDLE THIS WAY

This route maps the tidal channel I used to descend the Sélune, but as it's ever changing it's important to use your common sense to follow the river flow. Embark by the picnic tables just east of the bridge that spans the River Sélune between Pontaubault and Le Marais Gautier (/// certain.juiced.front). Note that there's not really a gentle slope to access the water, so it's a bit of a drop to get on to your board.

Begin by paddling under the bridge, then follow the tidal river as it meanders. They're large meanders, which have you looping around, almost doubling back on yourself at times, rather than travelling straight. The landscape here is flat and marshy, with muddy banks that slide into the water on either side, often with flocks of sheep grazing by the water. The grey, tidal sands all around you are quicksand.

After paddling for around 4km (/// unnerves.flicked.packages), you should get your first view of the spire of Mont Saint-Michel, out to sea to the west. This is the first point of reference on an otherwise flat landscape that changes little apart from the tides; seeing the spires gradually rise across the horizon is nothing short of magical.

Continue following the river. Another 6km on (/// databases. madmen.obstinate) you'll also be able to see the granite island of Tombelaine, 3km to the north of Mont Saint-Michel; at low tide pilgrims walk

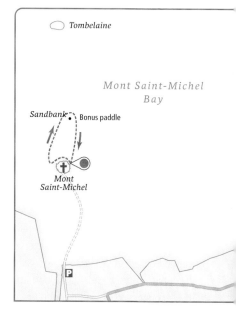

between the two. During the Hundred Years' War, the English had a fortress on Tombelaine and it was under English occupation for almost the full duration of the war as they repeatedly tried (and failed) to take Mont Saint-Michel. Only a few ruins are left from this time, but it's an excellent place for spotting seabirds, and Chemins de la Baie (⊘ cheminsdelabaie.com) organises guided walks to visit Tombelaine at low tide.

Once Mont Saint-Michel and Tombelaine are both in your eyeline, the bay widens for the final 4km of your paddle, as you meander west. By now, you've got the kind of panoramic view of Mont Saint-Michel that makes it look as though it has been stencilled on to the clouds, uninterrupted by the causeway, passing tour buses or – crucially – selfie-taking tourists. It has gone from being so small on the horizon that you could blot it out with your little fingernail to something that dominates the whole skyline. Despite the bay's width here, this is also one of the most shallow parts of the paddle, so it's very likely you'll have to alight at certain points. Hug the shore to your left (south) to avoid getting dragged out into the bay with the tide, and look for a little stone bungalow (/// undiplomatic. fraught.deflecting), the first building you've seen since leaving Pontaubault. This is where you disembark. There's no infrastructure so be prepared to haul your board up over the mud (take care, it's slippery!). Fortunately, the slope to disembark is much less steep than the access point in Pontaubault. The bungalow sits by a flat bike trail that goes towards Mont Saint-Michel, roughly 10km away; the wooden boardwalk is surrounded by flat, muddy ground full of samphire.

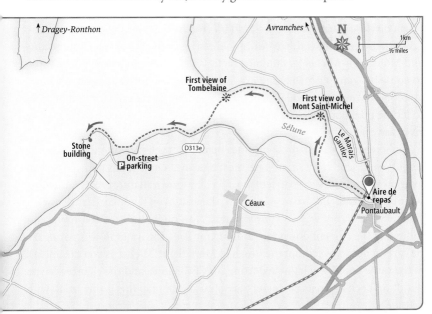

From here, it's still a short walk (10 to 15 minutes) to get to a place where it's possible for friends to pick you up. Follow the footpath to your east, with the sea behind you, to the intersection of Route de Roche Torin and the D313e (/// genie.ebbed.mushy).

BONUS PADDLE Paddling around Mont Saint-Michel as the sun rises, seeing it up close from every angle with only seals for company – it's the kind of thing travel dreams are made of and was one of the most memorable, surreal experiences I had while researching this guide. However, the tides around Mont Saint-Michel are extremely complicated, and this is not a route to do independently, even if you're an experienced paddler.

I recommend booking a trip with Ian Wood from the aforementioned Kayak La Baie (⌂ kayaklabaie.com), who has an unparalleled knowledge of the tides, the Mont Saint-Michel tidal bore (a wave that comes in as the tide rises), local wildlife, and how to get out of quicksand, even when it sets like concrete around you. Kayak La Baie is currently the only outlet running this trip.

This paddle starts between 1 and 2 hours before high tide and takes you a short distance north of Mont Saint-Michel towards Tombelaine, before riding the tide back in the same direction to the beach below Mont Saint-Michel. For me, this happily coincided with sunrise. If you're lucky enough to be paddling the sunrise golden hour, note that you'll arrive before the shuttle buses start running across the causeway, so will need to walk with your guide the 3km to Mont Saint-Michel with your paddle strapped to your back. Once there, inflate your board on a beach on the eastern side of the island (/// riverfront.plastering.windbreaker).

On the water, follow the retreating tide to a sandbank between Tombelaine and Mont Saint-Michel (/// outdoing.tactless.strain) to wait for the tide to begin to come in again. Fish will regularly jump out of the retreating water around your board. Your guide will instruct you to park up on the sand for a bit in order to let the tidal bore pass (unless you're a pro paddle surfer and used to surfing river waves).

You'll need to wait 15 or 20 minutes before you get back into the water. The tidal bore resembles a small, fast-moving wave. Once it has gone past, wait another five minutes or so to let the water slow down slightly before launching your board again, but when you take to the water you'll notice it's still moving much faster than it was on your way out. You might well see common seals following the current down too, looking for fish. The water flow is strong, so be careful not to overshoot the beach at Mont Saint-Michel as you disembark at the same beach you launched from. It's easily done, and the chances of you paddling back against the current are slim. I reiterate: this is one to do with a guide.

↑ Kayakers disembarking at Mont Saint-Michel (Ian Wood/Kayak La Baie) → Sunrise paddlers (Polly Waters)

ESSENTIALS

GETTING THERE Ferries run from the UK to Caen, from where it's a 1½ hour/135km drive to Mont Saint-Michel. There is a major train station and international airport at Rennes, about 80km away from Mont Saint-Michel.

There's free on-road parking at the start point for the main paddle (although it is limited), and plenty of flat, grassy areas for inflating your paddle. Parking for the disembarkation point is a 10- to 15-minute walk from the end of the paddle, at the corner of Route de Roche Torin and the D313e (/// genie.ebbed.mushy). Note that you'll need to organise lifts if you're paddling this route without a guide.

For the bonus paddle, parking is available at Mont Saint-Michel's extortionately priced car park; a shuttle runs regularly from here to the abbey from 07.30 to midnight daily. The timetable is available online via **Normandie Tourisme** (⊘ normandie-tourisme.fr). Otherwise, it's a flat 3km walk across the causeway.

HIRE & LESSONS A combination of tricky tide conditions, quicksand and a lack of public transport to and from the route start/end points means this is a place worth booking with a guide. For tours, paddle and kayak hire, contact **Kayak La Baie** (⊘ kayaklabaie.com).

WHEN TO GO The weather is more reliable during the summer (May–Sep), but the school holidays see peak crowds. Summer temperatures tend to hover around the low 20s. Mont Saint-Michel is open daily, with the exception of 1 January, 1 May and 25 December.

WHERE TO STAY & EAT Avranches, a 25-minute (22km) drive from Mont Saint-Michel has cheaper accommodation than the hotels clustered near Mont Saint-Michel's causeway, a plethora of restaurant choices and a view of the abbey from the ramparts of the town's castle. Here you'll find **Hôtel La Ramade** (⊘ laramade.fr), in a handsome building with a sunny conservatory and well-stocked bar. For a pre-paddle belly filler that won't break the bank, head to **Crêperie du Pot d'Étain** (🛈), also in Avranches – try their crêpe with stewed apples cooked in salted butter.

Kayaking guide Ian Wood, owner of Kayak La Baie, runs a gîte that sleeps six in Dragey-Ronthon, a 40-minute (35km) drive from Mont Saint-Michel; contact him for reservations (⊘ kayaklabaie.com).

TITBITS During the summer months there's an excellent sound and light show at Mont Saint-Michel (⊙ Jul & Aug 07.30–midnight). It retraces the history of the abbey and the legends that surround it, and the cloisters are lit in a multitude of colours. It's also much quieter to visit at night rather than during the day. Book online (⊘ normandie-tourisme.fr).

Roughly 25 people still live year-round on Mont Saint-Michel (canadastock/S)

6 PADDLING WITH PAINTERS

PADDLE THROUGH LANDSCAPE STRAIGHT OUT OF AN IMPRESSIONIST PAINTING AMONG SOME OF THE MOST DRAMATIC COASTAL SCENERY IN THE COUNTRY.

WHERE	Étretat, Normandy
STATS	2.8km return 🏄‍♂️🛶② or 16km return (extended version) 🏄‍♂️④🛶③
START/FINISH	Étretat Beach, 1 pl Victor Hugo, 76790 Étretat
	/// participated.viscose.diversify

When Monet first came to paint the cliffs of Étretat in February 1883, he'd regularly take a rowing boat and paddle out to secluded spots to capture the majesty of the rock formations. He painted the changing light over the Porte d'Aval, the Porte d'Amont and the Manneporte 20 times during that first visit, fascinated by the way different times of day changed his perception of the rock arches. It wouldn't be long before he returned. Having grown up in neighbouring Le Havre, this was an area he knew well, and in February 1886 he immortalised the cliffs once more, sending ten of the paintings he created to an exhibition in Brussels. He wasn't the first nor the last artist to be captivated by the curious cliffs. The chalky plateau of France's Alabaster Coast, formed over millions of years of erosion, was inspiration to Eugène Boudin, Gustave Courbet and Henri Matisse, among others, and in more recent years has been the muse for photographers and snap-happy tourists. Now it attracts over a million visitors each year.

The town of Étretat may be full of knock-off souvenir shops and overflowing, overpriced car parks, but from the water it's easy to see why this place inspired the Impressionists. Separated from the white cliffs of England's Jurassic Coast by a small strip of sea, the cliffs here feel as though they could slot together like a jigsaw puzzle. Instead of Durdle Door, this side of the Channel has the Porte d'Aval (Aval Door sea arch), and Étretat's Aiguille (needle) is reminiscent of the toothy Needles on the Isle of Wight.

Étretat may be three hours from Paris, but this doesn't stop it being enormously popular with daytrippers from the French capital and other nearby cities. Start your paddle as early as possible to avoid the crowds – I set off at 06.00 with the place to myself and returned very smugly at 09.00 to enjoy breakfast just as the first of the tour buses were arriving.

Although there were far fewer tourists in Monet's day than now, he still preferred to visit the cliffs in winter to paint them in tranquillity. If you can brave the cold, you'll likely have Étretat virtually to yourself on a clear day during the winter, but be aware that the watersports hire centre here is seasonal. Bear in mind too that since this is a sea paddle it can be dangerous in rough weather, particularly since getting the best views involves paddling through narrow sea arches.

PADDLE THIS WAY

Begin your paddle from anywhere on Étretat's main beach (/// participated. viscose.diversify). As you look out to sea, the hobbit-sized sea arch in Amont Cliff (/// sweeping.clinical.emerald) will be on your right, and the spindly sea arch of Aval Cliff (/// metronome.revel.unseated) on your left. The chalk cliffs

← Anna's view of the Needle at sunrise (Anna Richards)

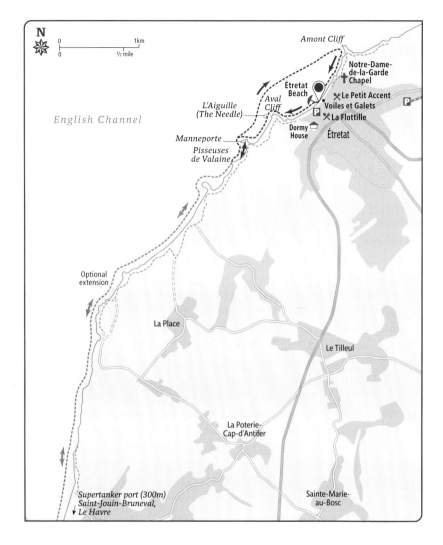

here are highly sensitive to erosion, which is how such unique shapes have been created along the coastline. Start your paddle depending on the wind direction: to Amont Cliff first if the wind is coming from the west, or in the direction of Aval Cliff if it's coming from the east – that way you'll be paddling with the wind on the return journey. I've given the directions for heading first to Aval Cliff, but simply reverse them to start with Amont.

A paddle of 1.5km west from the middle of the beach, sticking close to the coast, will take you to Aval Cliff. Look out for iron rungs and ladders dotted at intervals on the rocks en route. On a calm day, it's sheer joy to moor your paddleboard or kayak using one of the iron rungs and swim right through the

51m-tall Aval sea arch. Back on your paddleboard, just 20m further west is the conical-shaped L'Aiguille (The Needle /// feud.formulation.divots), towering 70m above you and almost as tall as the highest cliffs here. As soon as you've paddled away from it, turn around to look: L'Aiguille now appears to almost touch the arch. Another 300m of paddling takes you to a second sea arch, Manneporte (/// origami.withering.goldfish), which will have been visible once you passed Aval. Turn around again: once southwest of Manneporte, the arch acts as a natural frame for Aval and L'Aiguille – a ready-made painting. The final unmissable sight on this stretch of coast is the Pisseuses de Valaine (/// exert.dinghies.replant), 500m further southwest, which tastefully translates in English as the 'urinating' cliffs. Here, rivulets of water form several little waterfalls in the chalk; skinny little streams that tumble down on to the shingle beach below.

If you're feeling energetic, it's possible to paddle past the ivory cliffs and little shingle beaches right up to the supertanker port at Saint-Jouin-Bruneval (/// revel. oversell.shopkeepers), 8km from Étretat Beach and 5km further on from Pisseuses de Valaine. The long sea wall protecting the port signals that it's time to turn around. There's a small, sheltered beach at Saint-Jouin-Bruneval. If you're ready to head back, turn around and paddle back the way you came, hugging the coast to get the best views of the rock formations. As you paddle back from Saint-Jouin-Bruneval, keep your eyes skyward. On the left-hand side of Étretat Beach (as seen from the sea) is the Notre-Dame-de-la-Garde Chapel (/// improperly.unshaved. tenants), peering over the cliff edge. It's as pretty as a picture but, although it was built in 1854, before any of Monet's visits, it never made it into one of his paintings.

Once you arrive at Aval Cliff you'll be able to see Amont Cliff framing the other side of Étretat Beach directly in front of you. It's quickest to cut a straight line across the bay (northeast) to reach it. After exploring Amont Cliff, paddle back to the beach, which is clearly visible.

↑ Monet used to row out to paint Étretat from the water (Voiles et Galets d'Étretat)

ESSENTIALS

GETTING THERE Étretat is in northern France and easily accessible from the UK. Direct ferries run between Dieppe and Newhaven daily, and from Dieppe it's only 1½ hours by road to Étretat. Brittany Ferries used to run a direct line between Portsmouth and Le Havre (30 minutes by road from Étretat) and talks of reinstating the line have been underway for years, but at the time of writing there was no conclusive date for this.

The closest **train** station is in Le Havre (buses run from here to Étretat), and direct buses also run between Paris and Étretat, taking approximately 4 hours. If you're not travelling with a car, staying in Le Havre can be a good option as the choice of accommodation and restaurants here is far superior (and significantly cheaper) than in Étretat.

For drivers, the most conveniently located car park in Étretat is at place Victor Hugo (/// obviously.laughable.ghosted), but you'll be lucky to get a bay. There is also a car park at the train station, but ideally avoid bringing a car during peak season or aim to arrive early in the day (before 09.00).

HIRE & LESSONS Voiles et Galets (17 rue Adolphe Boissaye, 76790 Étretat /// relieves.dataset.lung ⊘ voilesetgalets.com ◷ Apr–Oct) hires paddleboards and double and single kayaks, and offers guided trips and lessons.

WHEN TO GO If you don't have your own kayak or paddleboard, make sure that you go in season (Apr–Oct) as hire shops are closed during the winter months. Even if you do have your own equipment, be aware that lifeguards don't patrol the beach during the winter and the likelihood of high winds and inclement conditions is higher.

↑ Taking to the water at Étretat allows you to escape the crowds (Runhart Fotografie/S)

Étretat is enormously popular during the school holidays and it seems that every tour bus for miles around descends on the small town during the day. Shoulder season (Apr– Jun and Sep–Oct) is calmer, particularly on weekdays, but arriving early is still advisable to secure parking.

WHERE TO STAY & EAT Hôtel **Dormy House** (⊘ dormy-house.com) in Étretat town centre has sea views from the garden and one of the best restaurants in the area. For cheaper accommodation with convenient transport links, opt to stay in Le Havre, 30 minutes away by car. **Hôtel Vent d'Ouest** (⊘ ventdouest.fr) is decked out like an old mariner's treasure trove – perfect for tired kayakers who've spent all day on the water. For hearty, unpretentious dishes in the centre of Étretat, **La Flottille** (⊘ restaurant-laflotille.fr) is a guaranteed belly filler, or pack a picnic from the selection of sandwiches and impossibly large cakes at **Le Petit Accent bakery** (◙ @lepetitaccent).

TITBITS Take trainers and go for a walk after you get off the water. The summits of Aval and Amont cliffs, either side of Étretat beach, will give the best views, but after the peace and tranquillity on the water they may feel hellishly busy. Note that as an area hard hit by coastal erosion, it's forbidden to take pebbles home as souvenirs as these act as a natural defence against the sea.

If you're looking for a culture fix, head to the modern art galleries in Le Havre. Don't judge the city on its concrete façade: the arts scene is booming, particularly during Un Été au Havre, the open-air art exhibition, which runs from late June to mid-September.

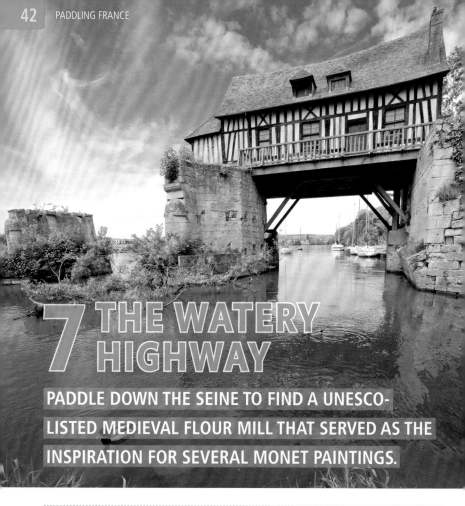

7 THE WATERY HIGHWAY

PADDLE DOWN THE SEINE TO FIND A UNESCO-LISTED MEDIEVAL FLOUR MILL THAT SERVED AS THE INSPIRATION FOR SEVERAL MONET PAINTINGS.

WHERE	Vernon, Normandy
STATS	16km round trip 🏃 🛶 ③
START/FINISH	Auberge les Canisses, 1 chemin du Halage de la Gare, 27600 Saint-Pierre-la-Garenne /// huddle.iodine.meaty

The Seine has been a working river for centuries, and the bridges that now mostly hold roads and railway tracks would have once been peppered with mills that harnessed the power of the water to turn their vast wheels. The 16th-century Old Mill of Vernon (Le Vieux-Moulin de Vernon) was used to grind flour before being abandoned in the mid 17th century when a flood made the structure too unsafe to use. It lay empty for the next couple of hundred years, during which time, in 1860, a new bridge was built further upstream. Amazingly, the Old Mill of Vernon outlasted the new bridge, which was blown up and rebuilt several times during the Franco-Prussian War before being completely destroyed towards the end of World War II, in

↑ Little of the original bridge over the Seine remains, but the Old Mill of Vernon has been standing for over 500 years (andre quinou/S)

1944. By this point, the Old Mill of Vernon had also suffered significant damage, but was still (just) standing. The local people rallied together to save the building, which they saw as an important part of their cultural heritage, not least because it had been immortalised several times by Claude Monet, who had lived just 5km further away at Giverny.

Starting from the waterside hotel-restaurant Auberge les Canisses, this paddle heads upriver (southeast), following a busy railway line, getting steadily more urban as it goes. It culminates in Vernon, now a busy commuter town, with a history that goes all the way back to prehistoric times, although it's best known for the old mill, which straddles the river. The return route edges the northern bank of the river as you paddle downstream, past a delightfully varied mix of groomed, waterside gardens and small châteaux, and river islands so thick with foliage they look positively Amazonian.

I recommend taking strong insect repellent for this route – I was nibbled to shreds by horseflies. You can paddle this route in either direction, but I prefer anti-clockwise as you save the nicest views for the second half. A paddleboard is better than a kayak here as you get views over the riverbank, which from the water level would be difficult.

There is a fair amount of pond weed in patches, but it's not enough to slow your progress or be much of a menace; you might just find that you have to unclog your fin fairly often. I'd still recommend going for a decent-sized, rigid fin over a flexi-fin as the river is very deep so you don't need to worry about it snagging on the bed.

PADDLE THIS WAY

Leaving Auberge les Canisses (/// huddle.iodine.meaty), turn your board to your right with the hotel behind you. You're going to be beginning by paddling upriver along the River Seine. Although it's one of the biggest rivers in France, it's not particularly fast-moving, so you shouldn't notice the current against you very much. What will affect you more is if it's a windy day: it's a wide river and most of the buildings along it are low, which – coupled with relatively flat ground – means the wind has plenty of space to gather speed.

You'll notice that you're following the railway track at first; it's interesting to see the trains speeding past on their way to Paris, as they do rather frequently. The road also runs parallel, a long, straight road that runs all the way from Auberge les Canisses to Vernon; as a result, this route feels like a distinctly urban SUP safari. In the middle of the river, starting from just after Auberge les Canisses, are a series of three islands: Île Emien, Île Chouquet and Île de la Madeleine, with only a narrow channel of water dividing each. They're so thickly caked in impenetrable plants that they look like giant bramble patches and completely obscure the northern bank, and they're on your left for over half the time you're paddling upstream. As you leave the last of the three, Île de la Madeleine (/// crystal.factory.teaches), to your left, behind you, the river widens further still.

On the approach to Vernon there's lots of old factory buildings. Many of them have been abandoned, and some have been made to look less bleak with colourful wall murals (/// suppose.gazette.casino). When you can see the town's large bridge cutting across the river ahead, look over to the left bank and you'll see the Old Mill of Vernon (/// deciding.bride.persuade); you can cut straight across the river to reach it (checking for other river traffic first, of course).

It's possible to paddle right underneath the mill, which is a very novel experience. Unsurprisingly, it's one of the most photographed sights in the area; it was built in the 16th century on top of a bridge that once crossed the Seine, which is thought to have been built as early as the 12th century. The mill looks wonky, almost tipsy, straddling the water on unstable-looking, rather dumpy, dark wood legs. Immediately on the other side of the mill is a pontoon with yachts and a large, green park, ideal if you want to have a break.

From here, head back under the mill and downriver. The current is very subtly with you here but, as I said earlier, wind direction and speed counts for more. Ignore the first little channel off to the right, which is usually dammed with trees

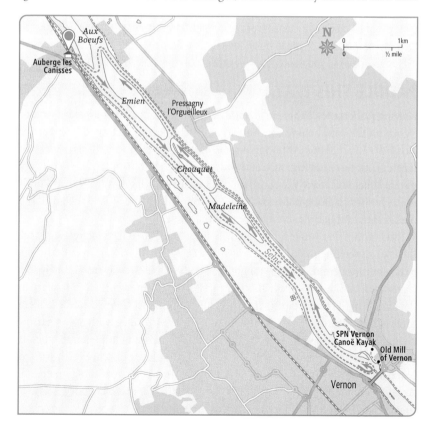

and foliage (if you do by accident paddle down it, don't worry too much as it's just a short detour before it comes out on to the Seine again). When you reach the first of the islands, keep well right. Paddling back on the right is much more pleasant than the way out; gone are the noises of passing trains and cars, and you'll pass beautifully manicured gardens on the riverbank, many of which have spinning model windmills. On your left, the islands that hide the bank you paddled up alongside are a tangle of thick foliage. After several picturesque gardens, the same wild tangle of plants dominates the riverbank on your right-hand side, too, creating the impression that you're miles from civilisation.

At the end of the second island (Île Chouquet), at Pressagny l'Orgueilleux (/// scholarship.eschew.denser), the dense foliage is replaced with a waterside château and village houses of golden stone. Paddle the length of the third and final island (Île Émien) and round it to the left (/// elated.lifeguards.distortion). Here, you're doubling back on yourself to cross the Seine through a channel between two islands, heading diagonally left across the river. Once you emerge, you need to keep heading upstream rather than downstream. You're between two leafy land bodies, Île Émien which you've just paddled past, and the southernmost tip of Île aux Boeufs, which is confusingly named as it isn't actually an island – it's attached to the bank by a narrow strip of land. Be sure to keep to the right again as you're back in the shipping lanes. As you round the headland of Île aux Boeufs, double back to go downstream, keeping it on your right. You should just about be able to see Auberge les Canisses from here, now on your left-hand side, which is your finishing point.

↑ Paddling a quiet stretch of the Seine (Coralie R./SPN Vernon Canoë Kayak)

ESSENTIALS

GETTING THERE Direct trains run between Paris and Vernon, taking under an hour. Both Vernon and Auberge les Canisses are easy to reach by road, with the D6015 going right past them. There's no public transport to Auberge les Canisses, but it's only a 10-minute taxi ride from Vernon train station.

HIRE & LESSONS SPN **Vernon Canoë Kayak** (⌀ canoekayakvernon.org) hires kayaks and paddleboards. They're just a stone's throw from the Old Mill of Vernon, so if you're just here to see the mill and don't want to do a 16km paddle, you can easily hire a board from here and hit the water for half an hour or so. If undertaking the whole route, hire your board from here and take it by car to Auberge les Canisses, the start point.

WHEN TO GO The seasonality matters much less than what the wind is doing on the day. Generally, May to September will have better weather, but since the Seine is such a wide, exposed river, strong winds can make your paddle difficult here.

WHERE TO STAY & EAT **Auberge les Canisses** (⌀ canisses.com) could not be more perfectly placed for this paddle, and this route disembarks from the hotel's own pontoon. The hotel restaurant is a little pricey, but has a lovely garden and the food is good quality. Just across the railway track, the boulangerie **Le Petrin du Goulet** sells decent sandwiches for picnic lunches.

TITBITS It would be a shame to paddle around this monument that inspired several of Monet's paintings without visiting the site of his most famous painting of all: Giverny (⌀ giverny.org). Monet's home and garden, where you can see the waterlilies for yourself, is 6km from Vernon and so kaleidoscopic in colour it could inspire even the most unartistic person to pick up a brush. It's always busy; visit early in the day to avoid day-trippers.

↑ The grassy banks near SPN Vernon Canoë Kayak make for a great picnic spot (Coralie R./SPN Vernon Canoë Kayak)

8 SEALS IN THE SOMME

NAVIGATE EVER-CHANGING CHANNELS OF WATER IN THE SOMME'S TIDAL ESTUARY, WHILE FAT SEALS SLIDE DOWN THE SANDS AMONG WADING BIRDS.

WHERE	Saint-Valéry-sur-Somme, Hauts-de-France
STATS	13km return 🚶 🏊 ④
START/FINISH	Metal slipway, 2 av du Général Leclerc, 80230 Saint-Valéry-sur-Somme /// reorder.crunched.twists

The Somme is a name that was etched into my mind from school history lessons. Before moving to France, I don't think I even knew the Somme was a river, and thought instead of muddy trenches, maimed soldiers and bloody battles. The Battle of the Somme is infamous as one of the most disastrous of World War I, seeing over a million casualties on both sides, and more than 300,000 fatalities.

Further inland, the battlefields, cemeteries and wartime memorials serve as a stark reminder of this region's tragic past. The Bay of Somme, however, looks so peaceful that it's hard to believe it was ever ravaged by war. The Somme River winds 152km a little to the southeast from the Fonsommes Hills near the Ardennes, to meet the English Channel at the Bay of the Somme. This is one of the most peaceful places in northern France, and over 300 species of migratory birds stop on the tidal estuary, as well as native ones; look out for egrets, geese, curlews, avocets, redshanks, herons and spoonbills, among many others.

Physically, this is not a challenging route, but it does require some planning and knowledge of the tides. I'd recommend it for kayakers and paddleboarders with a good level of experience; beginners should book on to a tour. Don't attempt this route in strong, offshore winds.

↑ The Bay of Somme is a haven for birdlife (Hemis/A)

I've done my best to give a comprehensive route here, but this should be used as a rough guide as the sandbanks are constantly shifting and fluctuating with the tides. It's a paddle that is best undertaken as the tide is going out, so that you come back in with the rising tide: set off approximately two hours before low tide. At the lowest point in the tide there can be very little water, so you might need to wait on a sandbank until the channels fill up again. Pack a snack and some warm layers.

PADDLE THIS WAY

Start from the launch point across the bridge from La Canoterie (/// reorder. crunched.twists). It's a steep metal slipway that gets very slippery in the rain, so watch your step. From here, paddle left towards the sea, through the lively port of Saint-Valéry-sur-Somme (/// muffled.bonded.intolerance), always full of yachts and motorboats. Directly after this, you'll begin passing the town itself (/// clogging.ratty.trivia); Saint-Valéry-sur-Somme is a funny place that looks somewhere between an English town in the Midlands and a Victorian seaside resort. It's composed of rather shabby buildings that would have been highly fashionable at the turn of the 20th century, plenty of red brick or whitewash with brightly painted half-timber.

Paddling on, the houses get grander and grander. This was where the richer merchants lived. Although most of these buildings date from the 19th century, Saint-Valéry-sur-Somme was an important port town as early as the 15th century

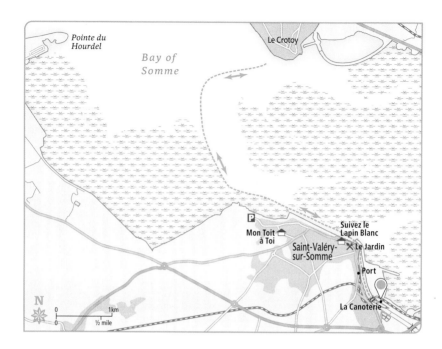

for its herring trade. Make sure you keep the dyke (/// intersect.revalue.swept) to your left, the water is deeper here and it also shelters you as you paddle – there's a big, open gravel car park that's a lovely spot for a night by the water if you choose to travel this part of France by van.

The dyke acts as a windbreak and is a great way to orientate yourself, as you can't get lost with this in your periphery the whole paddle. Continue for approximately 2km out to sea, keeping the dyke to your left, until you're two thirds of the way between Pointe du Hourdel and Saint-Valéry-sur-Somme. Look over the sand flats to your right: it's likely that you'll already be able to spot lots of wildlife. Wading birds pick their way peacefully over the muddy tidal sands, which often look slick like oil puddles, coated with what little water remains from the retreating tide. However much of a birder you are, though, the highlight has to be the seals. Common and grey seals both congregate here, beached on the gentle sandy slopes, often sliding inelegantly down to meet the water like fat, slightly fuzzy slugs. It's forbidden to approach the seals, and keeping a distance of at least 300m is recommended.

Paddle down the watery channel to your right (/// apart.forsake.supplemental), and, if you want to return with the rising tide, park up your board on a sandbank (/// occults.nursemaid.camcorder) and wait for 20 to 30 minutes for the tide to begin to rise again (this isn't obligatory, but it makes the return journey easier). As the tide begins to rise and flood the channel, paddle back the way you came, making for the dyke, which you can then follow all the way back to your start point.

ESSENTIALS

GETTING THERE Saint-Valéry-sur-Somme is 1½ hours (111km) from the Eurotunnel and ferry terminal in Calais. Public transport isn't great in this area so it's easiest to rent a car. If you are arriving by public transport, note that most local buses to Saint-Valéry-sur-Somme transfer via Abbeville.

HIRE & LESSONS La Canoterie (🌐 canoekayak-baiedesomme.fr) runs one to two guided tours per day on pirogue canoes, depending on tide times. They also have a fantastic clubhouse and restaurant.

WHEN TO GO Many places in the Bay of the Somme are closed outside of April to October. June, July and August are the best months for seal spotting (at low tide).

WHERE TO STAY & EAT Mon Toit à Toi (🌐 montoitatoi.com) has just two rooms and a beautiful courtyard garden. Quirky chambre d'hôte **Suivez le Lapin Blanc** (🌐 suivezlelapinblanc.com) has rooms themed on different movies, including *Mary Poppins* and *Laurence of Arabia*, in the centre of town. **Le Jardin** (🌐 bienvenueaujardin.fr) serves excellent seafood, salads and French dishes with a fusion twist, and has an enormous garden. Dining options are very good in town and there are many decent restaurants along the riverside walkway, which is an extremely pleasant spot.

TITBITS Hauts-de-France is the capital of *char à voile*, an enormously fun sport. Three-wheeled buggies equipped with sails are used to land sail the vast, flat beaches, and even amateurs can reach speeds of up to 60km/hour. You can try the sport through **Eolia** (🌐 eolia.info) at Fort-Mahon-Plage, a 30-minute (34km) drive from Saint-Valéry-sur-Somme. It's open all year, provided the wind conditions are right.

↑ Harbour seals are most frequently seen in the Bay of Somme, but you may spot grey seals, too
(Philippe PATERNOLLI/S)

9 ALLOTMENT ANTICS

PADDLE THROUGH THE URBAN OASIS OF AMIENS' VEGETABLE GARDENS, SPREAD ACROSS A WATERY NETWORK OF ISLANDS & CANALS.

WHERE	Amiens, Hauts-de-France
STATS	5km round trip 🚣 🛶 ②
START/FINISH	Club Nautique de Rivery, 13 Impasse Motte, 80136 Rivery
	/// splat.finest.monkey

This is a paddle that surprises you. It's almost Amazonian, with muddy-coloured, slow-moving rivers, twisted trees and tangled bramble bushes making walls of foliage so dense it's sometimes impossible to paddle down the smaller channels. Amiens is a nice enough city, with the accolade of having the largest Gothic cathedral in France (Notre-Dame d'Amiens), but as soon as you get into the *hortillonnages* (vegetable gardens), it becomes magical.

The hortillonnages are a network of criss-crossing waterways that branch off the River Somme, the large river that cuts through the centre of Amiens on its journey to the English Channel. They span 300ha with some 65km of canals, and everything looks so saturated in water as to create an illusion that the soil is bloated. The narrowest channels are barely the width of a human torso, and the largest make enormous, mud-coloured pools where – instead of hedges to separate their watery back gardens – the locals erect fences, with floating model ducks to replace scarecrows. Weeping willows trail fronds over the water, creating leafy curtains. There are hydrangeas everywhere throughout the summer, and community gardens, generally a hive of activity with dungaree-clad people of all ages mowing their lawns, digging the soil and ferrying dugout canoes from one garden to another.

↑ The hortillonnages in Amiens date back as far as medieval times (Mark Pitt Images/S)

The gardens are thoroughly lived in, a mixture of private residences, campsites, allotments and even farms (don't be surprised if you see a curious sheep peering out at you from the undergrowth!). At the waterside bistros, canoes park up like it's Henley Regatta. Closer to the Somme, the partially concealed smallholdings and country homes become like terraced houses, and there are people going about their daily chores and hanging out their laundry by the water (a warning: it's easy to accidentally set off their burglar alarms as you paddle past). It's magical, whatever the weather. I paddled this route on a grey and miserable day, but the hortillonnages themselves were far from grey and miserable – they were peaceful, colourful and utterly surprising. It was so nice I did it twice.

Here you'll see a lot of long, scull-like canoes made from dark wood, often equipped with motors, which are used for group tours. Sometimes some of the small streams are blocked with canoes like these and, at the risk of stating the obvious, this means that the waterway is closed. Respect any signs saying no entry and remember that these streams are people's back gardens. Tourism has boomed in the hortillonnages and many of the locals are extremely intolerant of trespass, however accidental.

I strongly recommend taking a phone with GPS with you, especially as many of the waterways have very little that distinguishes them, and it's extremely easy to take a wrong turn or overshoot the channel that you were looking for. For this reason I've numbered the different stops (in the text here and on the map) during the paddle to make it easier to navigate. Check What3Words regularly if in any doubt as it's difficult to get a sense of how far you've gone with no landmarks as reference points. As the route is so close to central Amiens (although it feels remote when you're on the water) the mobile signal is generally very reliable.

This route gives you a good flavour of the hortillonnages and includes the museum and riverside restaurant Ô Jardin, but don't be afraid to explore further and longer if you've got GPS – it would be easy to spend a full day paddling around these warren-like waterways. This route is well adapted to both paddleboards and kayaks, but personally I like it best for paddleboards. The rivers are fairly deep so there's no risk of snagging your fin on the bottom, and you get good views standing up.

PADDLE THIS WAY

Start from Club Nautique de Rivery (❶ /// splat.finest.monkey), which has (limited) free parking spaces just outside it, a really easy launching spot just by the metal bridge which spans the river, and a good flat tarmacked area by the water for inflating your board.

With your launch point behind you, paddle to the left for a couple of hundred metres, until you get to the first waterway (slightly wider than the one you're on), which branches out to your right (❷ /// daisy.teaching.applied). Until here, you'll have been paddling past moored canoes, but as you turn right you'll start to see flower-bedecked garden verges. At the 300m point, an even wider waterway goes to your left (❸ /// segments.monument.prepares). Follow this along fenced-off ponds that act as back gardens as the river widens and widens, admiring the garden displays as you go. It's like the Chelsea Flower Show on steroids, with elaborate scarecrows, windmills and flowerpot men.

Paddle alongside an étang (❹ /// verge.first.sprinkle), a shallow, muddy lagoon much wider than the other waterways you've paddled down, where the dense tree cover opens up so you're paddling under the sky, and then double back on yourself

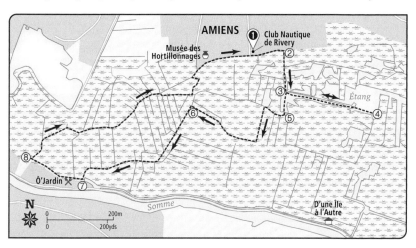

to get back to point ❸. Instead of turning right back to Rivery, turn left; the waterway almost immediately makes a sharp L-shaped turn to your right (❺ /// famines. hatter.rabble). The river gets slimmer here, but the little channels branching off to either side are skinnier still, so keep to the widest route. Eventually at a fork (❻ /// someone.revised.shirts), take a left; you should start seeing the skinny spires of Notre-Dame d'Amiens in the distance, as well as the Brutalist tower designed by concrete aficionado Auguste Perret, which vies unsuccessfully for your attention on the skyline. Keep these as reference points as you paddle – you're now heading almost directly for them. Where the waterway forks again, take a right and you'll immediately see Ô Jardin restaurant (❼ /// pebbles.retain.dynamic). This is easily the best place to eat in the hortillonnages, and it has a large, shady garden and an extensive menu; you can easily moor up your paddleboard on the jetty.

Leaving Ô Jardin, turn left and take any of the first three very narrow waterways on your right to join a wider waterway (❽ /// careless.voted.snooty). Keep following this waterway as it heads to your right. You should start seeing signs for the Musée des Hortillonnages; if not, when the river widens further, take the narrow channel directly in front of you (/// compound.caskets.zest), which will take you to the museum (/// foiled.editor.spinning). Moor up at the museum to learn about the history of the hortillonnages, traditional farming practices, and the region's biodiversity. Disembarking from here, turn left and carry on down the narrow strip of water for a few hundred metres, which will take you back to Club Nautique de Rivery.

↑ Perfect reflections on the water from Anna's SUP (Anna Richards)

ESSENTIALS

GETTING THERE Paris-Beauvais Airport is 50km away, with car hire available at the airport. Amiens is easy to reach by train from both Paris and Lille, with both journeys taking a little over an hour. From the train station, it's a 25-minute (2km) walk to Club Nautique de Rivery, which is the starting point for the paddle; Rivery is a suburb of Amiens. Coming by car, you can park at the club or, if the spaces here are full, you should be able to park on-street in Rivery.

HIRE & LESSONS Club Nautique de Rivery (⌀ hortillonnages-canoe. com ⊙ Apr–Oct) hires kayaks. Ô Jardin (⌀ o-jardin-amiens.fr) hires rowing boats that come with short paddles rather than oars, and they also organise guided trips of the hortillonnages.

WHEN TO GO The hortillonnages are colourful throughout the spring and summer, but go in the spring to see the flowers in full bloom. If you have your own board, this route can easily be paddled at any time of year, and it's even atmospheric in the rain, which adds to the Amazonian feel. From late May to mid-October annually, the Hortillonnages International Garden Festival showcases art installations on the islands on the hortillonnages, some created by local students. These can be visited on foot or by boat; for details see ⌀ visit-amiens.com.

WHERE TO STAY & EAT For a city of its size, Amiens' hotel selection is abysmal, and largely confined to international business hotels. Try to stay in the hortillonnages rather than in town. The options here are mostly *chambres d'hôtes* (bed and breakfasts): **D'une Île à l'Autre** (⌀ duneilealautre.fr) and **Au Jardin sur l'Eau** (⌀ aujardinsurleau.com) are perfectly located for paddlers.

Dishes at **Ô Jardin** (⌀ o-jardin-amiens.fr) are tasty and fresh, with plenty of vegetables. Their wine list is extensive and the garden practically spills down on to the water. Just along the river, the old *quartier*, Saint-Leu, has lots of good restaurants. Try **Le Quai** (⌀ restaurant-lequai.fr) for classic French bistro dining.

TITBITS Don't miss Amiens' immense Gothic cathedral, the largest in France. Construction of Notre-Dame d'Amiens began in the 12th century – you can climb the 300 steps up to the top of the North Tower to see the intricately carved gargoyles and spires from above.

The view towards the cathedral from the river (Alexandre.ROSA/S)

10 STARRY EYED

A PADDLE AROUND LILLE'S PENTAGONAL CITADEL PARK PROVES YOU DON'T HAVE TO LEAVE THE CITY TO ESCAPE THE CROWDS.

WHERE	Lille, Hauts-de-France
STATS	6.5km round trip 🏃🛶②
START/FINISH	Association La Deûle, 108 Quai Géry Legrand, 59000 Lille
	/// forks.twins.requested

Capital of the Chtis (the local term for people who live in Hauts-de-France), Lille must be one of the most fun places to live in the country. Sure, the weather is often distinctly British and the suburbs show clearly that this was a city built on industry, but the Lillois have turned factories into edgy places to eat and the opulent Flemish façades of the handsome old buildings glisten all the brighter under the rain.

Built on an island between the Canal de la Deûle and the Canal de la Haute-Deûle, Lille's pentagonal citadel was constructed in the 17th century to protect the city, as part of a network of fortifications that lined France's northern border with Belgium. Today, the citadel sits squarely in the middle of one of France's finest urban parks, which on a good day is full of cyclists, walkers, joggers and rollerbladers. There's a treetop obstacle course (similar to Go Ape! in the UK, but known in France as 'Accrobranche'), and a vast zoo complete with monkeys and white rhinos. This paddle takes you down a waterway off Canal de la Deûle, back up the canal, past Lille's port, and along a section of the Canal de la Haute-Deûle, skirting around the park, but you can't see the citadel from the water. What's more, if you'd like to visit the inside of the citadel you'll need to go with

↑ There is a strong paddling community in Lille (Meiqianbao/S)

your passport and visit on a Sunday afternoon, the only time it's open to the public, as the fort is now occupied by NATO.

Elsewhere in Lille, there's a thriving artisan beer scene, plenty of modern art and food markets that you could spend all day salivating over. What I wasn't expecting to find in an inland city was such a strong paddleboarding community: on a nice day you'll definitely see people on the water here and Association La Deûle, the watersports centre, is very proud to have turned out quite a few competitive paddlers who are ranked among France's best. The paddle route starts from the watersports centre, which offers canoeing, kayaking and paddleboarding, and has a large climbing wall inside. It's not just a watersports centre though, but also a charitable organisation that provides the homeless in the area with hot showers and a safe space.

Long ago, before Lille's citadel was built, the city was essentially an island, encircled by the Deûle River and its tributaries, and perhaps something of that island heritage has been retained, even though it's now the tenth biggest city in France. While paddling may not be a common form of transport for the average Lillois, it's rare to find a city centre watersports club with such a packed agenda (weather permitting, there are kayaking trips every Saturday, and members can often be seen playing kayak polo on the Canal de la Haute-Deûle). This must also be the only paddleboard club in France where, in summer and autumn, members go fruit picking on the water and return home with bags full of figs and blackberries for jam making.

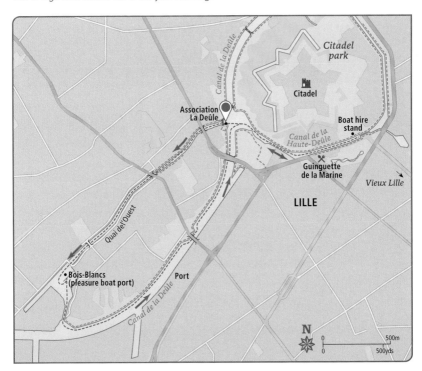

PADDLE THIS WAY

Launch from the pontoon just outside Association La Deûle (/// forks.twins. requested), which is on a waterway that bisects the Canal de la Deûle and Canal de la Haute-Deûle. With your back to the pontoon, turn left. This is one of the leafiest parts of the route, taking you past overhanging fig trees and blackberry bushes. After the second bridge (/// kitchen.herds.others), the scenery becomes more urban and the trees give way to red-brick buildings and *peniches* (barges). The Deûle and the waterways around it underwent a huge clean up about 30 years ago, following decades of heavy pollution from the textile factories that lined much of the river, plus the nearby coal mining industry at Béthune. Today, you'll still smell some factory fumes, but these are overwhelmingly pleasant: one of the old textile factories is now a coffee roasters, and the scent that wafts over the waterways is like fresh toast.

Pass under a series of small bridges (one so low that you'll need to bend double, or drop to your knees), before the sparkling, new pleasure boat port Bois-Blancs opens up to your left (/// loyal.values.drones). There are enormous peniches at mooring here, as well as lots of waterside bars and restaurants, and brand-new pontoons. This was previously a factory workers' quartier that has been rapidly gentrified over the last decade.

Keeping the pontoon on your left, paddle out to meet the main branch of the Canal de la Deûle (/// touches.pleasing.gulped), a much wider waterway than the one you've just been on, and take an immediate left. Stay on the left-hand side along this stretch of water – you'll soon see Lille's enormous port (/// economies. spinning.eyelid), stacked with Maersk shipping containers and cranes, on the right-hand bank, and it's best to steer clear of this. Just after the port, pass under a bridge, after which the left-hand bank becomes peppered with luxurious-looking new builds half masked by foliage. At the second bridge (/// brass.tangible.jumps), keep left. When you see a makeshift arena for kayak volleyball matches up ahead of you, follow the narrower waterway, Canal de la Haute-Deûle (/// depend. strongly.pavement), around to your right to skirt the outside of the citadel park. You'll see little day-hire boats and peniches as you paddle, many of which arrive from Belgium or the Netherlands. It's a very convivial atmosphere, and there are two waterside restaurants here, known as *guinguettes* (waterside watering holes, generally with restaurant services, music and dancing) and traditional in this area. Guinguette de la Marine makes a great lunch stop; it's easy to moor up at one of the iron rings on the canal wall and jump out to refuel.

From here, continue on as far as the boat hire stand (/// roaring.dates.miracle), and then turn around and paddle back the way you came. When you get back to the crossroads, take the channel directly in front of you, under a small bridge, to take you back to the pontoon at Association La Deûle.

↑ Lille's port sees lots of cargo boat traffic, so take care as you paddle (Hemis/A)

→ Lille's citadel is now used by NATO (Glenmore/S)

ESSENTIALS

GETTING THERE Eurostar runs multiple, daily direct services between London St Pancras and Lille Europe, taking just over an hour. From the Eurotunnel or Calais ferry port, Lille is a 1½ hour (115km) drive. Association La Deûle is just 3km, or a 45-minute walk, from the city centre; by public transport, the closest metro station, Bois Blancs, is a 1km (15-minute) walk away.

HIRE & LESSONS Association La Deûle (⊘ ladeule.com) hires canoes, kayaks and paddleboards and is open year-round.

WHEN TO GO Thanks to its large student population, Lille is lively any time of year, although August tends to be the quietest month as students return home for the holidays and the Lillois beat a hasty retreat to the coast. September is *braderie* (flea market) season, with Lille playing host to Europe's largest at the start of the month; this is followed later in September by a citywide beer festival. The city is in party mode, but accommodation is at a premium.

The weather in Lille is similar to southeast England, so – unless you have a good wetsuit – paddleboarding is more comfortable in the summer months, although the club is handily open year-round.

WHERE TO STAY & EAT For accommodation, **OKKO** (⌖ okkohotels.com) couldn't be more central and has complimentary tea, coffee and snacks, while **The People Lille** (⌖ thepeoplehostel.com) is a good budget option, within easy walking distance of the citadel. **Pâtisserie Meert** (⌖ meert.fr) is a Lillois institution serving waffles and other sweet treats. To try Lille's famous *carbonnade flamande*, a stew made from braised meat slow-cooked in beer, head to **L'Arrière Pays** (⌖ arrierepayslille. fr) – the rib-sticking portions are accompanied by chips that will put energy in your paddling muscles all day long. On the water, try **Guinguette de la Marine** (◘ laguinguettedelamarine), which serves regional specialities, plenty of vegan options, and fusion cuisine too.

TITBITS The **Fête Historique des Louches** (⌖ fete-des-louches.com) in early October in Comines, just outside Lille (45 minutes by bus from Lille Flandres station) literally translates as the 'ladle festival' and it originates from when a medieval lord imprisoned in his tower allegedly threw a spoon adorned with his coat of arms out of the window to alert the locals to his plight. His successful rescue is now celebrated with ladle decorating and throwing competitions, and the guzzling of enormous quantities of soup.

↓ Lille has a glowing reputation as one of the most friendly places in the country (Fortgens Photography/S)

11 THE GREAT MIGRATION

THE FLAT WATERS OF THIS LAKE IN THE HEART OF THE CHAMPAGNE REGION AREA PARADISE FOR BOTH PADDLERS & BIRDERS.

WHERE	Giffaumont-Champaubert, Champagne (Grand Est)
STATS	13km round trip 🚶② 🛶①
START/FINISH	Playa Regat'Ô, Presqu'île de Rougemer, La Folie, 51290 Giffaumont-Champaubert /// freebies.overexposed.correlation

When looking for paddling routes in Champagne, I initially drew a bit of a blank. It seemed that water was to be drunk sparingly between glasses of bubbles, rather than paddled and kayaked through. Until, that is, I discovered Der-Chantecoq Lake.

It's an artificial lake, and I must confess that I approached this with a certain amount of snobbery, which, as proved by this route and several others in the book, was completely misplaced. Der-Chantecoq Lake opened in 1974, having been in the works for a decade. The name comes from the region, Der, where the lake is located, and Chantecoq, one of three villages that were submerged to create it. At 48km², it is the largest artificial lake in France, constructed to hold excess water from the River Marne, which feeds into the Seine, to avoid the latter flooding its banks.

This paddle, which starts at the small stone beach of Playa Regat'Ô, is a little taste of what's possible on the lake and takes in the picturesque Saint-Laurent de Champaubert Church; if you're here for a few days, go exploring and launch from different spots around the lake. Most of the lake is fairly shallow, at between 4 and 7m deep, although at the deepest point it reaches 18m.

Der-Chantecoq Lake is splattered with islands. There are reeds and water lilies and, although the little towns around the water's edge have a distinctly resorty feel, this is the

↑ More than 140 species of bird call Der-Chantecoq Lake home year-round (Instantvise/S)

sort of place where you feel at one with nature. Lots of people go to Champagne for the bubbles, but others come for the birds, which are here in abundance. In particular, the lake is the site of a vast migration: from late autumn to early spring, tens of thousands of common cranes stop here as they travel between wintering grounds to the south and breeding grounds to the north. When the cranes migrate they're so numerous that the skies look like someone has enthusiastically shaken a pepper pot. The birdwatching zone (/// plates.stoves.masculinity) on the west bank of the lake is particularly good for birders.

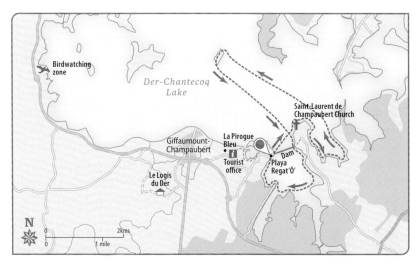

PADDLE THIS WAY

Disembark from Playa Regat'Ô (/// freebies.overexposed.correlation) and cross the dam to your left, heading across the water to the opposite bank to reach the church, Saint-Laurent de Champaubert (/// unnerve.memories.recap). Its waterside location makes the church extremely picturesque, but it was surrounded by dry land until Der-Chantecoq Lake was created. Little is known about its history, but it sat atop Champaubert, the largest of the three villages that were flooded to create the lake (the other two were Nuisement and Chantecoq), which was home to just over 200 inhabitants. A small stone wall now protects the church from the water.

Keeping the shore to your right, round the headland after Saint-Laurent de Champaubert and turn into the bay on your right (/// partygoers.handed.regard), fringed with dense reedbeds. Iridescent dragonflies skim over the water during the summer months and it's the perfect place for wildlife-spotting. Year-round, look out for white-tailed eagles, great egrets, grebes, ducks and geese. If your paddle coincides with the great crane migration, the best time to spot the birds congregating by the water's edge or taking flight above you in 'V' formation is early in the morning.

After circling the perimeter of this bay, paddle back out to the main lake and make for the island (/// tramples.toil.verve) in the middle of the water, 4km away

↑ The calm waters of the lake make it a great family paddling spot (Philippe JACQUEMIN)

to your left. It initially looks as though it is entirely covered in foliage, but as you approach you'll see a narrow channel cutting through the island, among the reedbeds. Paddle all the way through and out the other side.

Emerging from the island, the town of Giffaumount-Champaubert is straight ahead of you. Keep it to your right as you make for the mainland, and you'll arrive back by Playa Regat'Ô again. Instead of going straight back, however, cross over the dam and do a short loop in the bay, where there are some lovely, sandy beaches that you can pull up on (/// scuffled.steam.reaffirmed).

I realised after tracking this route that I'd drawn a phallic symbol. A perfect Chante-coq, if you will.

ESSENTIALS

GETTING THERE Reims-Champagne Airport (direct flights to London) is 90km away, and car hire is available at the airport. Somewhat of a public transport black hole, Der-Chantecoq Lake is nonetheless easy to access by road. It's an hour's detour (57km) from the main highway, the A26, which runs between Reims and Troyes.

HIRE & LESSONS Playa Regat'Ô (◧ regisregatostanduppaddle) is one of a number of paddleboard and kayak hire outlets on the banks of the lake, and perfectly positioned for undertaking this route. Hire spots are generally only open from April to October so, if visiting during the winter, bring your own board with you.

WHEN TO GO If you want to catch the great migration of common cranes, visit between mid-October and mid-March, but wrap up warm as the water will be much chillier at this time of year.

WHERE TO STAY & EAT Le Logis du Der (⟡ lacduder.com) is a quaint little bungalow full of character, with several self-catering rooms furnished with kitchenettes, just a short drive from the water. It's in the old town of Giffaumont-Champaubert, a picturesque little place that's much more traditional than the modern, lakeside complexes where the tourist office, casino and most of the local restaurants are found.

In Giffaumont-Champaubert's modern, lakeside complex next to the lake's tourism office there are plenty of bars and restaurants, with champagne at rock-bottom prices. **La Pirogue Bleu** (◧ lapiroguebleu) is particularly good.

TITBITS Toast your paddle with a champagne tasting (it would be rude not to when in the region). **Champagne Denis Chaput** (⟡ champagne-denischaput.com) is a family-run vineyard that offers tastings, a little under an hour south of Der-Chantecoq Lake.

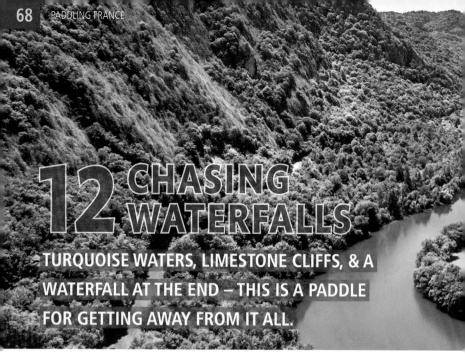

12 CHASING WATERFALLS

TURQUOISE WATERS, LIMESTONE CLIFFS, & A WATERFALL AT THE END – THIS IS A PADDLE FOR GETTING AWAY FROM IT ALL.

WHERE	Onoz, Burgundy (Bourgogne-Franche-Comté)
STATS	14km return 🚶③ 🛶②
START/FINISH	Plage de la Mercantine, 39260 Onoz
	/// kindled.censorship.therapies

The scenery in Jura always reminds me of *Jurassic Park*, and not just because this was once a land where dinosaurs roamed. It's often described as France's last wild heartland – the savage, verdant scenery here, as soon as you leave one of the little towns, is such that it feels as though you could be miles from civilisation. Which is especially curious when you think that it's in such close proximity to polished Switzerland and, from the southern edge of the region, Lyon is only an hour away.

I'd been to Jura many times before, hiking and cycling mostly, but deciding on a paddling route was a tough one, because this area has a huge number of waterfalls, many of them among the most spectacular in the country, and it was difficult to know which to choose. I decided on Cascade de la Pèle (Pèle Waterfall) because it gives you a decent arm stretch and goes through a really wild patch of river. You can't drive to the waterfall – even walking there is tricky – so by far the best way to access it is by paddleboard or kayak, and when you arrive you feel like an intrepid explorer discovering this spot for the first time.

The departure point for this route, Mercantine Beach, is basic in terms of facilities; nonetheless, this stretch of golden sand on the Ain River is a good spot to while away the afternoon, particularly after your paddle. Other than a watersports rental outlet and

↑ The River Ain, Jura – an area often described as the last 'wild' part of France (Leonid Andronov/S)

public toilets, there's nothing here except some campsites and holiday houses further up the hill; you'll need a car to get to cafés and restaurants. Once you leave Mercantine Beach there's no infrastructure until Cascade de la Pèle, so you'll need to be confident in your ability to kayak or paddleboard 14km. It's not a technical route, but prepare yourself for a considerable workout if it's windy.

PADDLE THIS WAY

Start from Mercantine Beach (/// kindled.censorship.therapies). With the beach behind you, turn left to go past several small bays. They all look as though they're going to open up into larger creeks, but none do. The craggy limestone here is almost completely covered with trees – a mixture of oak, beech and maple – and the canopy is so dense that it looks as though the cliffs are sprouting bunches of broccoli; just above the water line they stop in an almost impossibly straight line. The first landmark as you're paddling is a lone house (/// puppet.satchels.frizz)

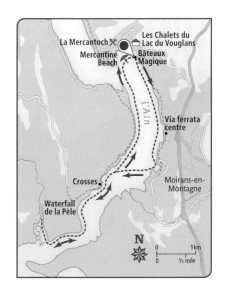

right on the top of the cliff on your left-hand side, which must have the most enviable view, and is a via ferrata centre. For easier navigation, depending on the wind direction, I recommend crossing the river to the right-hand bank here, which means you won't miss the turning to Cascade de la Pèle.

After several stony little headlands where the trees tumble down to meet the river and fallen tree trunks lie in the water like sleeping crocodiles, you'll come to a rocky headland where there's a small stone cross with a larger wooden cross in front of it (/// fishes.crown.origami). Keep paddling the same way and just under a kilometre later you'll go past the largest bay yet (/// vertical.viola.deflected); as you round another headland (/// boyish.rums.opinion) you'll have the impression that the river stops a few kilometres ahead of you, thanks to the large rock face directly in front. The rocks on the left-hand bank become increasingly devoid of trees, and they start to resemble the wider teeth on a cheese grater, with trees perched at the top.

The creek (/// anklet.bruisers.simulated) that leads to Cascade de la Pèle is just before that rock face, after the largest headland you've passed, and it's on your right-hand side. It should be obvious that all of the other creeks you've passed are dead ends as they're so short, and this is the only one you can paddle down. Round the headland, hugging it to the right and keep paddling right. You'll see blackish rocks forming a kind of semicircle on your left. As this body of water is heading in a different direction to the rest of the river you may find that the wind direction changes or varies in intensity. Jura is notorious for unpredictable weather, and since this route is less sheltered than it looks, the wind can create pretty big waves on the water when it blows strongly.

After paddling a further 500m, Cascade de la Pèle (/// informers.remakes. distinctive) towers in front of you. If you visit in summer, it's likely that there won't be much, if any, water at all. The rocks might just be slicked with small trickles of water. In winter it often freezes over.

↑ During the summer, there's little to no water in the falls (Anna Richards)

After you've taken the time to admire the waterfall, turn around and paddle back the way you came. After turning left out of the creek, pick the bank most sheltered from the wind. It's near impossible to lose your way on the return journey because you're retracing your paddle strokes, but if you reach a pleasure-boat port you've gone too far.

ESSENTIALS

GETTING THERE The closest airport is Lyon-Saint Exupéry (120km away), where there are numerous car rental outlets, and you'll need a car for this one. The nearest major train station is in Bourg-en-Bresse, from where a smaller train (taking 40 minutes) takes you to Lons-le-Saunier, where there's a **Hertz** car rental outlet (⌂ hertz.fr). Lons-le-Saunier is a 40-minute drive from Mercantine Beach. There's free parking at the top of the footpath to the beach (a stony 500m walk).

HIRE & LESSONS Bateaux Magique (⌂ location-bateaux-jura.com ⌚ mid-Jun–early Sep), which has a branch on Mercantine Beach, hires pedaloes, kayaks and paddleboards.

WHEN TO GO The prettiest time to go is in the autumn, when the foliage is russet coloured and the flame-hued trees that rise up around you make you feel as though you're in completely uncharted territory. There's also generally plenty of water spilling from the waterfall. However, hire centres are seasonal, so if visiting after early October, bring your own gear.

WHERE TO STAY & EAT Les Chalets du Lac du Vouglans (⌂ chalet-vouglans.com) is the closest accommodation, located by the car park above Mercantine Beach. It's a holiday village with cabins that can be booked on a full-board, half-board or self-catering basis. The sole restaurant near the beach is **Le Mercantoch** (⌂ le-mercantoch.fr), which sells burgers, salads and a menu heavy in meat. I recommend packing food for your paddle as it's fairly long and you won't find anywhere to buy snacks en route – but the stony beaches make for scenic picnic spots.

TITBITS Jura's 'yellow wine' is an acquired taste, but it's unique to the region. While most wine is fermented without oxygen, in Jura they allow their wine to oxygenate and a thin layer of mould forms on the surface. It makes for a wine that smells pungent, tastes fairly acidic and is golden in colour. It's best enjoyed with Comté, one of the most famous cheeses from the region. Comté and yellow wine are available from most restaurants in the area.

13 CASTLES IN THE SKY

IN THE HEART OF THE LOIRE, CHÂTEAUX TURRETS ARE REFLECTED IN THE WATER, GIVING THE IMPRESSION YOU'RE PADDLING THROUGH THE SKY.

WHERE	Saint-Dyé-sur-Loire, Loire Valley (Centre-Val de Loire)
STATS	11km one-way 🏄 🚣 ②
START	Val des Châteaux Canoë Kayak, chemin de la Croix Du Pont, 41500 Saint-Dyé-sur-Loire /// cleaned.lighted.scopes
FINISH	Loire Kayak, D951 Le Lac de Loire, 41350 Vineuil /// canyons.employ.positive

I was lured to this part of the Loire by the Château de Chambord, one of the most famous châteaux in the Loire Valley. Built on the request of François 1 in 1519, it has over a hundred turrets. Unfortunately, you can't paddle right up to that château, but this route takes you down the River Loire, past some spectacular, smaller châteaux and beautiful little villages.

At 1,020km long, the Loire is the second-longest river in France, and the longest solely in l'Hexagone (the Rhine is just over 200km longer but spans nine countries in total); I could have written an entire guide about paddling on this river alone.

The start point for this route is sleepy Saint Dyé-sur-Loire where life seems to move at a more languid pace than the river it sits alongside. Encircled by vineyards and tree-

↑ Some of the best views of privately owned châteaux are from the water (Pecold/S)

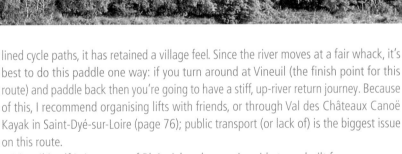

lined cycle paths, it has retained a village feel. Since the river moves at a fair whack, it's best to do this paddle one way: if you turn around at Vineuil (the finish point for this route) and paddle back then you're going to have a stiff, up-river return journey. Because of this, I recommend organising lifts with friends, or through Val des Châteaux Canoë Kayak in Saint-Dyé-sur-Loire (page 76); public transport (or lack of) is the biggest issue on this route.

Vineuil itself is just west of Blois. A handsome, riverside town built from a creamy-coloured limestone known as tuffeau, it's known for Baroque churches, a cathedral with extremely elaborate stained-glass windows… and magic. Several notable magicians lived here, including Jean-Eugène Robert-Houdin (1805–1871). Robert-Houdin, an illusionist and magician, took advantage of electricity being in its infancy – his most famous trick was with a 'light and heavy chest', where he'd ask a child to lift a chest (which they did with ease), before asking an adult male to do the same, changing the electromagnetism so that it was impossible to lift. His story, along with that of other magicians from Blois, is explored in the town's Maison de la Magie (⌀ maisondelamagie.fr) which is well worth a stop on your travels; you can paddle the 4km to Blois from Vineuil, but be aware that there's likely to be considerably more boat traffic.

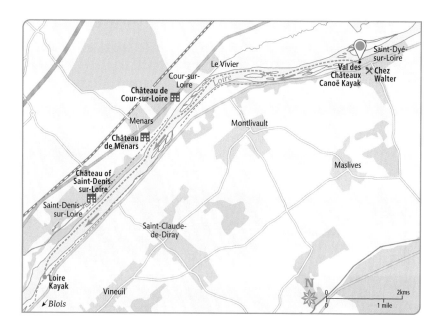

Magic isn't confined to museums in these parts; for me, it's most apparent in the reflections on the water. Although the Loire's current is powerful here, the river surface on a clear day is as smooth and untroubled as a mirror, and the châteaux you pass reflect off the water with such clarity that you could be looking at their double in a looking glass. There are several châteaux on this route, many of which are in private ownership, meaning the best way to snoop is from the water. The Château of Saint-Denis-sur-Loire (⌖ saintdenissurloire.com) is my favourite, and one of the few that is open to the public, although only on certain days during the summer. It's a UNESCO-listed building and the vaulted ceiling of the old church has some lovely paintings.

There are numerous sandy beaches that you can stop at en route to picnic or take a dip. A local man assured me that these were nudist beaches, but to the best of my knowledge, they're not officially, and I saw only one nudist during my paddle – the man in question himself.

PADDLE THIS WAY

The Val des Châteaux Canoë Kayak in Saint-Dyé-sur-Loire (/// cleaned.lighted. scopes) is an easy launch point. Keep left of the numerous small, sandy islands right at the start, where the water is deeper. After 2.5km, take the widest channel (/// apron.unforgiving.liquidation) that cuts between two islands, a little way before Cour-sur-Loire. There are numerous sandy beaches where you can stop to picnic or take a dip.

The river curves to your left and goes past the small agglomerations of Le Vivier and Cour-sur-Loire. A shallow island of trees and sand lies between Le Vivier, Cour-sur-Loire and your paddling route which skirts the southern bank of the river. At Cour-sur-Loire, you'll see a spindly church spire poking through the trees, and the slate roof of the Château de Cour-sur-Loire, built in the 15th century (open to the public with prior reservation only). However, the first really impressive château (/// ignorance.scuffled.interference) is 5km into your route, on the right-hand bank, in the town of Menars. I recommend hugging the right-hand bank from here because you'll get a much better view of the waterside châteaux. The Château de Menars was built between the late 17th and early 18th centuries, and has a creamy façade and slate roof. Originally, it boasted 400ha of forested land and was a major hunting ground; now much smaller, it's in private ownership so can't be visited, but that doesn't stop you from having a nosy from the water. In particular, you'll get a great view of the beautifully manicured gardens, which spill down towards the Loire and are decorated with water fountains.

A further 3km on, you'll pass the town of Saint-Denis-sur-Loire on your right. The Loire has over 3,000 châteaux, and the Château of Saint-Denis-sur-Loire (/// dodges.vest.that), also on your right, is even more impressive than the previous one. Equipped with a little arched aqueduct, it was built in a medieval classical style in the 14th century. The landscaped gardens, complete with a moat, separate the château from the river, but the slate-topped turrets are still easily visible from your board.

The final 2km to reach Vineuil are largely rural. Disembark at Loire Kayak (/// canyons.employ.positive), at a stony beach on your left-hand side. Look for a curious pavilion that looks like a circus tent but is in fact a restaurant, which is just behind Loire Kayak's modest cabin, or for the rows of kayaks on the beach. There's a swimming pool and campsite here too, ample parking, and often several food trucks.

↑ Saint-Dyé-sur-Loire (Philippe DEVANNE/S)

ESSENTIALS

GETTING THERE Tours Val de Loire airport has direct flights to London Stansted and is a 77km drive from the paddle start point (rental available at the airport). The closest major train station to Saint-Dyé-sur-Loire is in Orléans (52km/50 minutes away by road), but Blois (16km/15 minutes by road) has local TER links. The D951 between Orléans and Blois passes through Saint-Dyé-sur-Loire. A long, inefficient bus route links Blois and Saint-Dyé-sur-Loire, but it's best to hire a car (**Europcar** has outlets in both Blois and Orléans ⌀ europcar.fr). There's plenty of parking both at the start and the end of the route.

HIRE & LESSONS **Val des Châteaux Canoë Kayak** (⌀ vcck41.com ☺ Jun–Aug) hires canoes and kayaks and will pick you up at the end of the route if you hire with them. They can also suggest a number of itineraries, ranging from 5 to 30km

WHEN TO GO If not equipped with your own board, it's best to go during the summer when the watersports centres are open. Otherwise, in spring Château de Chambord is less crowded and the water levels in the Loire are higher.

↑ The château of Saint-Denis-sur-Loire with the village behind (Hervé Lenain/A)

WHERE TO STAY & EAT There's one luxury hotel in Saint-Dyé-sur-Loire – and not dissimilar to the châteaux you've paddled past. **Manoir Bel Air** (⌂ manoirbelair.com) has gorgeous river views, particularly from their on-site restaurant. Blois, 4km from the end point, has a huge choice of accommodation. **Le Clos des Péziers** (⌂ le-clos-des-peziers.com), in the countryside near Vineuil, is a 17th-century mansion with beautiful rooms. There are plenty of campsites along the banks of the Loire, including upmarket **Camping Sandaya Château des Marais** (⌂ sandaya.fr). In Saint-Dyé-sur-Loire, eat at **Chez Walter** (f Chez.Walter.41), which has a great-value three-course set lunch menu.

TITBITS Definitely make time to visit some of the Loire's châteaux on foot while you're here. Undoubtedly one of the most famous is the graceful – and unmissable – **Château de Chambord** (⌂ chambord.org), a 5km drive from Saint Dyé-sur-Loire. If staying in Blois, don't miss the **Château Royal de Blois** (⌂ chateaudeblois.fr). It may have fewer turrets than Chambord, but the stone façades are intricate beyond belief.

14 A ROYAL PADDLE

ZIGZAG THROUGH THE ARCHES OF A CHÂTEAU SPANNING THE RIVER CHER ON ONE OF THE PRETTIEST ROUTES IN THE COUNTRY.

WHERE	Francueil, Loire Valley (Centre-Val de Loire)
STATS	5km return 🧍②🛶①
START/FINISH	Car park/Canoë Kayak Chenonceaux, 37150 Francueil
	/// gobbled.tucking.greens

The king and queen of paddles, and one of the most photographed routes in the country, this trip takes you right under the vaulted arches of the majestic Château de Chenonceau. Unsurprisingly, this is a popular route, so you can get a lot of boat traffic: small motorboats, kayaks, canoes and paddleboards. The best way to avoid this is to go at either sunrise or sunset. Sunrise is particularly spectacular, as hot-air balloons often fly over this part of the river, and if you're lucky you might get low morning mist that clings to the surface of the water and gives the château a mystical feel. Sunset doesn't disappoint either, and at golden hour the last rays of light dance off the slate turrets and diamond-shaped glass panelling of Chenonceau's windows.

As I set off paddling this route, at approximately 6pm on one of the longest days of the year, I felt as though I had all the time in the world. That was probably quite a misguided idea, given the sun would set four hours later, but it's not a long paddle and there's something about this place that makes you feel as leisurely and languid as the part of the River Cher you're paddling.

↑ Chenonceau became known as the Ladies' Castle in hommage to the number of women who influenced its design (prosign/S)

Chenonceau is open to visitors daily all year round, except for a few public holidays. It was built in the 16th century on the site of an old mill, and Diane de Poitiers and Catherine de' Medici were among the famous women to contribute to its expansion, earning it the nickname 'Ladies Castle'. Although from my thoroughly unbiased opinion I'd say the best views are from the water, the gardens with their ornamental mazes, rose bushes and fountains are certainly worth a look. Inside, the wide, tiled hallways, wood panelling, portraits and colourful upholstery make a feast for the eyes. A high wall divides the gardens from the water, so rather than mooring up your paddle to visit, I'd recommend driving or walking there once you get off the water. As the crow flies it's only a couple of hundred metres from your launch point, but it's a 3km walk via Pont des Chisseaux (which you paddle under after the castle) or a 5km drive.

PADDLE THIS WAY

Launch your board facing Chenonceau from the little car park in the woods by the water (/// gobbled.tucking.greens). (If you've made a reservation with Canoë Kayak Chenonceaux, they'll meet you here with their trailer.)

Turn to your right as soon as you launch, paddling towards Chenonceau (already clearly visible directly in front of you), which spans the water only a couple of hundred metres away. The two arches on the far right of the château are reserved for motorboats, so it's better to cross the river and go under the arches on the left-hand side (/// limes.evaporating.scarfs). This is also where you'll find the most impressive architecture. There's a vast stone bridge going over the moat, which visitors cross to get to the château, and a tower that looks as though it's been pulled straight from the story of Rapunzel. The bridge reflects perfectly on the water, so take some time to zigzag under the arches on the left-hand side and in the centre. I could have stayed here for hours.

Leaving the château behind you, paddle on a kilometre further to pass under a bridge, Pont de Chisseaux (/// darkened.spur.profuse), crossed by rue de la Gare. If you're anything like me, you'll be turning around to ogle Chenonceau as you go, but you're coming back this way, so the views won't go anywhere.

ESSENTIALS

GETTING THERE Tours has an international airport (Tours Val de Loire) with direct flights to London Stansted. The closest mainline train station is Tours (30km), 40 minutes away by road, where there are several places to hire cars. A car is beneficial here, and Chenonceaux is just off the D976. Note that the car park where Canoë Kayak Chenonceaux launches from, and the starting point of this paddle route, is not gritted and the slightest rain turns it into a mud bath. It's not usually busy, so if you're driving with your own board this is the best place to park up. Also be aware that the car park is not signposted, so it's easiest to use the What3Words reference listed to find it.

HIRE & LESSONS Canoë Kayak Chenonceaux (⌂ canoekayakchenonceaux. fr ☉ Jun–Sep) hires kayaks and canoes and brings them by trailer to the paddle's starting point. Owner Morgan Bezard is a mine of information on the local area. Note that, as they're a mobile rental outlet, you should contact them in advance to reserve. There are several other kayak rental outlets in the area that may be easier if you're not travelling by car, but I can't vouch for them.

WHEN TO GO As with most watersports outlets in France, the kayak hire sites around Chenonceau are highly seasonal, usually open at best from April/May to September/October. If you've got your own board, consider coming off season to avoid the crowds.

WHERE TO STAY & EAT The best located accommodation spots are the two campsites at the far end of the paddle. **Camping Bar Restaurant de l'Écluse**

Pond weed causes a minor annoyance, just enough to clog your fin and slow you down.

After the bridge, the river curves slightly to the right and a kilometre later there are campsites on both sides, along with boat rental outlets. Disembark at the pontoon of Camping Restaurant de l'Écluse (/// eclipsing.unrestricted.pitchers) to refuel – whether it's for your morning coffee and croissant or an evening sundowner, it's a lovely stop in peaceful surroundings before you paddle back again.

On the return journey, look up at the steep walls on your right just before you reach Château de Chenonceau. Behind these is the Diane de Poitiers Garden (/// squadrons.supine.invariably), named after a French noblewoman who was the mistress of King Henri II of France during the early 16th century. She was significantly older than the king, and reputedly wooed him with her intellect; she made many changes to Chenonceau during her time here.

From here, it's only around 500m to disembark at the same spot you launched from.

(⟨⟩ campingbarrestaurantdelecluse.fr) has, as the name suggests, a bar and a restaurant, and pitches are extremely good value, especially considering the location. On the other side of the river, **Camping le Moulin Fort** (⟨⟩ lemoulinfort.com) is a little more luxurious, with a swimming pool, games room and a restaurant. If you're coming in a campervan, you can overnight in the car park at the start of the route, for free – and enjoy one of the most exquisite views in France.

TITBITS Chenonceau steals all the glory, but it's not the only château in the area located quite literally in the water. Also well worth visiting is **Château d'Azay-le-Rideau** (⟨⟩ azay-le-rideau.fr). During the 16th century, both of these châteaux belonged to François 1; Azay-le-Rideau is particularly impressive for its woodwork: the oak interiors (using wood from the Forest of Chinon) are so detailed and full of beams that they look like the inside of an old galleon.

↑ Navigating the languid waters of the River Cher (SS)

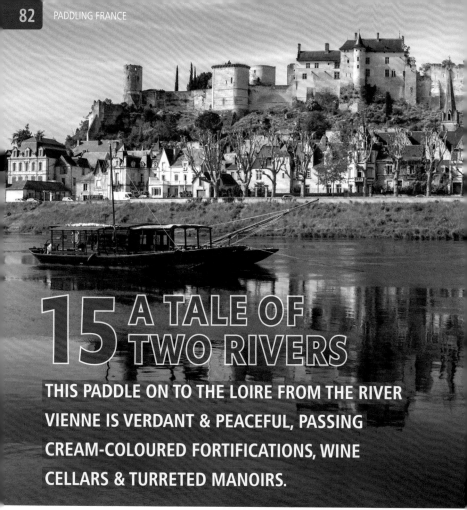

15 A TALE OF TWO RIVERS

THIS PADDLE ON TO THE LOIRE FROM THE RIVER VIENNE IS VERDANT & PEACEFUL, PASSING CREAM-COLOURED FORTIFICATIONS, WINE CELLARS & TURRETED MANOIRS.

WHERE	Chinon to Montsoreau, Loire Valley (Centre-Val de Loire)
STATS	16km one-way 🚶 🛶 ②
START	Chinon Canoë, Quai Danton, 37500 Chinon
	/// blackboard.discovers.frazzled
FINISH	Montsoreau slipway, 49730 Montsoreau
	/// tinting.chorused.sunbeams

This area reminds me of long, summer evenings with friends, the table groaning under the weight of produce we'd bought from the market, delicious scents from the barbecue permeating our nostrils. From here, and even when right up close, the Loire and Vienne look as though they move languidly, but when you're on the water, or even more so when swimming, you can feel the strong pull of the current, particularly when the Vienne merges with the Loire and gains speed.

↑ Joan of Arc met with Charles VII at Chinon's castle in the 15th century (Julen Arabaolaza/S)

This was one of only a few routes that I was lucky enough to test with a group of friends, and the memory of kayaking en masse will stay with me a long time. Regardless of whether you're in a group or not, it's a fantastic route. Technically it's not at all challenging, starting on the Vienne and finishing just after it merges with the Loire.

The route starts in Chinon, a particularly historical part of France. The town is reputed to be the place where Joan of Arc met King Charles VII of France in 1429, a meeting said to have been instrumental in encouraging the French to keep fighting during the Hundred Years' War against the English. It has also been linked to the Plantagenet dynasty, who held the English throne from 1154 (when Henry II ascended to the throne) until 1485, when Richard III was killed in battle.

That's recent history though for this area, which is also full of caves, the earliest of which date from prehistoric times. In the Middle Ages, labourers began to quarry tuffeau, a creamy coloured limestone found in this part of France, and used it to make the châteaux, manor houses and fortifications that line both the Loire and Vienne. As the labourers carved out the stone, they created yet more caves, and often labourers and their families would move into the husks they'd chiselled out. Today, many of the caves are used as wine cellars, either by big wineries or in private homes, adapted by the residents. Chinon, Candes-Saint-Martin and Montsoreau – the three main settlements passed on this route – all have caves.

The châteaux and majestic houses that you see from the river are picture-perfect and clean-looking in creamy yellow, making for an extremely scenic kayak. The other big attraction in this area is the wine, and it's particularly well known for Chenin. There's an impressive wine cellar in Chinon, Cave Monplaisir (/// reclaims.park.nests), which is under a kilometre after the start point and so large and multi-faceted it feels like a smuggler's cave. Tastings cost a pittance, although whether it's advisable to go here pre-kayaking is for you to decide. You do paddle right past it though, and it's easy enough to pull up your kayak on the bank…

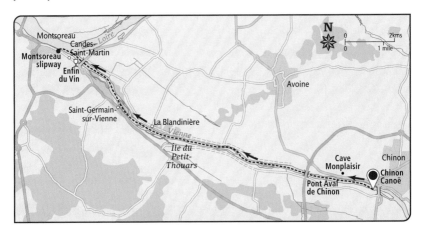

It's also worth taking the time to explore the sleepy town of Montsoreau at the end of the route; every street is so beautiful it almost catches in your throat as you try to take it all in. Window boxes spill over with flowers on the gorgeous buildings, and willows line the green walkways along the banks of the Loire. Many of the peniches (barges) look as though they're about to rot and sink into the river, but even this is picturesque. Montsoreau has a fantastic weekly market on Sundays, but other than that food options are fairly limited (particularly for vegetarians), although the bakery is good.

The beauty of this route is that you don't see too many buildings and towns along the way; there are plenty of small villages just a stone's throw from the water but, when you're on the river, you have the impression that you're miles from anywhere. It's bookended by two seriously impressive medieval towns: Chinon at the start and Candes-Saint-Martin at the end, both constructed from the pale tuffeau stone.

Reference points on this route are largely bridges and islands but, since you're going with the river, and it runs in a reasonably straight line, it's impossible to get lost. The Vienne's current is strong here, so if you're not plagued by headwinds the water carries you along easily. Particularly in the summer months the water can get exceptionally low, however, and there may be moments when you have to alight from your paddle and walk. For this reason, it's better kayaked than tackled with a paddleboard. If using a paddleboard, use a shallow, flexible fin.

This is a one-way paddle: if hiring kayaks from Chinon Canoë they'll pick you up from Montsoreau at the end of the route, otherwise you'll need to organise lifts as – although the start and end points are just 20 minutes' drive apart – there's no public transport connecting them.

PADDLE THIS WAY

Launch from Chinon Canoë (/// blackboard.discovers.frazzled) and turn left, following the direction of the current. You're in the heart of the Loire country here, though you're paddling down the Vienne. The first landmark you'll pass, 3km after Chinon, is Pont Aval de Chinon (/// horizon.implode.bribes). This bridge is also where you lose the road that runs along the riverside, and it feels as though you've left civilisation behind.

Just under 3km further on, you'll reach the first in a series of small islands. Only the largest of the group has a name, Île du Petit-Thouars (/// moderation. deregulated.tender). Some are joined to the land on the south bank of the river or only separated from land by narrow channels, so keep right and paddle along the north bank of the Vienne for deeper waters and to stay where the current's pull is stronger.

Just before the last island, paddle past the hamlet of La Blandinière (/// laptop. unhooks.festivities) on your right, barely visible from the water, although you should be able to spot the roofs of farm buildings. A kilometre further on is

↑ Candes-Saint-Martin from the water, where the Vienne joins the Loire (Julen Arabaolaza/S)

← Many of the tuffeau caves are used to store wine, pictured here at Cave Monplaisir (SS)

slightly bigger Saint-Germain-sur-Vienne (/// routs.snuggly.caved). Continue paddling and in 3km the Vienne joins the Loire River at a road bridge just before Candes-Saint-Martin (/// loosening.banter.muddier); you'll notice your speed pick up dramatically and the water become a lot deeper. Hug the left bank as the speed of the river means you risk overshooting your end point if you're on the other side of the river. In terms of beauty, Candes-Saint-Martin arguably blows both Chinon and Montsoreau out of the water. If you have time to disembark,

ESSENTIALS

GETTING THERE The closest major train station is in Tours (47km from Chinon) with TGV services. Tours also has an airport with direct flights from London Stansted. A slower train links Chinon to Tours (48 minutes), or there are plenty of car hire outlets in Tours, including a **SIXT** (⌂ sixt.fr) in the train station itself.

HIRE & LESSONS Chinon Canoë (⌂ chinon-canoe.fr ☉ Apr–Sep) rents kayaks for one to two people and organises multi-day river trips of up to four days. They also run tours that combine wine tasting, cycling and kayaking.

WHEN TO GO The Vienne generally has more water in the spring (Apr–Jun), but there's something very special about long summer days here, even if they do see the most crowds.

↑ Montsoreau's 15th-century château was built in a mix of Gothic and Renaissance styles (Florian Fortiera/S)

wander up to the top of the hill through arched streets and visit the church, which began construction in the 12th century. Practically on the waterside, wine bar Enfin du Vin has two gardens and is an excellent pitstop for refreshment; you can pull your kayak up on the shore (/// primes.brewers.luncheon).

Back on the water, it's a further kilometre to reach the slipway in Montsoreau (/// tinting.chorused.sunbeams), where you disembark. Owing to the river speed, the final kilometre flies by.

WHERE TO STAY & EAT Dutch-run **La Closerie Saint-Martin** (⚓ lacloseriesaintmartin.fr), just outside Chinon, has five themed rooms, a courtyard garden and pretty blue shutters. In Candes-Saint-Martin, **Enfin du Vin** (⚓ enfinduvin. net) does delicious pâtés and spreads alongside its extensive wine collection.

TITBITS Alongside the various wine cellars and wine bars listed along the route, there are an abundance of châteaux and cellars offering tastings. In Chinon, **Château de la Grille** (⚓ chateau-de-la-grille.fr) is particularly scenic, or head to **Domaine Filliatreau** (⚓ domaine-filliatreau.com), just after Montsoreau, for post-paddling refreshment. There's also an excellent wine bar at **Abbaye Royale de Fontevraud** (⚓ fontevraud.fr), a 10-minute drive from Montsoreau. The abbey was founded in 1101 by a Benedictine visionary, Robert d'Arbrissel. Don't just visit for the wine, the architecture is magnificent too.

16 THROUGH THE SALT MARSHES

PADDLE THROUGH NARROW CHANNELS, PASSING THE ÎLE DE RÉ'S OYSTER FISHERMEN & SALT HARVESTERS AT WORK.

WHERE	Île de Ré, Nouvelle-Aquitaine
STATS	3km round trip 🏄 🛶 ②
START/FINISH	Les Herbiers, 17111 Loix /// consumption.panoramic.uninvolved

The Île de Ré is another haven of childhood nostalgia for me, and usually the furthest south we'd make on our family road trips. Once safely installed in our campsite, the car would be forgotten and we'd go everywhere on two wheels, hopping from beach to beach.

At under 25km long, and 5km at its widest point, it's easy to get all around the island in a day, although I recommend taking much longer to explore. Île de Ré is neither as sleepy or as seasonal as many other French islands, in part due to the bridge that links it to the mainland; some 17,000 people live here, many of whom work across the water in La Rochelle. The island quite clearly survives on tourism, but it's not without its own produce. Salt is a big one, and you'll see the salt harvesters scooping neat, white heaps in the *marais* (marshes). Oysters are the other. The bungalow shacks you'll see on narrow strips of land in the middle of the marais are actually oyster shacks, generally only open at lunchtime. There's also a thriving wine industry here, though you'll have to head inland to see the vines; salt and wine were exported by the island in exchange for rocks to build

↑ The Île de Ré produces some 3,000 tonnes of salt each year (Ivonne Wierink/S)

fortifications, most of which were constructed in the 1600s. You'll paddle around the remains of these fortifications on this route.

The Île de Ré has many beautiful beaches and port towns that make for scenic paddleboarding and kayaking, but I opted for the marais as it's what makes the island so unique. Rectangles of salt ready to be harvested, edible seaweed growing in abundance on marshy banks and a kayak so muddy it feels a little like mud larking – it may not be physically demanding, but it's still an adventure. This round trip, from an unnamed beach near Loix (follow the what3words directions listed) on the northern side of the island, takes you into the belly of the Île de Ré's salt and oyster industry, and shouldn't take more than a couple of hours to complete.

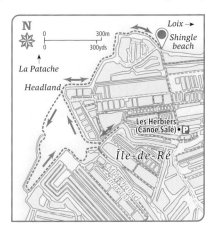

To reach the launch point, you'll be driving or walking on a road right

through the middle of the marais. Although this is an open-water route, it's in a well-sheltered bay, and it dips in and out of the tidal marshes. It's better kayaked than attempted on a paddleboard, as the water levels in the marais can be very low in some channels, and you'll be more restricted if you have a board with a fin. The seabed here is a thick, gelatinous sludge, so wear shoes that you don't mind getting dirty.

This is one of the least physical routes in the book, and an easy jaunt to do as a family, but you need to be aware of the tides and that the water level really varies in the little inlets, which means you risk getting stuck in the mud – as a result, it's a good idea to go with a guide. In addition, going with a guide means you don't have to drag your kayaks down to the beach.

PADDLE THIS WAY

Start from Les Herbiers (/// consumption.panoramic.uninvolved), a small car park near the town of Loix. This is the closest that you can park to your launch point – a 500m walk along a narrow spit of land to reach the beach.

From the little shingle beach, the leafy headland of La Patache will be facing you. Launch and turn left (west) and, keeping the shore to your left, kayak for a kilometre. At this point you'll round a little headland (/// bettered.bongos. anew). Just after this, enter the marais, inland, on your left. There aren't defining

↑ View towards Loix (christophe faugere/A)

landmarks here, so keep an eye on your GPS location – rather than shingle beaches, you're looking for muddy, marshy channels.

As you enter the marais, you'll reach a narrow channel (/// cheapens.paintball. follow) that heads east through mud banks that spill over with edible seaweed. *Salicorn* (samphire) is everywhere, and you can snack on it as you paddle around, provided that you know how to identify it. It's a fleshy green succulent, short, with multiple branches like a stubby tree, and you can collect it from late spring and throughout the summer. You can eat it raw in a salad, but it tastes better boiled or steamed and then served in butter.

After exploring here, turn your kayak around and head back west for around 300m. This is a great place to explore the labyrinthine little mud channels (/// discovering.retool.teacups), and you'll see the stone ruins of former dams and fortifications, many of which date from the 17th century. In 1627, an English fleet tried to invade the Île de Ré via Loix, led by the Duke of Buckingham. They were not successful as, having not properly researched the local tides, the English ships were left stranded in the mud when the tide went out, making them sitting ducks for the islanders to open fire on.

Exit the marais by paddling north towards open water; once free of the mud channels, hug the shoreline to your right to retrace your oarstrokes back to the beach you departed from.

ESSENTIALS

GETTING THERE The Île de Ré is connected to La Rochelle on the mainland via a toll bridge (one-off fee of €16 on the way in). La Rochelle has an international airport and excellent train links with Paris; there are several places to hire cars here. Bus line 3/3E runs between La Rochelle city centre and Île de Ré. There are cycle-hire outlets all over the island; the nearest one to this route is **Beach Bikes** (⊘ beachbikes.fr) in Loix. Île de Ré is a paradise for bicycles, with well-marked trails all over the island, which is almost entirely flat. Cars stop for bikes rather than the other way around.

HIRE & LESSONS Canoë Salé (⊘ ilederecanoe.com ⊙ Apr–Oct) runs guided trips through the marais on two-seater kayaks, lasting approximately two hours. They generally leave from Les Herbiers (/// consumption.panoramic.uninvolved), where there are a few parking spaces but I'd recommend arriving a little before your tour, because parking is extremely limited. On the southern side of the island, **Sup Evasion** (⊘ supevasion.com ⊙ Apr–Nov) rents paddleboards from the sandy beach of La Couarde-sur-Mer and also runs tours into the marais.

WHEN TO GO Île de Ré's season starts in April and usually runs to early October, although many islanders (most of whom work in La Rochelle) live here year-round. Avoid July and August if you can as this is a very popular destination for holidaying Parisians and it gets extremely busy.

WHERE TO STAY & EAT There are heaps of campsites on the Île de Ré, but if you prefer a hotel the best place to base yourself is in the fortified port town of Saint-Martin-de-Ré. **Hôtel la Jetée** (⊘ hotel-lajetee.com) has 15 rooms in the heart of town and an excellent breakfast buffet. For meals, **Madame Sardine** (🅕 RestaurantMadameSardine) has super fresh fish and *fruits de mer*, served with a view over the water. For late night dancing with sand between your toes, head to **La Pergola**, La Couarde-sur-Mer (⊘ lapergola-iledere.com).

TITBITS The battle for the best beach on the island is hotly contested, but Trousse Chemise takes some beating. It's on the north coast, on the headland of Les Portes-en-Ré, opposite Loix where you've been paddling. Although it's a popular spot, it feels undiscovered, as there's very little infrastructure and wooden boardwalks through the dunes take you to the beach. Surfers should head to Conche Beach, Lizay, which is on the northernmost point of the island, and catches some of the best swells from the Atlantic.

↑ A kayaking trip in the sheltered marais near Loix is perfect for families (Anna Richards)

17 MOUNTAINS MADE OF SAND

PADDLE OUT TO EUROPE'S LARGEST SAND DUNE, ON THE EDGE OF THE ATLANTIC.

WHERE	Dune du Pilat, Nouvelle-Aquitaine
STATS	8km round trip 🛶 ③ 🛶 ②
START/FINISH	Le Pilat Plage, avenue du Banc d'Arguin, 33115 La Teste-de-Buch /// anticipation.heartland.imbalances

Dune du Pilat is the largest sand dune in Europe, formed millions of years ago, when the Pyrenees (to the south) and the Massif Central (to the east) eroded. The sand from both was carried towards this part of the coast by river, where it was deposited, forming this giant sand dune. Just over 60km from central Bordeaux, on France's southwest coast, facing out to the Gulf of Gascony, it's an impressive landmark. Oddly enough, in spite of its size, unless you're approaching by sea you won't see the sand dune until you're almost on it, as it's surrounded by thousands of hectares of forest.

↑ The largest sand dune in Europe has fantastic sunset views out to sea (Mbgraphy/S)

Made up of 55 million cubic metres of sand, more than 100m tall and almost 3km long, Dune du Pilat has to be seen to be believed. It's more akin to something that you might expect to see in the Sahara. A bird's-eye view reveals a picture-perfect mound of sand, a bit like a giant loaf of bread, surrounded on three sides by trees, and on the fourth by the Atlantic Ocean, with another much lower sandbank, the Banc d'Arguin, acting as a shallow buffer between Pilat and the sea. When you land your paddle at Dune du Pilat, it rises above you with almost impossible steepness, looking taller than its 106m. You'll feel the burn in your legs climbing up it; if you've ever gone running on sand, you'll understand how much trickier it is – it's more like a step machine made out of sand.

This said, Dune du Pilat is under threat from coastal erosion following strong winter storms in recent years that have diminished it in both height and width. In January 2009, a storm with recorded windspeeds of 175km/hr lifted large amounts of sand from the dune. In the summer of 2022, an enormous fire raged across the forests surrounding the dune, burning thousands of acres of woodland. Homes and campsites were destroyed, and the giant sand dune smoked like a volcano. The recovery process is long, and still in progress, but the forests surrounding the dune are beginning to take shape again, once again carpeting the landscape in green.

It's difficult to say what's visually most impressive, the sheer scale of the sand dune, or the contrast it makes against the cerulean sea. The sand here is cream coloured, turning pale gold in the early morning and late afternoon light. The wind (usually present in some capacity) creates wave-like ripples on the sand. Unsurprisingly, it draws tourists from miles around, and the little towns surrounding the dune (Le Pilat Plage, Haut Pyla, and even Arcachon and La Teste-de-Buch further up the coast) have become tourist traps of over-priced cafés, hotelsand souvenir shops. Most people don't paddle to the dune though, which gives you the edge on escaping the crowds.

Navigation-wise, this is a really simple paddle. Once you can see the dune it's impossible to get lost – it comes into sight just a kilometre from your launch point. It's also a simple paddle on a flat day, but – as evidenced by this area's popularity with surfers – the seas here are often far from calm. When I did this, during the winter and in the company of a long-suffering friend, it was blowing a hoolie, and I almost lost said friend out to sea. Being on the Atlantic coast, with no land to act as a buffer against the elements between here and the Americas, the waves can get very big.

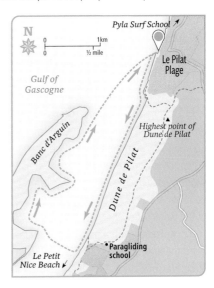

PADDLE THIS WAY

Launch from the little beach in Le Pilat Plage (/// anticipation.heartland.imbalances) at the end of avenue du Banc d'Arguin. From here, paddle to your left (south); it's a kilometre of scenic paddling before you see the dune, past villas and holiday homes largely obscured by trees. Remember to stay close to the coast. The edge of the Dune du Pilat (/// indices.reclaimed.progressed) is just after a crop of rocks, some of which have been graffitied; there are often sunbathers here escaping the crowds that congregate on the dune itself. You can beach your paddle here (navigate a few semi-submerged boulders close to shore) and climb up Dune du Pilat for the views (/// splays.sandwich.paralegal). It's 106m high, but it feels much more taxing as the sand is continually slipping and shifting under your feet; from the top you may still be able to see some of the damage the 2022 wildfire caused.

ESSENTIALS

GETTING THERE Fly or catch a train to Bordeaux. By road, Dune du Pilat is only an hour (66km) southwest of Bordeaux; take the A63 followed by the A660. There is plenty of parking near the launch point (free out of season), on avenue du Banc d'Arguin in Le Pilat Plage. Alternatively, you can take a train from Bordeaux to Arcachon (67km; 52 minutes), from where buses run to Le Pilat Plage, taking half an hour.

HIRE & LESSONS **Pyla Surf School** (⌀ pylasurfschool.com) is a family-run joint and hires stand-up paddleboards, kayaks and even giant SUPS. As the name suggests, they also run surf lessons, so – whatever the weather's doing – there's a watersport to keep you busy here.

WHEN TO GO During the winter the waves roll in, perfect for surfers but not so good for paddleboarders. I recommend sticking to the summer season here (Apr–Oct), but expect the roads to be very congested during the school holidays.

WHERE TO STAY & EAT **Villa Sunshine** (⌀ surfbiscarrosse.fr) is further down the coast from the dune, but it's well worth making the trek here for good-value, good-quality accommodation. The young owners are big surfers and full of ideas for outdoors adventures in the area. Self-catering is easy, too, as the four rooms on site share a kitchen. The owners also run their own surf school. They don't rent kayaks or paddleboards, but by taking surf lessons or hiring gear here you can still make the most of the water when the wind and waves roll in.

Dining comes with a price tag around Dune du Pilat – it's no exaggeration to say that I had the most expensive coffee of my life here. If you do decide to splash out, **Le Petit Nice Plage** (◼ Restaurant le Petit Nice), just south of Dune du Pilat and easily accessible

Run back down to launch again, and paddle to the end of the sand dune, 3km further on (/// burnt.disavows.thanks), to see it from all angles. The dune slopes more gently towards the sea here, and sparse trees create a more gradual gradient between the sand and the forest. Where the trees start to merge with the sand (you'll also see a paragliding school), turn your paddle out to sea and make for the sandbank opposite, Banc d'Arguin (/// weeknights.dinghies. abstraction), under half a kilometre away. This sandbank is continually shifting thanks to the tides and currents, but you can land and picnic on it, and enjoy a fantastic view of Dune du Pilat. From here, paddle a further 2km, all the way to the northernmost tip of Banc d'Arguin (/// twisted.passages.juke), and then head diagonally northeast towards the coast for a kilometre to return to Le Pilat Plage and your launch point.

from the water – just paddle for another kilometre after the end of the dune – is one of the more affordable choices. They serve hearty burgers, seafood platters and planches just a stone's throw from the sea.

TITBITS Sunset is the ultimate time to visit Dune du Pilat – as the Atlantic coast faces west, you can see the sun hit the sea behind the Banc d'Arguin sandbank. Take your own drinks for sundowners as the handful of cafés within walking distance come with a hefty price tag.

↑ Dune du Pilat is a popular spot for paragliding (SS)

18 PADDLING WITHOUT BORDERS

PADDLE BETWEEN FRANCE & SPAIN, EXPLORING CAVES OR SIMPLY STOPPING OFF TO DRINK SANGRIA & EAT PINTXOS.

WHERE	Txingudi Bay, Nouvelle-Aquitaine
STATS	8km round trip ③ ②; extended route 19km return ④ ③
START/FINISH	Atlantic Pirogue (inside Decathlon), 8 rue des Orangers, 64700 Hendaye /// dissolve.wiggles.rebirth

Divided by the narrow mouth of La Bidassoa River, it's impressive how different Hendaye (in France) and Hondarribia (in Spain) are. Both are Basque towns, with buildings characterised by whitewashed walls decorated with brightly painted timber beams – but this seems to be where the similarities end.

Hendaye is a surfing hub that in parts looks like a smaller, more run-down version of Biarritz, with high-rise buildings interspersed with derelict old mansions and a long, sandy beach where surfers catch breaks all year round. Surf shops are in ample supply and there are plenty of bars and restaurants, creating a decent buzz in summer, but out of season the main town feels a little forlorn, with many buildings standing empty. Outside of town, however, the hills quickly become some of the most idyllic scenery in the country. These are the foothills of the Pyrenees, so they're mostly softer than the higher mountains, with

↑ There's no border control when whizzing between France and Spain by kayak (MELBA PHOTO AGENCY/A)

verdant fields, but occasionally the slopes drop vertiginously, foreshadowing the mountain peaks just a few kilometres further back that divide the two countries.

By contrast, Hondarribia just across the border hasn't let surfing define its personality and it's altogether more lived in. Wander through the streets of Hendaye after dark out of season and it's a bit of a ghost town, whereas in Hondarribia, in classic Spanish fashion, the streets are alive. Supper time is just getting started at 22.00, children are playing in the streets, people of all ages are chatting on benches, and the sangria is free-flowing.

Strong offshore winds stopped us from paddling out to the caves on Spanish Cap du Figuier, so I've included two routes here. The first is a harbour paddle that zigzags across the French-Spanish border. This is a relaxing paddle that can have you sipping sangria in Spain one moment, and wine in France just half an hour later. The optional, extended route takes you out around the first headland in Spain, past a little island called Isla de Amuitz, to kayak in and out of caves. It goes past the long, sandy beach of Hondarribia, hugging cliffs rather than port walls. As the extended route is significantly longer and takes you out of the harbour into the open sea, it's a more challenging route. Don't attempt it in bad weather.

PADDLE THIS WAY

Kayaking outlet Atlantic Pirogue is based at the back of the large Decathlon store (/// dissolve.wiggles. rebirth); a pontoon out the back of the shop serves as the launch spot. With the store behind you, paddle straight ahead for 1.5km to reach La Caneta (/// sprays.pigment.workers), a quartier of Hendaye with its own port. There's a small island, Île des Faisans (/// emphasis.squares.curve) to your left, a blob of sand barely above the water. Make straight for the most eye-catching building on the water's edge, which is called La Maison Mauresque. It's the only one made out of exposed stone amid a sea of whitewashed houses with terracotta roofs, and has two symmetrical towers with a shorter building linking them, and a row of five vaulted windows that look like a

railway viaduct. This is the heart of La Caneta, but in spite of what the name might suggest, you're still in France here; it has had a turbulent history as a result of many conflicts between France and Spain. The ruins of an old Vauban fort are still defended by three cannons, pointed directly at Hondarribia just over the bay, and which can be seen from the water. Vauban, a 16th-century engineer and architect for Louis XIV, designed 165 forts during his career, including the UNESCO-listed 12 groups of fortifications around the French border.

The buildings are beautiful, and there are two in particular worth looking out for. The green and white Bakhar Etchea is just to the left of La Maison Mauresque; you can see it from the water, but if you want to disembark for a closer look, there's a wooden boardwalk that makes it easy to do so, and you can tie up your board here. The building isn't open to visitors, but what you can see from the outside is very pretty. Bakhar Etchea was the home of writer Pierre Loti between 1850 and 1923, and it's here that he wrote *Ramuntcho*, about a band of smugglers in the French Basque Country. La Maison Mauresque, right by the water, was formerly one of Vauban's forts. The five open vaults of the bridge-like part of La Maison Mauresque look over an inner courtyard, but since this building is now a private residence, the best views that you'll get of it are from the water.

From here it's only 400m to cross the Bidassoa and arrive in Spain. Make for the plane runway straight in front of you, a long strip of land so straight it's clearly manmade – it's the runway of San Sebastián Airport (/// topped.enhances. sticks), and you can practically feel your hair standing on end as the planes fly just overhead. Keep the runway to your left and paddle to the end of it, rounding it with the tip of the runway still on your left. Don't turn down the channel immediately after it, which leads straight to the airport. Instead, keeping the Spanish coast to your left, paddle on for another 1.5km to Portua (/// lighter. pins.reacting), Hondarribia's historic district, where you can disembark right in the middle of the town. Just after the car park, which juts out into the water, is a small beach (Pequeña; /// cook.powers.pity) where you can easily alight to explore the town and admire the architecture (read: eat tapas and drink sangria).

When you've had your fill, cut directly across the river again back to France to the Sokoburu dyke (/// desire.perform.talents), which shelters Hendaye's marina. Keep it to your left and paddle back to where you started. Alternatively, from Hondarribia you can follow the extended route, below.

EXTENDED ROUTE From Portua, paddle with Spain to your left for a further kilometre to the mouth of the river, exiting the bay into the Atlantic (/// commented.arrogant.raven). Follow the coast closely, keeping it to your left at all times, going past Hondarribia beach (/// paralegal.nightshirt.swab). Paddle a further 3km to reach the headland of Cap du Figuier (/// primly.shelters. collections). Around this headland and just around the corner to your left are numerous little caves (/// tropics.editors.disengage) that you can freely explore.

Afterwards, head back the way you came, roughly 4km, until you're back in the estuary. Another 1.5km, hugging the shore to your left along the Sokoburu dyke, takes you back on to the loop listed in the first route, and Atlantic Pirogue is on your left just after the harbour.

↑ Calm waters are great for paddling in Hendaye, but when a swell rolls in it's a surf paradise (Elisa Izco/DT)

ESSENTIALS

GETTING THERE The quickest way to get here from the UK is to fly to the Aéroport de San Sebastián, which is the runway you paddle past in Hondarribia. A small passenger ferry runs regularly between Hondarribia and Hendaye. Alternatively, travelling from Paris to Hendaye involves changing in Bordeaux.

HIRE & LESSONS Atlantic Pirogue (⌀ atlantic-pirogue.com) runs guided trips in the bay and further up the coast, and rents gear for autonomous adventures.

WHEN TO GO April to October is the best time to paddle here. While Hendaye isn't exactly dead during the winter season — because there are plenty of surfers making the most of the best swells — much of the hospitality industry shuts up shop.

WHERE TO STAY & EAT I could wax lyrical about the **Amama Baita** (⌀ amamabaita.com) for days. It might just be my favourite place to stay in France, a magical little oasis where chickens run free around the grounds and the excellent hosts cook up a different, sumptuous breakfast every day, always with a Basque twist. It's

under 10 minutes by road from Hendaye, but feels as though it's in the middle of the countryside, with a little sliver of the Atlantic visible from the top of the hill. Even if you don't paddle this route, book a stay at the Amama Baita, you won't regret it.

Hendaye has decent grub but, sorry France, Spain takes the biscuit here. Paddle over to **Bar Gran Sol** (⊘ bargransol.com) and indulge in a case of eyes bigger than stomach — there's so much to sample (all delicious) that this place warrants an over order. Note that it's so popular that even in off season you risk queuing for a long time to get a table if you arrive after 20.00.

TITBITS Château Abbadia (⊘ chateau-abbadia.fr) in Hendaye is an oddity. A turreted castle and observatory, it looks rather naff from the outside, but don't be put off — the interior is decadent. It was designed by eccentric explorer Antoine d'Abbadie in the 19th century, who collected objects, art and interior design ideas from his many travels to furnish his home. Most influential was his 11-year stint in Ethiopia, which influenced several of the rooms in the château, and much of the stained glass, tapestries and sculptures of exotic animals pay homage to his time there. A land-based activity not to be missed, and quite unlike anywhere else in the country!

↓ The last town in France before Spain, Hendaye also lies at the end of France's railway network
(Chromoprisme (null)/DT)

19 A LOT OF LIMESTONE

HEMMED IN BY LIMESTONE, A LEISURELY PADDLE ON THE RIVER LOT ALLOWS FOR STOP-OFFS AT MALBEC VINEYARDS EN ROUTE.

WHERE	Douelle, The Lot (Occitanie)
STATS	11km one-way ⚶ ② ⚓ ①
START	Nautinéa, Le Payras, 46140 Douelle /// claps.turkey.operative
FINISH	Caïx, 46140 Luzech /// prototype.splats.roses

It was late March when I paddled this route and there wasn't another soul on the water. The Lot still sees much less footfall than its neighbour, the Dordogne, making it perfect for people looking for a quiet break.

This river is like glass, still and slow moving with barely a ripple to disturb its surface, hemmed in by walls of limestone that protect it from the elements. I don't think I've ever paddled such a calm river. This is a trip to be savoured, as the river's wide meanders take you past châteaux and vineyards. While the châteaux may not rival the architectural grandeur of the Loire, there's a peace and tranquillity to this region, a kind of slow living and tourism that mimics the languid passage of the Lot itself. Even better, this is Malbec country, and the hill that I will die on is that this is the finest grape variety in the world (just don't tell the French I'm partial to the Argentinian version).

If you're going on an organised tour, book Nautinéa's paddleboard and e-bike combination. They'll meet you at your end point, Caïx Beach, and will swap your paddleboards for e-bikes to allow you to cycle back. The return cycle takes you right through the vineyards and along a green route with a bird's-eye view over the route you've just paddled. Nautinéa's base, located a kilometre north of Douelle, is also a great place to hang out, with a well-equipped semi-open-air bar and restaurant, plus spots for camping.

It's best to organise lifts with friends if doing this paddle under your own steam because, although this part of the Lot is relatively slow moving, be aware that you'll still have a tougher return paddle against the river. Regular buses run between Caïx and Douelle, so if your paddle packs down small, bussing back isn't complicated.

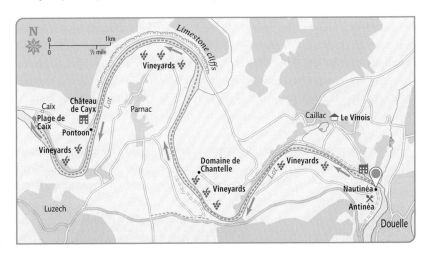

← Château de Cayx belongs to the Danish royal family (Anna Richards)

PADDLE THIS WAY

Launch from the slipway at Nautinéa (/// claps.turkey.operative); ahead you'll see a majestic turreted château on the hill. Turn to your left, and begin paddling along the river.

There aren't many major landmarks to pick out for the first 1.5kms because your surroundings are so green. The foliage tumbles down to meet the water at first and the river draws a relatively straight course, with electric blue dragonflies skimming over the water during the summer months and pond skaters dancing on the glassy surface. The trees that fringe the water's edge give the impression that you're in the middle of a forest, miles from civilisation, but just behind those trees are rows and rows of vineyards (/// curtails.tablespoons.ruined), the river meandering gradually to your left. After the second meander, which bears right, the trees thin, and on the right you can just about see Domaine de Chantelle (/// blotted. renewable.folks). They make five types of red wine (including a Malbec) and a rosé and are happy to organise tastings, just give them a ring in advance; it's easy to disembark here mid paddle.

Approximately 2km further on, dramatic limestone cliffs rise up to your right (/// adulthood.flattest.balanced), while your left-hand side is still dominated by neat rows of vines. Once you've passed the cliffs, look out for the square Château de Cayx (/// horizon.sauna.pivots) on your right-hand side, which looks like a medieval fortress, with a turret in each corner and one in the middle. Although the original building does date from the 15th century, it was all but derelict when

↑ Malbec is the best-known grape variety grown here (SS)

it was purchased by the Danish royal family in 1974, and they've spent years restoring it. The landscaped gardens, with many statues and trees, sweep down to meet the Lot, and there's a boutique on site where you can taste the wines they produce. Dock at the pontoon just after the château (/// copiers.cushioned. nominees) to visit from the water.

A final meander, a kilometre after the château and curving around to your right, takes you to the town of Caïx just after the river widens. Dock at Plage de Caïx (/// prototype.splats.roses), a long, grassy lido.

ESSENTIALS

GETTING THERE It feels remote here, but you're just 1½ hours (125km) by road from Toulouse, which has a major international airport and TGV connections. It's easy to hire a car from the airport or train station, and a car is advantageous in this area (there's ample parking at Nautinéa). If arriving by public transport, trains run from Toulouse to Cahors (1 hour 25 minutes), from where a bus leaves for Douelle (20 minutes).

HIRE & LESSONS Nautinéa (⌗ nautinea.fr ☺ Apr–Oct) in Douelle hires canoes, kayaks and paddleboards, and also organises e-bike and paddleboard trip combinations.

WHEN TO GO Visit between April and October, otherwise you'll find that there's not much open in this sleepy corner of France. Late August to early October is the prettiest time, as the vineyards that sweep down to meet the river are changing colour, with the little vine leaves curling and turning russet. Early autumn is also the *vendange* (harvest) season.

WHERE TO STAY & EAT Easily the best place in the area is **Le Vinois** (⌗ levinois.com) in Caillac, just across the river from Nautinéa (4km by road). The cosmopolitan owners travelled all around the world, living in Australia and London before falling in love with this remote French village after seeing it on a TV show, *SOS Village*, which highlights rural French towns in risk of becoming ghost towns. Le Vinois is a roaring success, with a restaurant that draws locals from miles around. The rooms are chic and modern, there's plenty of parking just across the road, and there's a small, seasonal swimming pool. **Antinéa** (⌗ antinea-lot.com), Nautinéa's beach-shack-style restaurant, dishes up rib-sticking burgers.

TITBITS There's no shortage of wine tastings in Malbec country, but it's worth leaving the countryside for a day to explore Cahors. Most people come to see the 14th-century fortified Valentré Bridge, which spans the River Lot. Of the many wine bars in town, **La Symphonie des Vins** (⌗ lasymphoniedesvins.fr) is particularly good, with sumptuous tapas spreads.

20 DILLY-DALLYING ALONG THE DORDOGNE

DRIFT PAST GOLDEN MEDIEVAL CHÂTEAUX, AMID SCENERY THAT LOOKS STRAIGHT OUT OF A FILM SET.

WHERE	Cénac-et-Saint-Julien, The Dordogne (Occitanie)
STATS	11km one-way 🧍③ 🛶②
START	Chemin des Pêcheurs, 24250 Cénac-et-Saint-Julien
	/// convoluted.barcode.swindles
FINISH	Impasse des Méraindiers, 24220 Beynac-et-Cazenac
	/// opening.jumble.predicament

This is a paddle that gets better and better as you go along, and the pièce de la resistance is the beautiful fortified town of Beynac-et-Cazenac at the end of the trip. The castle that crowns Beynac was built in the 12th century, and is one of the best preserved in the whole Dordogne. It's spectacular no matter where you view it from, but the best views are from the river approach.

The River Dordogne starts in France's Massif Central and joins the Garonne River near Bordeaux some 490km later. A region of immense importance during the Hundred Years' War, many of the châteaux that line the river are at least 800 years old – some several centuries older. Whether on land or afloat, you're voyaging through centuries of history here. On the 11km stretch between Cénac and Beynac you pass several of them, with the aforementioned Château de Beynac (which comes into view for the final couple of kilometres) the most impressive. That's not to say that the others aren't spectacular too:

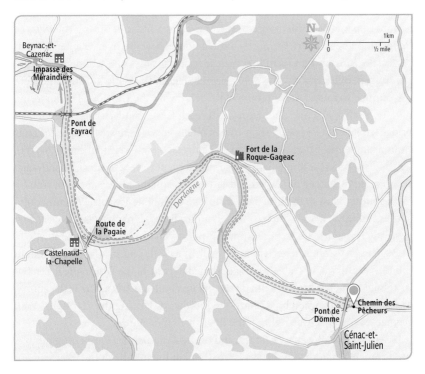

← Anna paddling towards Château de Castelnaud-la-Chapelle (Michelle Tucci Studio/michelletuccistudio.com)

from the water you'll also see the 13th-century Château de Castelnaud-la-Chapelle, which has so many layers it looks like it's built from Lego, and Fort de la Roque-Gageac, a 12th-century construction built into the caves on the cliff face.

In Cénac at the start of the paddle, the river goes really fast. You begin just before the bridge and you fly under it. As a consequence, this is definitely a one-way paddle. Organise lifts with a friend or go with a guide/public transport.

This part of the country is known, now rather controversially, for the Route de Foie Gras, a fatty liver pâté made by force-feeding ducks and geese. The markets and *épiceries* here are full of it, but luckily there are plenty of other specialities too, including truffles, walnuts and Rocamadour cheese.

PADDLE THIS WAY

Begin from chemin des Pêcheurs (/// convoluted.barcode.swindles), a dirt road by the river with plenty of free parking, just east of Pont de Domme in Cénac; it's easy to launch from the grassy bank here. Paddle to your left, or west – as soon as you begin you'll notice how strong the current is here and you'll positively whizz under Pont de Domme. The river follows a reasonably straight line for the first 3km, past arable land. Another kilometre on, it makes its first large meander past Fort de la Roque-Gageac (/// blinkers.collectively.autopilot), built into a series of caves in the ochre-coloured cliff. Dating from the 12th century, it's difficult to imagine a more impenetrable fortress, and it was used as a hideout during the Wars of Religion. Below the fort, terracotta-roofed houses line the river in a neat row, so perfect-looking and uniform that their identical façades and wooden doors are reminiscent of houses on an advent calendar. It adds to an already dramatic view.

Continue to follow the contours of the river, with the Dordogne meandering back on itself again, and after 3km you'll reach Castelnaud-la-Chapelle's arched bridge (route de la Pagaie; /// leggy.carton.intelligent). There are two small islands running under the bridge (/// pack.uncool.lodgers) – try to stay to the right of them for the fastest current. From here you get an excellent view of the angular and squat 13th-century Château de Castelnaud-la-Chapelle on the hilltop ahead of you.

It's another 2km to the little railway bridge of Pont de Fayrac (/// mannequin. aptness.bumpy); before you pass under, notice how Beynac-et-Cazenac castle is perfectly framed in its arches. From this point you can also easily see the town of Beynac-et-Cazenac itself, your end goal. The castle you see today was built in the 12th century as a strategic point designed to control the Dordogne River, but it's thought that the first castrum on the hill was built as early as the 11th century, and was once occupied by Richard the Lionheart. During the 100 Years' War, Beynac-et-Cazenac was right on the English-French border.

Disembark on the slipway at the end of rue de la Balme (/// opening.jumble. predicament), before you reach a large island in the middle of the river.

↑ The Dordogne is a popular spot for watersports (Antoine2K/S)

→ Anna paddling the Dordogne on a cold winter's day (Michelle Tucci Studio/michelletuccistudio.com)

↓ Beynac's château dates from the 12th century (rui vale sousa/S)

ESSENTIALS

GETTING THERE The easiest way to reach the region is to fly or get the train to Bordeaux and then rent a car to explore. From Bordeaux, it's a good 2½ hours of driving to reach Cénac-et-Saint-Julien, but this is a region which was made for road tripping, with every medieval town prettier than the last. There's a large car park at the starting point (campervanners often spend the night here). This is a linear route, so you'll need to organise lifts with friends. A bus does run between Beynac-et-Cazenac and Cénac, but it makes several detours and takes 40 minutes to cover what would be just 15 minutes by car.

HIRE & LESSONS SUP Perigord (⏁ sup-perigord.com ☉ Apr–Oct) organises paddleboard descents (guided or independently) of the Dordogne, including this section, with lifts back to base included.

WHEN TO GO April to October is the best time to explore the Dordogne, particularly as it's difficult to hire paddleboards and kayaks for the rest of the year and daytime temperatures in the depths of winter hover barely above freezing. Even in the height of summer, it doesn't take a big detour to avoid the crowds.

WHERE TO STAY & EAT La Treille Périgord (⏁ latreille-perigord.com) in Cénac is a hotel that looks like it hasn't changed in years, and that's all part of the charm in the historic Dordogne. It's under 5km from the paddle start point, on the north bank of the river, and the waterside views are hard to beat.

It's probably a sacrilege to recommend a Thai restaurant on the Route de Foie Gras, but hear me out. **Sawadee** (⏁ restaurant-thai-dordogne.com) is incredible, and it's right by the launch point. Portions are extremely generous, and service is with a smile. Can't wait to get back to base for your feed? **La Petite Tonnelle** (⏁ la-petite-tonnelle.fr) is a much more traditional choice in Beynac-et-Cazenac, with local produce like duck and boletus mushrooms featuring heavily on the regularly changing menu.

TITBITS After finishing the paddle in Beynac, stick around for the evening and climb up to the castle after dark. The floodlit narrow streets are enchanting, like something out of a Brothers Grimm fairy tale. Don't miss the **Château des Milandes** (⏁ milandes. com), less than 5km further down the river from Beynac. Châteaux may be more common than unhappy geese in this area, but Milandes is unique. Built in the 15th century, when many of the châteaux around here were austere, functional and made to be impenetrable, Château des Milandes was built to be light and aesthetic. In the 1960s, the famous cabaret dancer, actress and singer Josephine Baker lived here, and these days Milandes hosts art exhibitions and birds of prey flying demonstrations.

21 CATALAN COLLIOURE

PADDLE AMID BRIGHTLY COLOURED WOODEN BOATS NEAR AN ANCHOVY FISHING PORT TURNED ARTISTS' PARADISE.

WHERE Collioure, Languedoc (Occitanie)
STATS free paddle 🧍‍♂️🏄‍♂️ ①
START/FINISH Collioure Beach (Platja de Cotlliure), 1 boulevard du Boramar, 66190 Collioure /// oceans.indented.trails

---

My first visit to Collioure was aged 20, during my first experience of living in France when I au paired for a Parisian family who had a holiday home just down the coast at Sainte-Marie-la-Mer. So many things about that summer were magical. Other than looking after the kids and giving them the odd, very rudimentary English class, all I did was eat and swim and go for trips on their motorboat. But my favourite trips were to Collioure's Sunday market.

We'd get up before sunrise and arrive in Collioure Bay just as the market was setting up, bringing the boat through the narrow harbour wall to be greeted by rows of brightly coloured Catalan fishing boats. By this point we'd be ravenous and in need of a pain au chocolat and a croissant each, and the ones they served at the market were as big as saucers. Then we'd potter and swim and potter some more and swim some more before cruising home at sunset, salt-covered and sun drenched.

↑ View of Collioure from the water (Travelling-light/DT)

Collioure appears on records as early as the 7th century, but the oldest building still standing is the waterside castle that sits between the town's two beaches, Collioure and Porte d'Avall, and dates from the 13th century. Until the Treaty of the Pyrenees in 1659, this part of France was Catalonia, a separate nation comprising of parts of modern-day Languedoc-Roussillon and northeastern Spain. The Catalan pride is still evident to this day – in the road signs (all in Catalan as well as French) and the red-and-yellow striped Catalan flag that seems to be hung or pasted on every available space.

Tourism is now the town's lifeblood, and during the summer holidays the population swells from around only 2,500 inhabitants to more than 15,000. It wasn't always the way – during the 19th century and the first half of the 20th century, Collioure was a thriving fishing port, principally for anchovies, which were then salted at large salting plants in town. You'll still see Catalan fishing boats in the town's harbour – these *barques catalanes* once made up a fleet of 350 or so used for anchovy fishing. In the 1960s and 70s, overfishing meant that anchovies all but disappeared from these waters, and the fishing trade collapsed. The barques catalanes were left to fall into a state of disrepair, and by the turn of the millennium there were only around ten of the boats

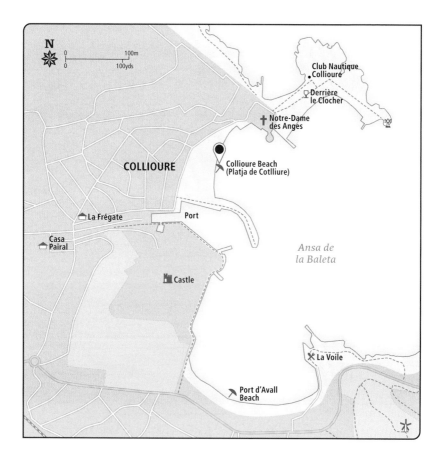

left. Thanks to the efforts of local boatbuilders, the last 20 years have seen more and more beautifully restored barques catalanes take to the water again, although now they're used for leisure rather than fishing.

Returning for this book, Collioure was exactly as I remembered it – the windmill on the hill, the brightly coloured artists' residences, the anchovy shops – with the exception that, paddling in early April, I was battered by the mistral, a fierce wind that made paddling complicated. Most of the time, however, the harbour walls protect the bay, sheltering it from the worst of the elements.

I've kept this as a free paddle, partly because it mimics the languid days I used to experience in Collioure, with nowhere to be and nothing to do, but also because the coast, flanked by the foothills of the Pyrenees, makes for a stunning paddle should you wish to go further. When you've had enough, and are back on shore, take the short hike up to the old windmill, eat sardines in the cobbled streets, and dip into each and every art gallery. I hope that you find it as magical as I did, aged 20 and living abroad for the very first time.

PADDLE THIS WAY

The most practical place to launch from is the main beach, Collioure (/// oceans.indented.trails). To your left is the much-photographed tower of Notre-Dame des Anges Church (/// accented.restructure.ovation), which was once a lighthouse; it's now a Catholic church, with an interior that's decadently decorated in gold leaf. On the little beach (accessible from the water) behind the bell tower is one of the finest bars in town, Derrière le Clocher (/// primers.aquarium.tightly). Just after is a small lighthouse (/// outdoing.chips.sultans), which can also be reached from the water or via a stone walkway along the wall from the church.

Collioure's bay is less than 500m across, so it's an easy paddle over to the other side, where luxury hotels look down over a section of the bay named, Ansa de la Baleta (/// bustled.unrelated.graciously; interestingly, *anse* is usually used in French to refer to a creek). On the little strip of land by La Voile restaurant, tangled strings of fishing nets and buoys are a reminder of the town's proud fishing heritage.

Port d'Avall Beach (/// crumbs.pricked.painful) is a long, sandy stretch of beach lined with palm trees, restaurants, boutiques and galleries, 500m south of Collioure Beach. From here, you can follow the stone wall of the castle on your left to arrive in Collioure's little port (/// tattoos.suppertime.unless). At berth are brightly coloured red-and-yellow barques catalanes, masts angled like jaunty berets.

↑ The harbour wall protects Collioure's bay from the elements (Hervé DONNEZAN/A)

ESSENTIALS

GETTING THERE The closest major transport hub is Perpignan, which has international flights to various airports in the UK, and direct TGV trains from Paris (5 hours). From here it's just half an hour (30km) to Collioure by road, or 20 minutes by train. Parking in town is tricky and expensive. If coming by car, it's often a good idea to book a parking space at your hotel in advance, but be aware that the costs can be eyewatering.

HIRE & LESSONS Club Nautique Collioure (⊘ ecole-de-voile-collioure.fr) rents paddleboards, giant paddleboards, canoes and kayaks by the hour, half day or day.

WHEN TO GO May and June are lovely months to visit, before the hordes of summer holiday tourists descend. September is also much quieter.

WHERE TO STAY & EAT There are many hotels in Collioure, but my favourite is **Casa Païral** (⊘ hotel-casa-pairal.com). It's inside an old anchovy salting factory, but you'd never guess that from the vibrant, beautifully furnished rooms, and the courtyard garden that looks more like a Moroccan riad than a French hotel. The pool is overhung with wisteria – simply idyllic. **La Frégate** (⊘ fregate-collioure.com) has laid-back dining, a menu heavy in tapas and a pretty mosaic-tiled ceiling. **Derrière le Clocher** (☉ derriereleclocher), the beach bar behind Collioure's iconic belltower, is an unmissable paddling pitstop.

TITBITS Don't leave Collioure without trying the anchovies. Although they are no longer fished from the town itself, there's still a long-standing tradition of salting them here, a process that takes around six months, with the anchovies laid out in neat spirals between layers of salt and compressed in barrels. The most famous anchovy company in town is **Anchois Roque** (⊘ anchois-roque.com), which has several outlets and was first established in 1870.

↓ The brightly coloured boats you will see in the harbour were once used to fish anchovies (Irina Papoyan/DT)

22 THE HERCULEAN WAY

FOLLOW THE OLD ROMAN WINE ROUTE TO MILLENNIA-OLD AQUEDUCTS & THE IMPOSING HILLTOP CATHEDRAL OF SAINT-NAZAIRE.

WHERE	Béziers, Languedoc (Occitanie)
STATS	6km return 🚶② 🛶①
START/FINISH	Ancien Moulin de Bagnols, 37 route de Murviel, 34500 Béziers
	/// vegans.human.searches

Research shows that Béziers dates from 575BC, making it one of the oldest cities in the country. It looks old, too. A vast stone aqueduct is one of several bridges that link the old town, perched on top of a hill as if in a kingdom from a fantasy novel, with the outside world. The bridge is so worn and pockmarked that you can practically sense the millions of feet, hooves and wheels that have traversed it over the centuries. As you climb the hill to the Cathedral of Saint-Nazaire, which is situated squarely in the centre of the old town and dominates the skyline (the cathedral took almost 200 years to build and has a 48m-high tower), steep staircases and higgledy-piggledy cobbles create the layered effect of a city that has been added to bit by bit over the ages, like a patchwork quilt.

The city really rose to importance under the Romans, when wine was transported all the way from Béziers to Rome along a route which has become known as the Herculean Way. Archaeologists found earthenware *dolias* (pots used for storing wine) near Rome that were inscribed with texts such as 'white wine from Baeterrae' or 'I am from Baeterrae and I am 5 years old'. Baeterrae was the Roman name for the city. Béziers and the surrounding area is

↑ Béziers is one of the oldest cities in France (LianeM/A)

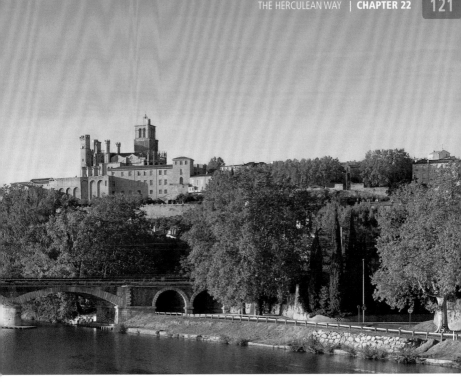

still excellent for wine, and is best known for reds and rosés. Coteaux de Béziers, the local speciality, is made from blended Carignan, Grenache and Syrah grapes.

Some of the traditions in Béziers feel distinctly Spanish. A lively little city of some 80,000 people, it really comes alive during the annual Féria de Béziers. Spanish-style bullfighting still takes place during this festival, flamenco, salsa and local folk music reverberate through the streets, and food stands serving Occitan and Spanish delicacies are on every corner. Despite this, Béziers is a good 100km north of where the border used to sit between France and Catalonia, and 150km from the present-day border between France and Spain. But it's just a stone's throw (15km) from the Mediterranean, between Montpellier and Perpignan.

This there-and-back route has almost continual views of the Cathedral of Saint-Nazaire and passes under Béziers' old and new bridges. Although you wouldn't know from the water, one of the bridges, Pont-Canal de l'Orb, carries a waterway, the Canal du Midi, that passes over your head as you paddle down the Orb River. The river itself is slow moving, so it's not difficult to paddle upstream.

PADDLE THIS WAY

Launch your board just north of the dam by the Ancien Moulin de Bagnols (/// vegans.human.searches), an old mill and hydraulic plant that supplied clean drinking water to the citizens of Béziers in the early 19th century, making it one of the most sophisticated drinking-water systems in France at the time.

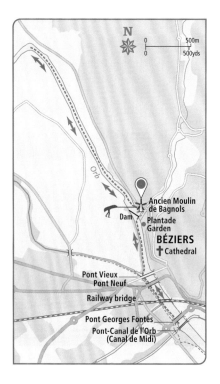

From here, paddle northnorthwest 2.5km to the first major river meander (/// restrict.sweetly.renting), which turns to your left. The paddle upstream is verdant and leafy, a contrast to the urbanism of Béziers; the river is sheltered by numerous trees and the current is slow-moving against you. Try to resist the urge to admire the view behind you as you head up – the idea is that you get your first view of the Cathedral of Saint-Nazaire from a distance.

At the meander, turn your board around and begin your descent down the river. There are a couple of small pontoons and private boat houses that you'll pass. It won't be long before you see the tip of the spires of the Cathedral of Saint-Nazaire up above you to your left, silhouetted against the sky.

Once you reach the dam that you started from, it's safest to paddle to the bank on your left-hand side, get off the water and take your paddleboard on foot along the bank – only for about 15m or so – to avoid the dam, after which point you can launch safely again. From here it's only half a kilometre to Bézier's old bridge, aptly named Pont Vieux (/// deflate.nibbled.painter). This bridge was originally built in the 12th century, but the present structure is a mishmash of stones placed in the 15th, 16th and 17th centuries. The 15 arches are all quite clearly different sizes, creating an effect a bit like bubbles when they reflect on the water.

Just after is the next bridge, named, very originally, Pont Neuf or New Bridge (/// dragons.golf.touched), which is where the D11, one of the main roads from the west, crosses to Béziers. The water is much shallower here and your fin may run aground on the stones. If water levels allow, continue paddling under the railway line (/// book.marriage.boomers), another road bridge (Pont Georges Fontès; /// bluffs.jeep.funds) and finally the Pont-Canal de l'Orb (/// object.swells.fills), where the Canal du Midi crosses the river. The Orb is extremely shallow here, so you may find it's not possible to descend this far.

Turn around and paddle back to Jardin de la Plantade (/// chats.glorious.dusted), a pretty waterside park just before the dam, to disembark thus avoiding crossing the dam again.

ESSENTIALS

GETTING THERE Béziers Airport (20km from the city centre) is served by international flights, and its train station has direct services from Paris (4 hours).

HIRE & LESSONS Smile Kayak (⏂ smilekayak.com ☉ Jun–Aug) hires stand-up paddleboards, but is highly seasonal.

WHEN TO GO Unless you've got your own boat, you'll need to visit during the summer. With your own board, you could in theory paddle at any time of year, as winter temperatures are fairly mild here, but it's most pleasant between April and October.

WHERE TO STAY & EAT **Hôtel des Poètes** (⏂ hoteldespoetes.fr) is in the heart of Béziers, with small but comfortable rooms. **Le Cèdre du Liban** (⏂ lecedreduliban. fr) does excellent Lebanese food and portions are hearty, with plenty for vegetarians. The covered market, **Les Halles**, is great for picking up a picnic lunch.

TITBITS Whatever else you do in Béziers, don't miss the enormous Gothic **cathedral of Saint-Nazaire** that dominates the skyline for the majority of your paddle, and is visible from its hilltop location for miles around. Particularly impressive are the six enormous iron bells kept in the bell tower. Also worth a visit is the **Maison Natale de Jean Moulin**, France's most famous World War II Resistance fighter. He was born in Béziers in 1899 and led much of the French Resistance under the Vichy regime, before being captured in Lyon in June 1943. Upon capture, he was tortured by the notorious SS officer Klaus Barbie (who was so brutal he became known as the 'butcher' of Lyon) and died just days later.

↑ The Orb passes beneath five bridges in Béziers (SS)

23 THE NATURAL HISTORY MUSEUM

KEEP YOUR EYES SKYWARD AS YOU PADDLE THROUGH THIS CANYON THAT'S HOME TO FALCONS, VULTURES AND EAGLES.

WHERE	Tarn gorges, Massif Central (Occitanie)
STATS	10km one-way 🛶 ③ 🛶 ②
START	Canoë 2000, La Malène village, 48210 La Malène
	/// fats.unpacking.starkest
FINISH	Grassy car park 700m east of Pas de Soucy Belvédère, D907BIS,
	48210 Massegros Causses Gorges /// eternal.tourism.erudite

I originally planned this as a night paddle. The Tarn gorges are home to a large beaver population, and they're much easier to spot at dusk. However, as has been my luck with beavers to date, they eluded me. Water levels were exceptionally low in 2023 so there were no night paddle tours going – and, with rapids to navigate, I wasn't going to attempt this one solo during the night. Beaver disappointment aside, I'm really glad that I saw the gorges in daylight because they are ridiculously pretty. They were formed millions of years ago when the Tarn River eroded two enormous limestone plateaux, the Causse Méjean and Causse de Sauveterre. At 53km long and 600m deep at their highest point, the gorges are certainly imposing, whether you spot the local fauna or not. Rock faces form all sorts of shapes: the wizened, lined face of an old man; chess pieces; gnarled knuckles.

The villages around here are what I'd call chocolate-box, almost too decorative to seem real. The houses cling to the hillside at impossible angles, looking as though they've been superglued to the precipitous cliffs and could fall into the gorge at any moment. The roads that wind into the canyon are steep and full of hairpin bends – not for anyone with vertigo.

Don't forget to look up while you're paddling as, among all the other incredible biodiversity, the gorges are home to griffon vultures. With wingspans of up to 2.7m, you can spot them from far away; they've got beigey-brown feathers that turn black at the tips, and are distinguishable from golden eagles (another healthy resident population here) by their short tails. Look out too for peregrines, kestrels and short-toed eagles – just a few of the bird species that call this place home.

As well as low water levels, the gorges have suffered in recent years from overtourism. As a result, in high season you might find kayak spots limited, and it's best to avoid visiting in July and August if you can. Pack water as you won't pass anywhere for refreshments in

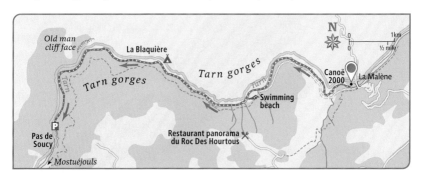

← Anna paddling down the Tarn (Michelle Tucci Studio/michelletuccistudio.com)

the belly of the canyon. Provided that you're confident, this route can be undertaken on a paddleboard, but if you don't have much experience, opt for a kayak. There are some rapids, but they're fairly small and calm – a smooth ride in a kayak. If you do paddleboard, use a shallow, flexible fin to avoid damaging it on the rocks.

As you're going through the gorges you'll see very little civilisation until the end of the itinerary, so pay attention to the What3Words references to track your progress. This is a one-way paddle, so it's best to organise lifts with friends and leave a car at the end point (by Pas de Soucy). There's also a bus that runs between Pas de Soucy and La Malène village, but you'll have to time your arrival carefully as it only runs every couple of hours.

PADDLE THIS WAY

Launch from Canoë 2000's wide stone slipway (/// fats.unpacking.starkest), just after the bridge in La Malène. This turreted little village is fairytale-like and has large weeping willows that trail their tresses in the water. Turn your paddle to your right after launching to follow the direction of the river.

The first meander that curves around to your left is a shallow one. After this, the river widens and bends around in a loop to your right, the gorge, already towering, getting higher around you. Three kilometres after you launch, on your left-hand side, there's a sizeable stretch of beach that is good for swimming from (/// sneezed.impiety.passing). The varying water depths here are really fascinating. One minute you're in a really fast-moving, often shallow patch of river that hurtles you along, the next you're in a virtually stagnant, deep pool, often before a river meander.

Another 2.5km downstream you'll pass La Blaquière campsite (/// retriever.circus.financially), partially obscured by the trees. Here too there are plenty of places to beach your kayak or paddleboard and go for a dip. Up above you, all but hidden from view, a scenic road traces the route you're following. It's likely the one you took to arrive at your start point, with numerous belvederes over the gorge.

The cliff faces get ever more elaborate in shape, and on the right-hand side (about 7.5km in) there's a rock up at the top of the canyon that I think looks like an old man looking down over the river (/// verging.splays.hamburgers). You're still passing shallow rapids and deep pools of slow-moving water as you go; I recommend taking the time to stop and swim in the deliciously cool depths.

The river turns more languid over the last 2.5km until you reach Pas de Soucy, a gnarly waterfall that shouldn't be attempted on a paddleboard, or even a kayak, unless you're seriously professional. Shortly before Pas de Soucy (/// eternal.tourism.erudite), after several boulders in the river, signs are hung all the way across the water, telling you to disembark on your right. Do not ignore these signs as the waterfall is just 200m further along. A stone road comes down to the grassy area where you've disembarked and there's plenty of parking (/// eternal.tourism.erudite).

↑ In summer, water levels can get very low in places (Sarah_Dias/S)
← Griffon vultures are a common sight in the Tarn gorges (SS)

Anna admiring the immense cliffs in the Tarn gorges (Michelle Tucci Studio/michelletuccistudio.com)

ESSENTIALS

GETTING THERE This is another remote corner of France; the closest big transport hub is Montpellier (TGV connections and an international airport), two hours (161km) to the south, via wild and rugged scenery. Public transport is scarce so you'll need to hire a car.

This is a one-way route, so you'll need to organise a lift with friends – bus line 258 runs between Pas de Soucy Belvédère and La Malène village, but look up the schedules in advance as services are infrequent. There's plenty of parking at Canoë 2000, although if you're not renting through them it's polite to ask if you can park there, and you may need to find alternative parking in La Malène village. At Pas de Soucy, the end point, there's a large grassy car park.

HIRE & LESSONS Canoë 2000 (⌂ canoe-kayak-gorgesdutarn.com ☉ Apr–Oct), right at the start point of the route, rents canoes, kayaks and paddleboards, and organises guided trips down the river.

WHEN TO GO During the winter, there's precious little open in the Tarn gorges. If you're prepared to be self-sufficient and are equipped with your own board/kayak it's a pleasant time to come, because you'll have the river all to yourself, but be aware that even the supermarkets close at funny hours and are few and far between. Peak crowds descend during the summer holidays – visit in May or June to escape the worst of it – restaurants and accommodation should all be open for the season by this point.

WHERE TO STAY & EAT Le Soleilo (⌂ lesoleilo.com) in Mostuéjouls (15km south of Pas de Soucy) is in the kind of surroundings you'd expect to see on a Christmas card: higgledy-piggledy stone houses, with stone-tile roofs and streets that meander up and down the steep slopes of the gorge. The rooms are spacious and there's a spa in the basement as well as a lovely outdoor pool.

There's no menu at **Restaurant panorama du Roc des Hourtous** (⌂ panorama desgorgesdutarn.fr), but that's how you know everything's fresh. It attracts customers from far and wide, and the view is exceptional. It's a 15-minute drive west from La Malène village, where you start the paddle, and it overlooks a section of the river you paddled down, but since the gorge is so steep you can't access it from the water. Book in advance.

TITBITS Tarn gorges are sandwiched between two *départements*, Aveyron and Lozère. Every region of France has a cheesy speciality, but Lozère's is particularly interesting. *Aligot* is essentially cheesy mashed potato, but with a ratio heavily weighted to cheese. It's traditional to ladle a little aligot on the heads of diners before serving it. You'll find it on many restaurant menus but, fortunately, most don't adhere to the local tradition…

24 A GALAXY FAR, FAR AWAY

AN OTHERWORLDLY LAKE WHERE THE RED ROCKS & BRIGHT BLUE WATER MAKE YOU FEEL AS THOUGH YOU'VE BEEN TRANSPORTED STRAIGHT TO MARS.

WHERE	Lake Salagou, Langedoc (Occitanie)
STATS	10km round trip/free paddle 🏃 ② 🛶 ①
START/FINISH	Base de Plein Air du Salagou, Route du Lac du Salagou, Rives de Clermont-l'Hérault, 34800 Clermont-l'Hérault
	/// stones.habitat.unwired

The colour of Salagou's rocks make this artificial lake look like the setting of a sci-fi film. It was created in the 1960s, but the rock colour is natural – a deep, rusty red formed by *ruffes* (clay-like sediments heavy in iron oxide) and black basalt. The colour pops, particularly on a blue-sky day. Sandwiched between the Grandes Causses Regional Park, a rocky, rural landscape of limestone pillars and gorges, and the Mediterranean Sea, Lake Salagou's Mars-like landscape is like nothing else in the country, and a surprising contrast to the green forests all around.

↑ The soil around Lake Salagou is a curious red (Lianem/DT)

At 7km², you could paddle the entire lake in a day if you're feeling energetic. I've suggested a 10km route that goes to a gorgeous, sheltered little beach (don't pack your favourite beach towel, it will get covered in red dust). Equally, you could choose to free paddle – the views won't disappoint wherever you go. Dusty red beaches, curious crimson boulders contrasting with the vivid blue of the lake and smattered, scrubby foliage on the shore create a striking colour palette.

During the summer months the lake gets extremely busy. As it is a lake paddle, the only weather you have to watch out for is high winds: it's reasonably exposed, so on a windy day you could quickly get buffeted around. Other than that, it's straightforward to paddle and the conical peninsula jutting out into the middle of the lake makes a good orientation point. With so many beaches, there's a plethora of launch spots meaning that, if you have your own board, you can hit the water from virtually anywhere around the lake.

If you're free paddling or looking to go further than the route below, the Guinguette du Relais Nautique (/// filed.decide.accumulation) has a scenic garden and decent grub.

I highly recommend exploring the hiking trails around Lake Salagou after you get off the water. Mourèze (15km southwest of Base de Plein Air du Salagou) is particularly special, with freestanding limestone pillars so covered with holes that they look as though they've been nibbled into shape by millions of termites.

PADDLE THIS WAY

Launch your board from the sloping beach at Base de Plein Air du Salagou (/// stones.habitat.unwired). There's quite a bit of pond weed in the shallow water you pass through at the start of the paddle, which can be a menace on your fin.

With the watersports centre behind you, paddle to your right and round the wooded headland, Mont Redon (/// disables.unsuited.affair), one of the greenest parts of the lake. Once around the headland you'll see the vast Lake Salagou dam (/// robs.lacy.bout) at the far end of the lake, on your right-hand side. (It's possible to paddle over to it, though I haven't included it as part of the route.)

Cross over to the opposite bank after the headland (/// harvester.unexplained. painting) and begin paddling west. There are lots of tiny little red beaches here, which are among the quietest you'll find owing to their relative inaccessibility

and distance from the villages around the lake.

From the northern shore, it's about 3.5km to reach Les Vailhés, a hamlet with a handful of campsites, on the lake shore. There are fewer trees on this stretch of the lake, allowing for uninterrupted views of the red rocks.

Hugging the shore, keeping it to your right, paddle for a further 1.5km from Les Vailhés to find a gorgeous little beach (/// enjoyment.tinge. rollover) encircled by trees. It's a good place to stop for a dip and a picnic.

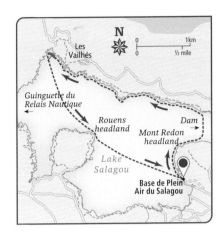

From here, beat a straight line across the centre of the lake to return to Base de Plein Air du Salagou. You'll go right past the conical-shaped headland of Rouens (/// receive.anymore.deduction), which resembles a squished party hat. From the water, it's easy to mistake it for an island, but it's attached to the mainland by a narrow strip of land – you'll significantly lengthen your paddle if you try to loop around it.

↑ Conditions on the lake mean it's a good spot for a family adventure (Base de Plein Air du Salagou)

ESSENTIALS

GETTING THERE Just a few kilometres from the A75, Lac du Salagou is easy to reach, provided you have a car. It's only an hour from both Montpellier and Béziers (both 55km), each of which have international airports, high-speed (TGV) rail services and numerous car-hire outlets. There's a decent-sized car park just above the watersports centre.

HIRE & LESSONS Base de Plein Air Destination Salagou (⌂ basedusalagou. com ⊙ Apr–Oct) hires all the gear you need, from kayaks and paddleboards to windsurfing and catamarans. They also offer archery on site.

WHEN TO GO If you've got your own board, visit out of season to have the whole place to yourself. Winter temperatures tend to be fairly mild here, rarely dipping below 10°C, but you'll need to be pretty self-sufficient as cafés, restaurants and even most hotels don't open until Easter. April to June, September and October are the most pleasant times to enjoy warmer temperatures and fewer crowds than during the summer holidays, with the majority of restaurants open too.

↓ It can be hard to believe that prior to 1969 there was no lake here (Pixemac/DT)

WHERE TO STAY & EAT Les Hauts de Mourèze ( hotelmoureze.fr), hidden away in the limestone pillars of Mourèze, has exceptional views and a large outdoor pool (this area is a suntrap, so it's appreciated). Dining in Mourèze's town is limited, but you can reach **L'Art de la Flamme** (art-de-la-flamme.fr) on foot, where their firepits and well-stocked bar will ensure you're there for the night. On the lakeside, opt for **Guinguette du Relais Nautique** (guinguettesalagou Apr–Oct) for cold beers, tapas and fresh fish.

TITBITS Too many people come to see Salagou's curious red rocks without exploring further. Mourèze and the surrounding villages are a cyclist's paradise, although routes are hilly, so take plenty of water. A 24km loop goes through the mountains above Lake Salagou and returns close to the lake. Start in Clermont-l'Hérault and make your way to Mourèze before looping right at Salasc, passing through the lakeside village of Liausson and returning to Clermont-l'Hérault. You can hire bikes from **Ozone VTT** (vtt-salagou.com Apr–Oct Sat & Sun; Jul & Aug daily). It's a kilometre before you reach Base de Plein Air du Salagou, on the right-hand side of the road, opposite Camping Club Lac du Salagou.

25 PADDLES & PEARLS

A VAST SALTWATER LAGOON, FILLED WITH OYSTERS, MUSSELS & OTHER FRUITS DE MER, MAKES FOR A GOURMET PADDLING EXPERIENCE.

WHERE	Sète, Languedoc (Occitanie)
STATS	14km round trip 🚣④ 🛶③
START/FINISH	KayakMed, 79 chemin Château de Villeroy, 34200 Sète
	/// pads.hooked.sitting

It was my belly that led me to the Étang de Thau, an enormous saltwater lagoon. Actually, it was my belly that led me to several of the itineraries in this book, but hungry paddleboarders, like armies, paddle on their stomachs. I first visited this area with a group of friends, when we spent our days sailing on the Étang de Thau and feasting on deliciously fresh seafood. Returning, I found the distance I'd covered was ideal for working up an appetite to consume all the seafood on offer here. You could say this is the most gourmet lunch paddle in the book.

The Étang de Thau is more than 70km^2, so conditions here are very similar to the sea. Waves can reach quite a size, and the wind frequently tears across the surface. A narrow strip of land separates the lagoon from the Mediterranean Sea, running between the seaside towns of Marseillan Plage and Sète for 18km. It can be driven or cycled, and from parts of it you can see the water on either side of you.

Sète, where this paddle begins, just 30km from Montpellier, is punctuated by a network of canals that link the lagoon with the Mediterranean. A fishing port, Sète's buildings may have changed over the centuries (now distinctly high-rise and modern, with lots of

↑ Many of the oysters sold all over France come from the Étang de Thau (KayakMed)

holiday rentals), but the town's main industry has remained unchanged. It's still a large commercial port, from where the Étang de Thau's oysters and mussels are shipped far and wide.

It's hard to believe that the lagoon isn't the ocean when you're paddling in the middle of it, and it's so immense that you often can't see the opposite bank, or only just. Around the edges are a mixture of palm-fronded fishing towns, pleasure boat marinas, and bland, uniform-looking holiday houses. It's also a popular spot for scuba diving, largely thanks to a healthy population of long-snouted seahorses at Ponton de la Bordelaise ((/// mayor.candle.clearances).

Long-snouted seahorses, which are only around 10–15cm long, thrive here thanks to the artificial reefs around the pontoon. I haven't included this as part of the paddle route, but if you'd like to make the detour, it adds 4km to the route outlined (and don't forget to don your snorkel if you want a chance of spotting seahorses!).

Note that there are two KayakMed outlets in Sète – the one you need faces the lagoon (the other faces the Mediterranean).

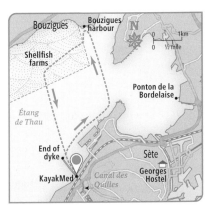

PADDLE THIS WAY

Launch from the KayakMed (/// pads.hooked.sitting) outlet in Sète, facing the Étang de Thau, on the banks of the Canal des Quilles. After launching on to the canal, paddle to your left. The first couple of hundred metres follow a narrow inlet with some of the most desirable-looking waterside houses along it.

Emerging from the inlet out into the lagoon, you'll see a long stone dyke immediately to your left. To avoid running aground in shallow water, follow this all the way to the end, keeping it close to your left-hand side. When you reach the end of the dyke (/// river.general.minute), turn right and make for the rectangular chunk of land directly in front of you (/// manhole.guessing.roofer), which is full of rather ugly houses that look like concrete railway cottages. This headland is just over a kilometre long. Once you reach the end of it (/// deflecting.unseeded.decree), turn left, out to the open water, and begin your crossing to Bouzigues, directly in front of you. The crossing is deceptively long – it looks close, but getting to the other bank involves a paddle of around 3km, and it's very exposed to the elements.

The little harbour of Bouzigues (/// floral.ties.pillowcases), with its many pontoons and yachts, is an easy place to moor up your paddle. Here are many

↑ These wooden structures are oyster and mussel farms (Olivier Tabary/S)

different waterside restaurants from which you can sit outside and keep an eye on your paddleboard or kayak while you eat. It's a seafood lover's dream: moules frites, oysters, clams, scallops, sea snails and giant prawns.

Refuelled, take to the water again, and paddle a short distance offshore from Bouzigues to take a wide channel on your right through the shellfish farms ((/// steer.enrage.argument). It's really important that you stick to the main highways, which are clear to spot in the shellfish farms as you risk ruining the farmers' nets if you start zigzagging through them. Equate it to tramping through a farmer's vegetable field, and don't do it. Oysters and mussels are the main shellfish cultivated here, and they flourish in the lagoon's nutrient-rich, brackish waters.

After a 3km paddle down the oyster motorway, take the wide channel to your left, out towards the centre of the lagoon. As you emerge from the shellfish farms ((/// twinkles.superficial.esteem), you're much more exposed to the elements. Keep going straight on; the final 2.5km across open water takes you back to the end of the dyke (keep it to your right this time) and your start point.

ESSENTIALS

GETTING THERE Direct TGV (high-speed) train services run all the way from Paris to Sète, taking only 3½ hours. Once there, it's easy enough to explore by bike – the cycle trails are largely flat and well marked, but be careful when cycling along the trails over the lagoon as many of them are dead ends. Hire bikes from **Tech Move** (⌀ tech-move.fr ☉ Wed–Mon). The closest airport is in Béziers, from where you can hire a car.

HIRE & LESSONS KayakMed (⌀ kayakmed.com) is one of the friendliest operators in the country, and a mine of information on local wildlife. They have two branches, so be sure to go to the one on the Étang de Thau for this paddle.

WHEN TO GO Summer is when Sète is in full, festive atmosphere, but it's also at its busiest. In late July and early August, world music festival Fiest'A Sète sees large, open-air stages erected by the water to welcome artists from all corners of the globe. During the winter months (Nov–Mar) many of the restaurants around the lake are closed, and the lagoon often gets buffeted by high winds. For optimal weather but minimal crowds, opt for May, June or September.

WHERE TO STAY & EAT There's no shortage of accommodation in and around Sète, and waterside campsites positively line the narrow strip of land between the Étang de Thau and the Mediterranean. One place that deserves a mention, though, is **Georges Hostel** (⌀ georgeshostel.com). There are private rooms and dorms of up to ten beds, it's very bike friendly, and extremely convivial.

Of course, having marketed this as a foodie paddle, I should give you at least several restaurant recommendations. **À la Voile Blanche** (⌀ alavoileblanche.fr) in Bouzigues is an excellent lunch stop. Their portions of moules frites are so generous that you risk sinking your kayak when you relaunch, and their cooked oysters are delicious too. On the other side of the Étang de Thau, Sète's long, sandy beach looks out across the Mediterranean, and beachside restaurant **L'Essentiel** (⌀ lessentielsete.com) makes a great lunch spot with a view; most of the seating is outside. The menu changes all the time, but always features plenty of fresh vegetables, and there's no better place to enjoy a sundowner. On the other side of the lagoon (not on this paddle route), there's an excellent seafood restaurant in Marseillan: **La Pacheline** (☎ 04 67 09 40 17), overlooking the yachts in the port, serves seafood platters that make the table groan under their weight.

TITBITS There are so many 'extras' I could give around Sète, but something unmissable is the Saturday morning market in the historic town of Pézenas, just 20km from the north side of the lagoon. Stalls piled high with Marseillais soap, towers of oysters and free-flowing wine from 09.00; it's beautiful and absolutely massive.

↓ Paddleboarders on the Étang de Thau (KayakMed)

26 ROMAN RELIC

PADDLE UNDER A 2,000-YEAR-OLD ROMAN AQUEDUCT ONCE USED TO TRANSPORT WATER TO THE ROMAN CITY OF NEMAUSUS.

WHERE	Pont du Gard, Languedoc (Occitanie)
STATS	10km one-way ③ ②
START	Kayak Vert Pont du Gard, 8 chemin de Saint-Vincent, 30210 Collias /// choker.sufficiently.flunk
FINISH	Natu'Rando, route d'Uzès – place de la Madone, 30210 Remoulins /// scopes.sullen.maximum

The lovely thing about this paddle is that it is exceptionally varied. The three-tiered Roman aqueduct Pont du Gard is probably what you're here to see, but the scenery around it is ever-changing – shallow limestone gorges interspersed with farmland, woodland and pretty little villages. The Gardon River varies in depth too; in places, the water is really deep and forms little pools known as *vasques* that are perfect for swimming in, while the flat rocks around them seem made for picnicking and sunbathing. Other parts are much shallower, creating little rapids that descend over the rocks. I recommend taking your time on this route so that you can go for plenty of swims along the way (and I've marked a couple of my favourite spots on the map).

A UNESCO World Heritage Site, the 48m-high Pont du Gard is one of the best preserved, most impressive Roman aqueducts in France, composed of three tiers and 48 arches. The Romans began conquering Gaul (modern-day France) in the second century BC. The later invasions were led by Julius Caesar, and between 58 and 50BC the Romans won many victories over Celtic tribes. Particularly important Roman cities were Lugdunum

↑ Pont du Gard is one of the most recognisable landmarks in the country (Eric Isselee/S)

(now Lyon), Vienna (Vienne, just south of Lyon and not to be confused with the capital of Austria), and Nemausus (Nîmes). Pont du Gard was used to transport water from the Eure spring, near Uzès, to Nîmes, and it's one of the best-preserved legacies of the Roman Empire in France today. It hasn't been used as an aqueduct since the 6th century BC, but during the Middle Ages it began to be used as a road. It was included on the UNESCO list in 1980, and now a hiking trail passes over the bridge, forming part of two 'Grand Randonnées' (the term for France's multi-day hiking trails).

This paddle takes you from the sandy-coloured town of Collias through a rural landscape of shallow limestone gorges and farmland, passing under the Pont du Gard to arrive in Remoulins, a historic town first mentioned in records in the 4th century AD. It was once fully fortified but now only the remnants of the rampart walls remain.

Navigation-wise, this route is straightforward, as it follows the direction of the river. The only technical aspect is a smattering of rapids. They're not too severe; if you are on a paddleboard I recommend using a shallow, flexible fin and dropping to your knees if you feel unsafe.

As this is a one-way route with the current, it's best to either organise lifts with friends or to book through a tour company, who will organise transfers for you.

PADDLE THIS WAY

Launch from the stone slipway by Kayak Vert (/// choker.sufficiently.flunk) just below Collias town. The river is particularly shallow here, which makes it easy to embark. Turn left to follow the direction of the river. You'll pass under a bridge almost instantly.

It may seem a sacrilege to stop so soon, but there's an ice-cream shack, À la Guinguette de Collias (/// blanking.names.apelike), on your right after travelling along the river for just under a kilometre (yes, I am a paddleboarder guided by my stomach). It also serves snack lunches and beers.

From here, continue for another 3km, following the gentle meanders of the river as it winds its way through a shallow limestone gorge covered in trees to

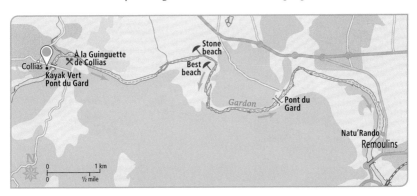

reach an excellent spot for swimming (/// bookkeeping.flitting.pavement), one of the widest shingle beaches on your route. Two kilometres further along, a narrow inlet on your left (/// crush.sturdily.trinket) is the best swimming spot of the paddle, offering sheltered and quiet bathing in idyllic surroundings. The road access to this spot is tricky, so you're only likely to be sharing it with other paddlers; the trees fringing the inlet make you feel hidden away from the world. The limestone cliffs get a little higher here, cocooning you from any wind, and continue to shelter you until you reach Pont du Gard.

Pont du Gard (/// neared.traced.elitist) is 1.5km further along. You'll see it several hundred metres before you reach it, and you'll also notice your quiet stretch of river get significantly busier. Day-trippers line the beaches just before the aqueduct, and there are likely to be kayakers who have hit the water purely to paddle under the numerous arches. The river's current will be pulling you towards the bridge, so if you want to take plenty of photos you'll probably need to back paddle a bit.

Pass right through any of the arches of Pont du Gard. Look up as you float underneath to drink in over 2,000 years of history above your head. This part of the river flows faster than most of the route, so it's often over all too quickly! Once you pass Pont du Gard, it's a little over 3km to reach the end point. The limestone gorges disappear here, making the river much more exposed to the elements so, if there's any wind, you might notice that it suddenly hits you here and makes your paddle much harder work. A kilometre from the end, the riverbank becomes leafy and green, a mass of foliage. As there are several kayak operators in the area, you'll see disembarkation signs every couple of hundred metres; alight on the left for Natu'Rando (/// scopes.sullen.maximum) – it's easy to miss, a little wooden ladder hidden among the trees with (as of the latest check) no sign to identify it, although this may well change.

↑ The Gardon is a popular spot for watersports, largely because of its peerless views of the three-tiered Roman acqueduct (Novinit Images/S)

ESSENTIALS

GETTING THERE The start point is less than a 40-minute (33km) drive from the city of Avignon, which has regular TGV (high-speed) train links around the country. There's also an airport (Avignon-Provence), and car hire is available from both the airport and the train station. Follow the N100 all the way from Avignon to Remoulins, the end point. From here it's a 10km drive to Collias. There are two sizable car parks just above the start point, in Collias town (chargeable); it's a short walk of 5 minutes or so to reach the water's edge from there. There's a large car park up the top at the end point, and the pretty sand-coloured town of Remoulins on your doorstep. If booking with Natu'Rando, they'll organise your transfer to the start point for you, otherwise organise lifts with friends.

HIRE & LESSONS There are several hire sites in the area, but the team at **Natu'Rando** (natu-rando.com), at the end of this route, know their stuff, and there's ample parking on site. At the start of the route, **Kayak Vert Pont du Gard** (kayakvert.com) hires sit-on kayaks, and is a 5-minute walk downhill from Collias's car park.

WHEN TO GO Shoulder season is best for paddling the Pont du Gard (Apr–Jun or Sep–Oct). This is a dry part of the country that frequently sees some of the hottest temperatures in France, so the water level can get low during the summer months. Alternatively, try to coincide your visit with the famous Festival de Nîmes, held in Nîmes' amphitheatre from late June to late July and just 29km (30 minutes) south of Remoulins, the route's end point.

WHERE TO STAY & EAT Much of the accommodation near Pont du Gard is self-catering. **Aux Berges du Pont du Gard** (masdemonpere.fr) has cute, characterful rooms with plenty of wooden furnishings, and an outdoor swimming pool.

Crêperie Bulle de Crêpes (Bulle de Crêpes) is a good pit-stop in Collias before you hit the water, with an extensive sweet and savoury menu and outdoor seating. At the end of the route, **Hostellerie du Moulin Remoulins** (Hostellerie du Moulin) has a garden shaded by weeping willows, and (a novelty in rural France) plenty of vegetables on the menu.

TITBITS It's not just Nîmes that's in festival mode here in July. Nearby Avignon hosts the month-long Avignon Festival. It's similar to the Edinburgh Fringe in that theatre, music and dance all feature, with some ticketed events and plenty of free performances on the street.

27 THE SAINTS' WAY

PADDLE PAST CENTURIES-OLD CHURCHES & UNDER BASALT ROCK PILLARS IN THIS LESSER-KNOWN CORNER OF FRANCE.

WHERE	Langeac, Massif Central (Auvergne-Rhône-Alpes)
STATS	11.5km one-way ☂④ ☂③
START	Domaine du Pradel, 43300 Saint-Julien-des-Chazes
	/// longingly.obviously.coughing
FINISH	TONIC Aventure, 43300 Langeac /// bubbly.sagas.bagpipes

The rural Auvergne has always held a certain magic for me. Squarely in the middle of what the French refer to as the *diagonale du vide* ('the empty diagonal'), it's one of the least populous areas of France. It's also one of the most historic – a region where many of the hidden chapels and churches are a thousand years old, and where hiking trails trace the routes religious pilgrims would have walked wearily hundreds of years before. Cutting through the middle of it is the River Allier, which here slices shallow basalt gorges. The 421km-long Allier begins in the Lozère before joining the Loire near Nevers.

Don't expect five-star hotels and tourist offices with staff speaking perfect English (in fact, opening hours are so laidback here that often the tourist offices aren't open at all). This is a place for Slow tourism, where everything around you is an impossibly green, and where mealtimes are for indulging in football-sized slabs of local cheeses you've probably never heard of.

Paddling through the Allier gorges feels a little like travelling through a landscape out of *Jurassic Park*. The basalt rock creates mythical-looking shapes that tower up above you, and there are very few people here. It almost surprises you to see signs of civilisation, usually in the form of little hilltop towns dominated by ancient church spires.

The start point is remote: Domaine du Pradel is a hiking gîte with poor road access. From here you paddle past isolated little churches in France's religious heartland. Although France is now officially a secular country, many people still come to this region of the Auvergne, around Le Puy-en-Velay, to undertake pilgrimages. The most famous is the Camino de Santiago, which starts in Le Puy-en-Velay itself and goes all the way to Santiago de Compostela in Spain, but numerous, lesser-known hiking trails join up ancient churches like a giant dot-to-dot, tracing the paths allegedly trod by saints in years gone by.

Aside from a couple of small villages, there's very little infrastructure on this route, and the rapids, which are frequent, can be quite gnarly as they feature large boulders. Only very competent paddlers should attempt this, otherwise take a kayak – though novice kayakers may still find it a bit hairy. The section of the Allier River just above this route is used for whitewater rafting, which should give you an idea of what you're getting into!

What's more, this route isn't an easy one to access independently, because it's in a public transport void. If booking a tour with them, kayak-hire centre TONIC Aventure, where you finish the route, will drop you off at the start point, but if you're coming in your own car, you'll need to organise lifts with your travel companions. You could also try hitchhiking (taking the usual precautions of course), but be aware that this is a tiny, stony track with very little footfall.

← Sainte-Marie-des-Chazes Chapel is a highlight on the route (Tonic Aventure)

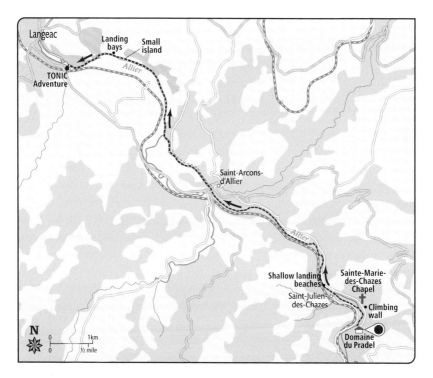

PADDLE THIS WAY

Start from the small car park opposite Domaine du Pradel (/// longing.obviously.coughing), a large gîte for hikers. Launch your board and turn right, following the direction of the river. Stay on the right-hand side as you paddle downstream and after 500m you'll pass an open-air climbing wall on the boulders on your right. Another 500m along, where the river forks, take the much wider, more obvious channel to the left and you will see one of the highlights of the route: Sainte-Marie-des-Chazes Chapel (/// triangular.resells.removing), on the right-hand bank. A little church built from volcanic stone, it is sandwiched among enormous boulders and forests, making it look like something out of a fantasy film. Its history is comparatively unknown, but it's thought to have been built between the 12th and 13th centuries. Its interior is simply decorated, but there are still some original, albeit rather faded, wall frescoes and stained-glass windows.

On the other side of the river, just after Sainte-Marie-des-Chazes Chapel, is the village of Saint-Julien-des-Chazes (/// memo.sandwiches.unfreeze), which you get great views of thanks to a relative absence of foliage. A red metal bridge crosses the river as you pass by the village.

After paddling under the bridge, the basalt rocks start off vertically scored on the lower level, like church organs, before bulging out like toadstools on the upper level. If you want a break, there are a couple of shallow landing beaches to your left. The river then gets skinnier, and just after a block of land that juts out on your left-hand side and causes the river to meander, you hit the first set of several rapids. They aren't particularly dangerous, but the boulders are big enough to bump your kayak around quite considerably and give you a good shower. Keep paddling as you pass through each set of rapids to help you to move with the current. The rapids are interspersed with calmer patches of river, as it passes farmland and wooded copses, and you'll often see cows coming down to drink by the water's edge.

Some 6km into the route, the hillside town of Saint-Arcons-d'Allier (/// purples. savings.distorting) will appear on your right. Most of this town is significantly higher than the Allier River, and the terracotta-roofed houses have window boxes that spill over with flowers like alpine chalets, making it all exceptionally scenic. Paddle under the stone bridge that leads to the town.

The rapids are frequent after leaving Saint-Arcons-d'Allier, and no sooner have you left one set behind then another appears, but it means that your travelling speed increases with the current. When you reach a small island in the middle of the river (/// listens.shopped.airlock) 4km after Saint-Arcons-d'Allier, keep right where the water is deeper. If you get tired, there are landing bays along the right-hand side of the river. Some kayaking clubs end their trips here, so you may see signs telling you to disembark. Ignore these and keep paddling.

The basalt gorges soften as you approach Langeac, giving way to a flatter, softer pastoral landscape where large fields and scattered farmhouses dominate the views. Rounding the river meander at the 10km mark, the higher buildings in Langeac start to appear. TONIC Aventure's kayak base (/// bubbly.sagas.bagpipes) is just before the town; look for the pontoon on the left.

↑ This part of the Allier is very wild (Tonic Adventure)

ESSENTIALS

GETTING THERE The closest airport with direct flights from the UK is Lyon-Saint Exupéry, 2½ hours away (car hire available). This is a really rural part of the country that you'll need a car to access. The nearest place of any size is Le Puy-en-Velay (40 minutes/31km) from the start point. The town's station has regular – but none of them high-speed – trains from Paris; car hire is available here from **Hertz** (⊘ hertz.fr). There's free parking both at the start and the end of this route, but make sure you organise lifts if not booking through an organised tour. I can't stress enough how much of a public transport black hole it is here.

HIRE & LESSONS TONIC Aventure (⊘ tonic-aventure.fr ☉ Apr–Oct) is an excellent operator that hires kayaks, as well as organising canyoning and white-water rafting trips further upriver, plus multi-day camping, kayaking and fishing trips. They'll also drop you off at the start point.

WHEN TO GO Water levels are highest in May and June, making these the best months to visit. Hire centres are open from April to October and, while you can attempt this route outside of this time period if you have your own board, be aware that snow isn't uncommon in this part of France and the water is freezing in winter.

WHERE TO STAY & EAT B&B **Maison Charivari** (⊘ maisoncharivari.com) has so much character and sits right on the Allier River, 13km after your end point. **Les Jardins d'Anna** (⊘ lesjardinsanna.com) is 31km away and has just a handful of rooms; the breakfast spread is excellent, with croissants bigger than dinner plates. **Le Trèfle à Quatre Feuilles** (⬛ Le-trèfle-à-quatre-feuilles) in the heart of Langeac is the sort of place I'd travel miles for, and a real rarity. Their menu is limited, but they serve great home-cooked food with plenty of vegetarian options.

TITBITS The GR470 hiking trail, which starts in Brioude, 44km north of the paddle start point, follows the Allier River all the way to its source in La Bastide-Puylaurent in Lozère. The full hiking trail is 190km and typically takes 11 days to complete, going past little-visited, centuries-old churches in France's former religious heartland.

← Aerial view over Saint-Arcons-d'Allier (Hemis/A)

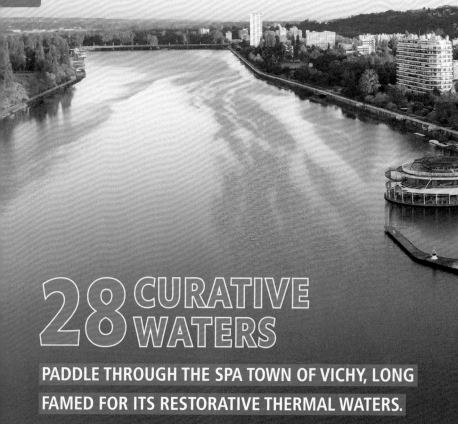

28 CURATIVE WATERS

PADDLE THROUGH THE SPA TOWN OF VICHY, LONG FAMED FOR ITS RESTORATIVE THERMAL WATERS.

WHERE	Vichy, Massif Central (Auvergne-Rhône-Alpes)
STATS	10km round trip ⛵ ③ 🛶 ②
START/FINISH	The beach next to Beaurivage campsite, 15 rue Claude Decloitre, 03700 Bellerive-sur-Allier /// builds.juggle.badly

Vichy owes its very existence to the sulphurous waters that bubble underground. Unsurprisingly, spa culture arose around these waters that promise to cure ills, drawing the sick and worried here in equal measure, particularly from the 19th century, when the French and British upper classes had enough time and disposable income to entertain the idea of a holiday. This was of course facilitated further by the invention of the steam locomotive, which came to Vichy in 1862. Spa culture boomed: resort hotels were built above the underground springs and visitors checked in for days or even weeks at a time. Even after Vichy's notoriety and fallen reputation as capital of the regime, which collaborated with Nazi Germany during World War II, the city's spa industry clung on (and it's certainly an image the city is keener to promote than unedifying wartime involvement).

↑ Vichy is known for its naturally thermal waters (Hervé Lenain/A)

It may be some people's cup of mineral water, but my visit to Vichy's spas left me cold. Literally. A 'Vichy Shower' involves a massage on clinical plastic sheeting under four tepid jets of water, and I was shivering the whole time. But Vichy's riverbanks – that's a different story.

As with the previous chapter, this route explores a section of the Allier, this time cutting between Vichy and the suburb of Bellerive-sur-Allier across the river, where the paddle begins. This part of the Allier may just be the finest riverbank for bons vivants in the country: waterside bar after waterside bar; reasonably priced restaurants with terraces spilling over the banks; leafy walkways and endless trails for walkers and joggers. Much of the route is extremely green, particularly for an urban paddle, but heading down a smaller water channel in the heart of the city also allows you to admire some of Vichy's Belle Époque architecture.

I'd recommend wearing closed shoes for this paddle, particularly because of this urban channel. As with most city waterways, people sometimes chuck their rubbish in here, and if you run aground at any point and need to get out and wade you'll want adequate foot protection.

PADDLE THIS WAY

Launch from the little beach next to Beaurivage-sur-Allier campsite (/// builds.juggle.badly). Just to your right is an island covered in trees; opposite, across the river, is one of Vichy's enormous urban parks, des Bourins. Cross the river, making straight for the park, and once on the other bank turn left to paddle alongside des Bourins Park. After around a kilometre, you'll arrive at Tahiti Plage (/// guess.gone.daylight), one of the best waterside bars in the area, with an extensive cocktail menu and cheap, picky bits to eat. Keep paddling north with the river (with or without an apéro break, that's up

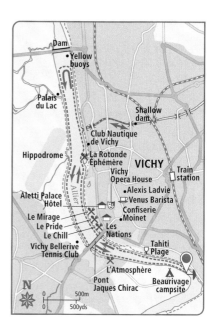

to you). This part of the Allier is slow moving, like paddling a lake, so, unless it's windy, you don't need to worry about having a tricky paddle back to base. Even if it is windy, however, the numerous trees provide plenty of shelter.

If you're visiting in season, just before you get to the bridge, Pont Jacques Chirac, you'll see an inflatable obstacle course. Keep going beyond the bridge to go past numerous waterside restaurants, including Le Chill, Le Pride and Le Mirage on the riverbank of Napoléon III Park. Behind the trees are five Swiss-style chalets commissioned by Napoléon III after his first spa retreat here in 1861, though you'll only get a glimpse of the roofs at most from the water. The chalets are well worth a visit when you've finished your paddle – or you can disembark at one of the aforementioned restaurants to explore on foot.

Another 300m further upriver from the chalets, you'll see a round building jutting out into the water on your right; this is La Rotonde Éphémère (/// fork. kept.hobbit), a restaurant. There's a marina here and a kayak club, and from here you'll see yellow markers counting down from ten to one on the banks of the river, which are used by Vichy's rowing team.

Just half a kilometre further upriver from La Rotonde Éphémère, a tributary of the Allier branches out under a road bridge on your right (/// wallet.hoping sourced). It's an interesting urban section, past some of Vichy's handsome buildings; it's just 500m before you get to a shallow dam (/// recent.onto.region), passing under several bridges as you go. You'll most likely see families of ducks crossing the river. It's much shallower here, so be aware that rigid fins might catch on the rocks.

Retrace your paddle strokes to the Allier, then turn right and carry on north along the river, past the yellow number signs for rowers, which are still counting down, until you reach a line of yellow buoys (/// infinite.things.locate). Cross the river here to the other bank and don't attempt to paddle further as there's a large dam just ahead.

Paddle back the way you came, this time along the eastern bank. The first building you'll see is the Palais du Lac, decorated with flags; it looks like a governmental building, but it's actually just an events space in a sports complex. After another 500m is the start of Vichy's vast hippodrome (/// beamed.boom. wink), where horse races have been held since 1903. After the hippodrome, you'll pass a kilometre-long and very pleasant stretch of greenery, where walkways are peppered with picnic benches, and then Vichy Bellerive Tennis Club (/// stunning. appetite.readers), before going under Pont Jacques Chirac again. Approximately 500m later is Vichy's best waterside bar restaurant, L'Atmosphère (/// kennels.lofts. rams). It's very paddleboard friendly and serves plenty of fresh fish, salads and cheese spreads, in addition to an extensive wine menu. It's just over a kilometre south from here to return to the point you launched from.

↑ This stretch of the Allier is slow-moving, which make conditions good for paddleboarding (Hugh Williamson/A)

ESSENTIALS

GETTING THERE Vichy is easy to reach by train, and the station is a 20-minute walk from the river. The nearest airport is an hour's drive away in Clermont-Ferrand (73 km); car hire is available here. If coming by car, there's plenty of free parking on allée des Belles Rives (Bellerive-sur-Allier), located across the river from Vichy, and just a couple of minutes' walk from the start of the paddle.

HIRE & LESSONS The **Club Nautique de Vichy** (⌖ clubnautiquedevichy. com), on the riverbank in the north of the town, is open year-round. They hire out stand-up paddleboards, with discounted rates for groups, but I strongly recommend contacting them in advance, especially if visiting in low season (Nov–Mar). Although Vichy welcomes a lot of tourists coming for the spas, the watersports centre is a locals' clubhouse and sailing club first and foremost, and paddleboard rental is very much secondary.

WHEN TO GO Vichy comes alive in the warmer months (Apr–Oct), but many people leave town in August for the summer holidays, so some restaurants will be closed. It's a lively town and, provided the weather is fine, paddling is possible here all year (with your own board).

WHERE TO STAY & EAT The best hotels are in Vichy rather than Bellerive-sur-Allier, and you have a greater choice of restaurants on your doorstep too if you choose to stay there. **Hôtel les Nations** (⌖ hotel-lesnations.com) has fresh, airy rooms, a great breakfast buffet, and a friendly resident dog that looks like a bear. The **Aletti Palace Hôtel** (⌖ hotel-aletti.fr) is well located with plenty of character but is in dire need of a lick of paint.

Aside from the numerous bars and restaurants listed in the route, Vichy has plenty of good grub away from the water. **Venus Barista** (⌖ venusbarista.fr) has managed the remarkable feat of being a great café during the day and a pub with excellent vibes and draught beers in the evening.

This is a town for sweet tooths, with pâtisseries and sweet shops seemingly on every corner. The pâtisseries at **Alexis Ladvie** (◙ patisserie.alexis.ladvie) are almost too pretty to eat. To try Vichy's famous digestive mints, go to **Confiserie Moinet** (⌖ confiserie-moinet.fr).

TITBITS Unmissable from Vichy's Belle Époque days is a trip to the **Opera House** (⌖ opera-vichy.com), which is so bedecked with gold it looks as though Midas went on a rampage. Check the schedule to see a show, or organise a walking tour through the tourist office. The 'curative' water is freely available from drinking fountains in pavilions in each of Vichy's many parks. It comes out of handsome brass taps smelling and tasting like rotten eggs.

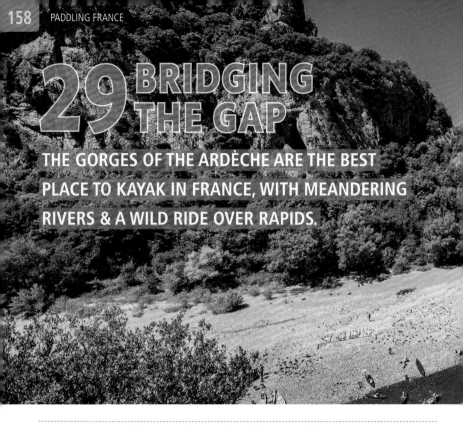

29 BRIDGING THE GAP

THE GORGES OF THE ARDÈCHE ARE THE BEST PLACE TO KAYAK IN FRANCE, WITH MEANDERING RIVERS & A WILD RIDE OVER RAPIDS.

WHERE	Vallon-Pont-d'Arc, Ardèche (Auvergne-Rhône-Alpes)
STATS	32km one-way 🚶 ⑤ 🛶 ④
START	Embarcadère public, 07150 Vallon-Pont-d'Arc
	/// myself.unproved.frosted
FINISH	Car park after Sauze, 07700 Saint-Martin-d'Ardèche
	/// selfish.sluggish.headstone

I f you only do one route in this book, make it this one, where the sheer scale of the cliffs rising up around the Ardèche River will leave you speechless. There are more kayak rental outlets in Vallon-Pont-d'Arc than you can shake an oar at; if you so much as mention visiting the Ardèche to a French person, the first question you'll get is 'are you going kayaking?' The main reason for this is the Pont d'Arc, a huge natural rock arch formed by thousands of years of erosion, which spans the Ardèche River. The river would have once meandered around this rock, before it eventually carved a hole right through the middle. Elsewhere on the river, where meanders are particularly windy, you'll see other rocks gradually being eroded by the power of the water – the beginnings of Pont d'Arcs for future paddlers.

The limestone gorges of the Ardèche once sat under the ocean, and the porous sedimentary rock was formed by the compressed bones of millions of fish. As a result,

↑ This archway was formed by thousands of years of erosion (Rolf E Staerk/S)

you can see the layers in it, and these rocks are littered with holes and caves. One of the most famous, the Chauvet Cave, has paintings that have been dated as at least 30,000 years old. The people who lived there left behind handprints and paintings of the prehistoric animals that used to roam these lands, including cave bears and cave lions.

This is a rare route where you can spend one or even two days on the water without seeing a human settlement, with vultures wheeling overhead and wild goats coming to drink on the shingle beaches below the gorges. It's the kind of kayaking trip where your neck will hurt from constantly craning upwards to marvel at the scenery above you, and it's one of my favourite places in France, on or off the water.

The Ardèche gorges are a nature reserve, and once you leave Vallon-Pont-d'Arc there are no villages, towns or human settlement of any kind until 32km later at Sauze where this route ends. If you don't have the energy or inclination for such a long kayaking route, many rental outlets offer shorter versions of the itinerary outlined here (8, 13 and 24km routes) with pick-ups at the end. If undertaking any of them independently, make sure you organise lifts with friends as you're not going to find much in the way of public transport. Every route offers passes under Pont d'Arc so, if you're tackling the 32km, it's best to start as early in the day as possible to avoid feeling as though you're kayaking the London Tube at rush hour. The other option is to split the 32km over two days, and camp at one of two designated bivouac spots. Other than the legality of it,

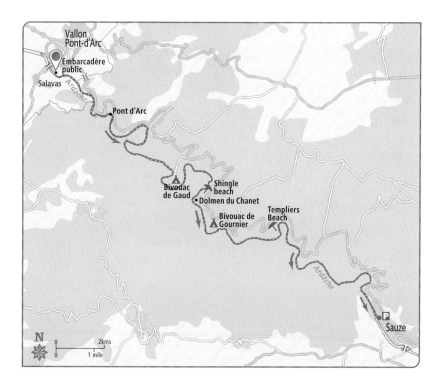

there's little difference between camping at these spots and wild camping, so you'll need to be self-sufficient. Bivouacking needs to be pre-booked via the tourist office in Vallon-Pont-d'Arc, and spaces are limited so book well in advance. You'll need to carry all your camping gear on the kayak(s) with you, and rental companies generally only supply one waterproof container – there are several rapids on this route, so good quality dry bags are an essential. Note that wild camping isn't permitted anywhere outside of the two bivouac spots.

In recent years, little rainfall has meant that the water levels in the Ardèche River are getting increasingly low. For a faster-moving current and to ensure that you can do the full 32km it's best to visit early in the season (between April and June). Officially the two designated bivouac spots are open between April and September, but often the opening is delayed until late April or early May.

If you're attempting the full descent in a day, make sure that you've crossed at least the first bivouac site, Gaud (12km in), before you stop for lunch. If you've the luxury of two days, take your time. Both bivouac sites are extremely basic in terms of facilities. Gaud is the largest of the two sites and gets fewer visitors, being just a third of the way down the river.

Pack suncream, plenty of water and more snacks than you think you'll need. Consider wearing a wetsuit if visiting out of season – the gorges of the Ardèche are up to

300m deep in places so much of the descent is shaded from the sun and, since you're frequently soaked by the rapids, it gets chilly quickly. Unless you're an extremely confident paddleboarder, I recommend a sit-on kayak for this route. Reasonably confident, fit kayakers should be able to tackle the route without too much difficulty.

As this is a one-way paddle, you'll need to organise lifts to get back to base (there's no public transport), unless booking with a rental outlet. All of the rental outlets in Vallon-Pont-d'Arc will pick you up at the end, but make sure you meet the cut-off time they've given you as they won't wait for you and it's a long walk back!

PADDLE THIS WAY

Launch from Vallon-Pont-d'Arc (/// myself.unproved.frosted), just after the bridge that links the village with the pretty medieval town of Salavas across the river, and head to your left, following the current. This is the most urban part of your paddle, and the road hugs the river here, with plenty of belvederes. Occasionally you'll be able to see people, as small as fruit flies, looking down from above. It won't take you long to reach the Pont d'Arc (/// nobler.postnatal.plump), 4km away. This is one of the widest stretches of the river, and goes past wooded riverside campsites and the biggest road that cuts through the gorges. There's a series of shallow caves on your left within the rock arch; from here you'll get a view of the entirety of the arch, and it makes for particularly dramatic photos with a wide-angle lens. Rapids are frequent the whole way, and give the kayaks quite a bashing. Remember to keep paddling as you traverse them to keep your momentum going.

↑ Anna following a friend down the Ardèche River (Anna Richards)

↑ A view of the Ardèche from one of the belvederes (Anna Richards)

Continue through and beyond the Pont d'Arc, and you'll find the kayaking crowds soon disperse somewhat; 1.5km later, the river meanders so strongly it almost doubles back on itself. Keep an eye out for caves high in the cliff face on your right-hand side. During World War II many of these were used for hiding in by members of the French Resistance.

A little over 5km after the big meander, the river meanders sharply again, to your right. Just after this you'll reach the first of the camping spots on your left-hand side, Gaud (/// softies.drive.foyer), around the 12km mark. It's easy to miss as the only landmark is a shingle beach, and there are several of these on the Ardèche River. If you're attempting the full 32km in a day, it's a good idea to push on rather than stopping for lunch here, but if you're splitting over two days then it makes for a decent lunch spot.

The river takes two sweeping meanders to your left just a kilometre after Gaud. As the second meander straightens out, there's another shingle beach on your left (/// ritzy.enticed.bruisers). By beaching the board or kayak here and taking the goat track (often overgrown) leading off the beach you can reach the curious structure of a flat stone balanced on two standing stones, Dolmen du Chanet (/// cooker.gust.melons), which looks like the stone table from C S Lewis's *The Lion, the Witch and the Wardrobe*.

Back on the river, continue for 4km, the river meandering to your right at first before following a fairly straight course, to reach Bivouac de Gournier (/// sunscreen.bendable.chunky). Trees shade the campsite and hide it from the river, and if you're visiting in season and the weather is fine, the atmosphere here is really jovial. If tackling the full descent in a day, this is a good place to stop for lunch, as it's roughly at the halfway point on your itinerary.

Shingle beaches become more frequent after Gournier. Templiers Beach (/// roosts.impiety.ourselves) is a particularly good place for a dip, with flat rocks to sunbathe and dry off on afterwards. At this point, you're a little over 21km into your descent.

Right after Templiers Beach, the river makes a sharp meander around to your right, almost doubling back on itself as it did after the Pont d'Arc. Continue for another 6km through the gorges, at which point the river begins to widen (/// drowsing.hive.condition). The gorges that have enclosed you since Vallon-Pont-d'Arc become wider and shorter here, allowing more sunlight in – but it is also more susceptible to wind. This final stretch of the river just north of Sauze is free of rapids and much more adapted to paddleboarders, so you'll likely see a few people paddling upstream.

Just before Sauze, hobby fishermen line the banks. It feels almost strange to see buildings again after the pure wilderness you've just traversed. Alight at the car park (/// selfish.sluggish.headstone) on your left, just beyond the main town.

ESSENTIALS

GETTING THERE The closest airport with direct flights to the UK is Marseille Provence (two hours, car hire available). Buses run to Vallon-Pont-d'Arc from Montélimar, which has a TGV train station and numerous car-hire outlets. Having a car is invaluable here, as public transport services are few and far between. The start point at Vallon-Pont-d'Arc is around an hour from the A7, otherwise known as the Autoroute du Soleil, which runs between Lyon and Marseille. There are plenty of car parks in both Vallon-Pont-d'Arc and Sauze, generally paid in the former and free in the latter.

HIRE & LESSONS Numerous hire outlets in Vallon-Pont-d'Arc offer similar packages, but I was very impressed with the professionalism of **Aigue Vive** (⌂ aigue-vive.com). They also organise canyoning trips as well as canoe and kayak hire. Bonus points for their vibrant, fuschia kayaks, which mean you don't risk losing your paddling companions.

WHEN TO GO If you want to bivouac and split this route over two days, don't arrive before late April. Increasing droughts in the Ardèche are affecting the river's water levels, so May and June are the best months as the levels still tend to be high. During the summer holidays, the Pont-d'Arc itself gets very busy.

↓ The Ardèche is one of the most popular kayaking spots in the country (Julia700702/S)

WHERE TO STAY & EAT There's a plethora of accommodation in and around Vallon-Pont-d'Arc, from campsites to five-star hotels. I've been to the Ardèche many times, and while Vallon-Pont-d'Arc has the convenience of numerous restaurants, shops and kayak hire outlets on your doorstep, it feels like what it is: a tourist town. Just across the river, the smaller town of Salavas has managed to retain its charm, with cobbled streets, shuttered windows and medieval stone towers. It's also much easier to park. **Hôtel des Sites** (⚓ hoteldessites.com) is a five-minute walk from the river, providing a slap-up breakfast to set you up for a long day of kayaking and colourful rooms.

La Mia Pizzeria (🆕 La-Mia-pizza), just opposite Hôtel des Sites, has an extensive menu of pizza to go or enjoy on site, and sells carafes of arguably the cheapest wine in France (careful, after a 32km kayaking trip it hits hard). Across the river in Vallon-Pont-d'Arc, tapas and cocktail restaurant **O'Tapas'oif** (🆕) has a huge patio bedecked with brightly coloured hanging models of llamas and parasols.

TITBITS Kayaking is the thing to do in the Ardèche, but if you've a head for heights check out one of the numerous via ferratas in the area. The precipitous limestone gorges give some pleasingly challenging scrambles. I particularly like Pont du Diable in Thueyts, a 48km drive north of Vallon-Pont-d'Arc, through the gorges, which has a zipline over the river and some good overhangs.

30 COMING ROUND THE MOUNTAINS

THE WILD WATERWAYS OF THE DRÔME ARE FULL OF CAMPSITES, BIODIVERSITY & GREAT KAYAKING.

WHERE	Saillans, Drôme (Auvergne-Rhône-Alpes)
STATS	11km one-way 🚶 ③ 🛶 ②
START	Car park off the D135, 26340 Espenel
	/// pursue.inroads.span
FINISH	Car park off the D93, 26340 Saillans
	/// clarifies.ruthlessly.vibrato

Where the mountains of Vercors Regional Park meet Provence, the softer, green hills of the Drôme are sliced through by the 111km Drôme River. A tributary of the Rhône, the Drôme flows down from the Alps to meet the Rhône between Valence and Montélimar, and the white stones that the water courses over make it look chalky in its shallower parts, and a startling blue where it runs deeper. The river travels through a hippie heartland of quirky little towns, lavender fields much less frequented than in southern Provence, and Vercors Regional Park, and descends 1,000m in altitude. For me, this is quite possibly the most underrated part of France.

Rapids are frequent, but not generally gnarly enough to throw you out of your kayak — it's more likely that you'll get stuck on a rock and need to back paddle. Unless you're very competent, you may struggle if tackling the route on a paddleboard; make sure you use a shallow, flexible fin. More of a nuisance is the water level, which at times is so low that a flat-bottomed kayak works much better than a paddleboard.

Fish are in abundance in the Drôme, and you'll likely see a few, particularly if you stop to swim en route. Particularly special is the *Zingel asper*, an endangered species that now only exists in the Rhône Basin, but there are also brown trout, eel, perch, pike, carp

↑ The Drôme has remained relatively under the radar for British tourists (niceartphoto/A)

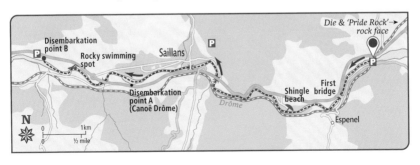

and clawed crayfish. Dozens of beaver families are starting to recolonise the river – look for evidence of gnawed trunks as you descend. Then there are coypu and otter, and, on land, roe deer, chamois, wild boar, badger and even wolves coming down to drink at the water's edge. Overall, there are more than a hundred animal species here and 680 plant species, including wild tulips, lily of the valley and gentian.

The town of Die, just upriver from this route (unless tackling the extended version with Canoë Drôme described on page 168) is a quirky little place, drawing an eclectic band of young people looking for a more grassroots lifestyle. Unlike many towns in the French countryside, where life centres around the bakery and PMU betting bar and the average age seems long past retirement, Die buzzes with frequent live music and theatre, and rainbow-coloured harem pants are the attire of choice; cigarette smoke often smells distinctly herbal. Die is nationally renowned for Clairette de Die, a sweet, sparkling wine that is said to have been invented when a shepherd tried to chill a bottle of white wine in the river, inadvertently turning it fizzy.

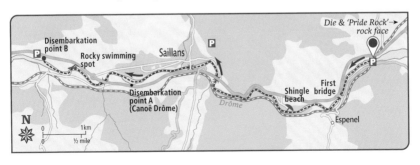

Paddling the Drôme feels like a detox, where the verdant green on either bank seems to oxygenate your every stroke and buildings are few and far between. Take your time and land on plenty of shingle beaches as you descend to swim in the river.

If water levels allow, Canoë Drôme organises a two-day, 49km descent from Pont de Quart to Crest, including the stretch of the Drôme River included in this itinerary, with an overnight camp at the 30km mark. Owing to widespread droughts, in 2023 this was only open in May, although it should generally be doable between April and June. As a result, I wasn't able to test it out.

PADDLE THIS WAY

From the tiny car park (/// pursue.inroads.span) off the D135 (running northeast from Espenel), on the river's south bank, uneven stone steps take you down to a shingle beach. Launch and turn left to follow the direction of the river. As you set off, look behind you to see one of the enormous limestone rock faces of Vercors behind you, shaped like Pride Rock in 'Lion King'; it's still visible at the end of the 11km route. After a kilometre, you'll pass under the first of several little bridges (/// unsolvable.stardom.shunning) that you'll meet en route.

Keep following the river for 1.7km from the bridge as it runs a reasonably straight course, to reach a long shingle beach (/// outwork.bickering.snapping) that splits the river in two. The right-hand side is wider, and looks more tempting to go down, but take the left-hand fork that hugs the treeline instead. At the end is a slalom (/// bookmark.courses.scissors) made of stones to rejoin the main river, which is really fun to go down and a good test of your turning skills. At the bottom of the slalom, bear left and keep paddling with the river.

Three kilometres on, arrive at the edge of the town of Saillans (/// vintage. struggles.verses). A handsome building towers over the river, and on a fine day the beaches here are busy, but it's still worth disembarking for a swim. As you

↑ Rapids on this stretch of the Drôme are fairly gentle (Andrew Wood/A)

paddle out of town, ignore the signs for disembarkation point 'A' for Canoë Drôme (/// everything.associate.crash) – your route continues further.

Just after a light set of rapids, 2km after leaving Saillans, the river meanders to the left and, on the right-hand bank, a series of flat rocks create a natural staircase into the river (/// ruin.songwriting.trappings). This is a wonderful place to swim. From here, a final kilometre among the trees takes you to your end point, marked with a letter 'B' on the right-hand bank (/// clarifies.ruthlessly.vibrato), where crudely cut steps give access up to a little car park.

ESSENTIALS

GETTING THERE The closest airport with direct flights to the UK, Lyon-Saint Exupéry, is two hours away (car hire available). TER trains run from Valence to Saillans, taking just under an hour, but to make the most of this part of France it's really helpful to have a car. It takes the same time by road and there are plenty of car-hire outlets in Valence. Saillans is right on the D93, which runs from the Rhône Valley to Vercors Regional Park. From here it's a 5km drive east to the car park in Espenel to start the descent, or the same distance west to reach the little car park where you finish. Public transport is all but non-existent, so you'll need to organise lifts with friends.

HIRE & LESSONS Canoë Drôme (⌖ canoe-drome.com) hires canoes and kayaks, and also organises multi-day descents of the Drôme River (water levels permitting). Snacks and refreshments are available at the base.

WHEN TO GO In the summer the weather is generally lovely and the cool waters of the Drôme make a welcome respite from the Provençal heat, but be aware that – particularly in August – you'll likely have to walk and drag your kayak in certain sections, and paddleboarding the river becomes all but impossible. May to early July is the best time for this route.

WHERE TO STAY & EAT La Maison Rose (⌖ maisonrose-saillans.com) in Saillans has a swimming pool and pretty gardens. There are also heaps of campsites along the banks of the Drôme, which make a convenient base. **Camping les Tuillères** (⌖ tuilleres.com) is a good one with a large swimming pool, run by Dutch owners.

Le Rieussec (⌖ le-rieussec-saillans.eatbu.com) in Saillans has good value four-course set dinner menus and serves typical French specialities (vegetarians will struggle).

TITBITS Go to **Domaine Long** (⌖ domaine-long.com ⏰ 09.00–19.30 daily) to taste the region's famous sparkling wine. All of their produce is organic and they also make rosé and red wines. It's advisable to ring/email in advance if you'd like to do a tasting.

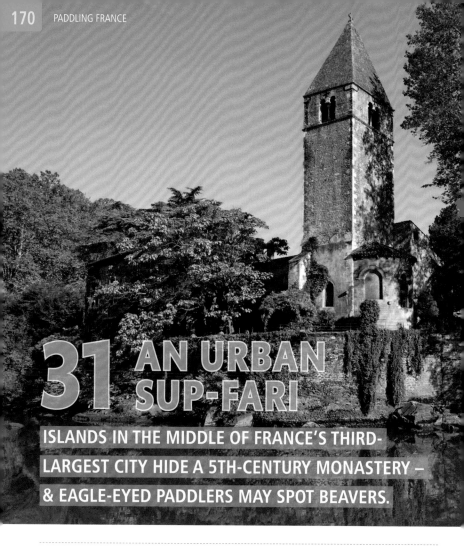

31 AN URBAN SUP-FARI

ISLANDS IN THE MIDDLE OF FRANCE'S THIRD-LARGEST CITY HIDE A 5TH-CENTURY MONASTERY – & EAGLE-EYED PADDLERS MAY SPOT BEAVERS.

WHERE	Lyon, Auvergne-Rhône-Alpes
STATS	12km round trip 🏄 ③ 🛶 ②
START/FINISH	Go Captain, Rochetaillée-sur-Saône, 829 chemin de la Plage, 69270 Rochetaillée-sur-Saône /// downturn.monkeys.regard

Lyon is my home, a pulsating mix of vibrant street art, live music played anywhere from ancient Roman amphitheatres to the roofs of old sugar factories, and a gastronomy scene that is arguably the best in the country. It's also a major metropolis, so it sometimes feels frenetic. I grew up beside the sea and, whenever I miss the water, this is my go-to paddle route. It starts on the Saône just below the gentle hills of the Monts d'Or and is so lush and green most of the way that it's easy to forget you're in a huge city.

↑ The abbey on Île Barbe was founded in the 5th century (SS)

The two parallel rivers that flow through Lyon, the Rhône and the Saône, converge at La Confluence in the city centre, creating a half island in the middle (known as Presqu'Île). The difference between the two waterways reminds me of the tortoise and the hare. The Rhône is France's most powerful river, a watery motorway with strong currents that starts in Switzerland and, after merging with the Saône, flows down to join the Mediterranean Sea to the west of Marseille. The Saône, by comparison, moves so languidly that it can be tricky to see which direction the water is running in. But this slow and steady flow makes it ideal for paddling, even for beginners.

Lyon's size and density hasn't stopped it from having an abundance of green spaces (Tête d'Or Park in the city centre is a whopping 117ha and comes complete with giraffes and flamingos in an open-air zoo) and – with two major rivers – the city isn't just green, it's also staggeringly blue. On the river itself, the most exciting wildlife you might see is beavers. In the early 20th century they had almost been eradicated in Europe, but thanks to conservation measures they've naturally recolonised both the Rhône and the Saône rivers. The beavers themselves are tricky to spot, but you're likely to see felled trees and evidence of dams.

Lyon city centre is full of boat traffic: *bateaux-mouches* (pleasure boats with restaurants on board that take tours up and down the river), cargo ships and passenger ferries. As a result, paddleboarding is forbidden in the centre, but you can still arrive there by water, so long as you disembark at the end of this paddle. The start point of this trip, Rochetaillée-sur-Saône, is some 12km north of the city centre by road, but only 6km by river. I've designed this as a round trip but, should your arms be weary mid-route or you don't fancy the return leg, you can alight on the south bank of the river, across from Île Barbe, and catch a bus back (line 40).

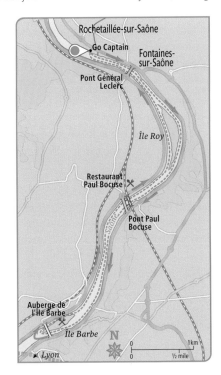

This is a simple route to follow, with only the length and boat traffic posing any difficulties. Don't paddle right in the middle of the river as cargo ships regularly come up this far. Both paddleboards and kayaks work well – choose your favourite. Although the Saône is slow moving, you'll meet more resistance on the return journey (and it will take you a little longer). Pay attention to the wind direction, as a northerly that blows you downriver will be a tough paddle back.

PADDLE THIS WAY

From the launch point (/// downturn.monkeys.regard), head left downriver, hugging the left-hand bank. After just over 500m, you'll pass Fontaines-sur-Saône on your left, a pretty Lyonnais suburb dominated by a copper-spired church made from *pierre dorée* (a golden stone found in the Monts d'Or), stencilled on the skyline behind you. Pass under Pont Général Leclerc (/// resist.slings.triangle), the first of three bridges you'll see on this route. Île Roy (/// reclaim.steps.villas) is 500m after the bridge and only accessible by boat or SUP – a good kilometre in length, the island obscures the northern bank of the river with thick foliage. Bar a distinctly average restaurant, there's not much to it, but the wooded island has become a haven for wildlife and, if you're lucky, you might spot beavers or kingfishers.

After leaving the island (keep left), you'll pass under two further bridges in quick succession, the first of which is the railway line; from the second bridge, Pont Paul Bocuse (/// tagging.holdings.grapes), it's another 3km of paddling past leafy suburbs that become increasingly peppered with the grand mansions and turrets of some of Lyon's wealthiest quartiers. The foliage on the banks is mostly broken only by jetties and launch points, with the low rumbling of the major roads that run either side of the river the only indication that you're so urban. As you round the river bend it reveals your first view of Île Barbe (/// hydrant.placed.bumpy), an abbey first built in the 5th century situated on an island whose name translates as 'Isle of Barbarians'. Although no-one knows for sure, its name suggests that it resisted civilisation for longer than the rest of Lyon. What is known is that Charlemagne himself donated a library to the abbey, and the original abbey was burnt down by Protestants in 1567 during the French Wars of Religion so the building that you see today was largely rebuilt after this. Half of the island is accessible to the public, but the other half is private residences, so by far your best view is from the water where you'll see virtually the whole lot – and it's magical.

This is as far as you can legally paddle before entering the busy city centre, but there's no signs telling you to disembark, so make sure you follow the guidance in the text that follows. Round Île Barbe and turn around to paddle upstream along the north bank, back the way you came, but hugging the other side of the river. Île Barbe is linked with bridges to the mainland, where there are bistros, boulangeries and supermarkets just a hundred metres or so away on either side, making this a good place to stop if you're peckish. The restaurant on the island, the Auberge de l'Île Barbe, is run by Relais & Châteaux and therefore comes with a champagne price tag.

As you reascend the river, keep the bank on your left. After you pass under the first two bridges, look out for the gaudily painted green and pink Restaurant Paul Bocuse, which is just visible from the water and one of the best-known restaurants in France. From here it's a gentle 3km paddle to return to your start point in Rochetaillée-sur-Saône.

↑ Views towards central Lyon (Hemis/A) → Lyonnais chef Paul Bocuse became one of the most famous in the world and his restaurant is visible from the river (ricochet64/S)

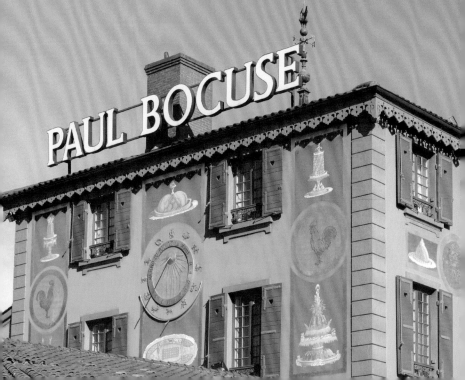

↑ Boat cruises ply the Saône (ldgfr photos/S)

ESSENTIALS

GETTING THERE From the UK, Lyon can be reached by taking the Eurostar to Paris and then the TGV to Lyon Part Dieu or Perrache, both of which are well placed for this paddle. Alternatively, Lyon-Saint Exupéry airport is served by international flights; from here, the Rhône Express runs straight to Lyon Part Dieu, taking under half an hour.

Bus 40 runs from Saint-Paul in Vieux Lyon to the launch point at Go Captain boat rental in Rochetaillée-sur-Saône. Parking in Lyon is notoriously bad, so take public transport if possible. The closest car park to the start of the paddle is on the other side of the river and a steep 3km walk largely uphill, so if driving, try to find on-street parking.

HIRE & LESSONS Go Captain (go-captain.fr) offers paddleboard, canoe and motorboat hire and lessons.

WHEN TO GO The most comfortable temperatures are in spring or autumn. During the winter months temperatures are regularly in minus figures for days on end, and sometimes there's snow (although it rarely settles in the city). In July and August, temperatures can get as high as 40°C. This might not bother you while you're out paddling, but it's not particularly comfortable for sightseeing in the city.

WHERE TO STAY & EAT Hôtel Lyon Métropole by Arteloge (lyonmetropole.com/en) overlooks the Saône just below Île Barbe so you won't quite be able to paddle past your window. It has the largest spa in the entire country. Head into the city centre for dinner. My personal favourite is **Les Assembleurs** (lesassembleurs. fr), a tapas bar with local wines on tap that turns even the most amateur wine drinker into an oenologist.

TITBITS To experience Lyon from the water in the evening, go to one of the peniches (boat bars) on the other river, the Rhône, and enjoy a glass of Côtes du Rhône, the local wine, with a view.

32 THE MOUNTAIN JEWEL

PADDLE AROUND AIGUEBELETTE, A LAKE SO VIBRANT IT FEELS LIKE THE COLOURS HAVE BEEN SUPERIMPOSED.

WHERE	Lake Aiguebelette, Auvergne-Rhône-Alpes
STATS	Free paddle 🚶 🏄 ①
START/FINISH	Port de Plaisance, 73610 Aiguebelette-le-Lac (/// united.sloths.highlights)

Lake Aiguebelette used to be the under-the-radar alternative to Lake Annecy, and while it can't quite claim that unknown status anymore, it's still much quieter than its more famous neighbour. The colour of the water is what first astonishes you here: a mix of teal and emerald, it positively glows – it's not surprising that the lake has been called the 'jewel' of the region.

Unlike many lakes in the foothills of the Alps, Lake Aiguebelette has remained remarkably undeveloped. Much of the lakeside has tangled foliage that tumbles down to meet the water, and there's no footpath, let alone a road, running around its whole perimeter. You can easily explore the entire lake, which measures just under 5.5km², by paddleboard without fear of getting lost.

↑ Picture-perfect Aiguebelette is a nature reserve (Hemis/A)

Here you'll find some of the calmest paddleboarding conditions possible – though the water is so inviting that you may well voluntarily take a tumble. I came here with a friend one weekend in July – Lyon was too hot, but here the slight elevation (373m) meant that the weather couldn't have been more perfect. There wasn't a ripple on the lake, and mornings still had that nip in the air that I'd been missing in the city. Off the water, hiking and biking routes up in the hills are excellent, and sunset views over the glass-like lake take some beating.

You need to have a permit to paddle here as this is a Ramsar wetland (designated for protection under the internal Ramsar convention in 1991), which can be purchased online via the CCLA (ccla.fr) and costs €7 per day, or €20 for the whole year. Not having a permit risks a hefty fine, but you can easily buy it online on the day.

PADDLE THIS WAY

The pontoon at the Port de Plaisance in Aiguebelette-le-Lac (/// united.sloths.highlights) is a good launch spot, with the lake's originally named islands, Grande Île (/// vivacious.uneasy.hummed) and Petite Île (/// envies.enticed.breath), almost directly in front of you. On Grande Île there's a pint-sized chapel, Saint Vincent Chapel, but it's virtually impossible to see with all the foliage. It's forbidden to land on either of the two islands and little wooden markers outline how closely you're allowed to approach them. The lake is considered to be of international importance owing to the birdlife and fish species that reside in this pristine habitat, hence the Ramsar designation.

There are seven lidos to explore around the lake. One of the nicest beaches is just north of Saint-Alban-de-Montbel: Sougey Beach (/// checkpoint.rebutted.coated). The sand here is so white that it makes for a startling contrast with the teal and emerald water. The beach has a fenced-off area for swimmers, and is also a popular launching point for paddleboarders. The northern half of the lake has fewer beaches, but is also less developed; north of La Combe, save for one lakeside road, the greenery of the mountains is uninterrupted.

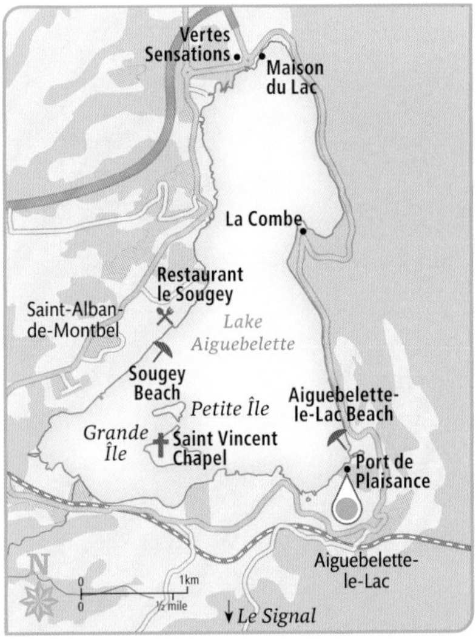

Don't worry about following the lake perimeter, it's perfectly possible to zigzag to and fro across the lake, and it's small enough that it's very difficult to lose your way.

ESSENTIALS

GETTING THERE The closest major train station is in Chambéry, from where it's a 20-minute (19km) drive to the lake. Chambéry Airport is served by international flights to various UK airports, and car hire is available from the airport. Buses run from Chambéry city centre to Aiguebelette-le-Lac, taking half an hour.

HIRE & LESSONS Vertes Sensations (⌀ vertes-sensations.com ☉ Apr–Oct), on the northern shore of the lake next to the Maison du Lac, hires paddleboards, canoes and kayaks.

WHEN TO GO Summer is a great time to go to Lake Aiguebelette, when the slight increase in altitude makes for cooler temperatures than in the cities. During the winter, air temperatures regularly drop below freezing and there's frequent snow, particularly from November to March. You'll need your own gear if you want to paddle during the winter months.

WHERE TO STAY & EAT Le Signal (☎ 04 79 36 07 29) in La Genaz is an excellent campsite and as cheap as they come, with panoramic views over the lake from the approach. It's under 5km uphill from Aiguebelette-le-Lac. There are resident chickens, and the friendly owners sell fresh eggs and their own homemade jam. Other accommodation around the lake is largely in self-catered gîtes.

Dining options are somewhat limited and pricey around the lake. There's a Lidl at Le Pont-de-Beauvoisin to stock up on provisions, and Sunday morning markets in Novalaise and Chambéry. **Restaurant le Sougey** (🅵 Auberge-du-Sougey-plage-lac-Aiguebelette) in Saint-Alban-de-Montbel is one of the best options and has a hearty menu of Breton galettes and wood-fired pizzas with views over the lake.

TITBITS Lake Aiguebelette is a popular paragliding spot, and views over the lake and surrounding mountains are spectacular. There are paragliding operators in Novalaise and Saint-Paul-de-Yenne, 5 and 10km from the lake respectively. **Aiguebelette Parapente** (🖉 aiguebeletteparapente.fr) in Novalaise does induction flights and runs courses.

↓ The calm waters here couldn't be better for stand-up paddleboarding (Hemis/A)

33 ALPINE ADVENTURE

FRANCE'S CLEANEST LAKE, ENCIRCLED BY MOUNTAINS, PROVIDES CRYSTAL-CLEAR PADDLING CONDITIONS.

WHERE	Annecy, Auvergne-Rhône-Alpes
STATS	Free paddle 🚣 ⛵ ①
START/FINISH	Skiwake74, 120 route de la Plage, 74210 Doussard
	/// needier.verging.repeats

Annecy is beautiful no matter the season. A teal-coloured Mexican wave of a lake undulating through the lower Alps, framed by mountains that shelter it from the elements and medieval architecture at water level – a mixture of châteaux, former prisons and higgledy-piggledy streets that tell the story of a turbulent history. Until the 14th century, Annecy was ruled by the Counts of Geneva, before coming under the control of the House of Savoy. During the 17th century it yo-yoed between French and Savoyard jurisdiction, and only permanently became part of France in 1860. As a result, the architecture of Annecy's main town is a hotchpotch. Savoyard houses that look like mountain chalets have been picked up and relocated to town and, now fighting for space, have become tipsy. There are imposing-looking medieval castles and former prison buildings with iron grills in the windows, and Belle Époque tower blocks from when Annecy started to become the popular tourist destination it is today. There's plenty of modern construction too, as more and more people swap larger cities for proximity to the mountains. It's particularly popular with young Parisians looking to live a more outdoors lifestyle and French commuters working in Geneva; Annecy, although one of the more expensive places to live in France, is still much cheaper than Switzerland, so many enjoy the more economical living costs while earning a Swiss salary.

A victim of its popularity, Annecy town has begun to outgrow the modest amount of land assigned to it. It still makes a convenient base, thanks to all the hotels, restaurants and easy public transport – remarkably for a city of this size, there are no fewer than seven Michelin-starred restaurants. However, the real charm here lies in the area's natural beauty, which is best discovered by escaping the main town for the lake.

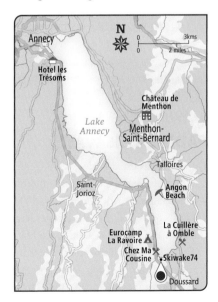

As you leave Annecy town behind, grassy lidos spring up at intervals on the lakeshore. Towns are frequent, but considerably smaller than Annecy itself, and the pace of life becomes slower. The southern end of the lake is quietest, a sleepy stretch of water where reed beds tangle along the shore and the mountains

← Family-friendly Annecy was home to France's first paddleboard club (AU74LOU/S)

framing the lake look like camel's humps. Paddling up the eastern bank, past Talloires and Menthon-Saint-Bernard, feels like discovering how Annecy must have looked in centuries gone by, where little church spires and château turrets peep out amid the trees, shaded by the mountains.

Lake Annecy is an outdoor sports paradise, and paddleboarding or kayaking is just one part of it. In winter, you could ski in the morning and paddleboard in the afternoon – taking care not to fall in as the water temperature hovers at a distinctly refreshing 4°C at that time of year. (Wrap up warm, the lake is glacier-fed and even in summer the waters are chilly.) January is a particularly fun time to visit to experience the annual Glagla Race, a 15km cold-water stand-up paddle race across the lake, while all of your surroundings are covered in snow. In summer, there's no better way to cool off after a sweaty mountain hike or cycle than by plunging into the cool depths of Lake Annecy.

While Annecy town may have become much more desirable over the last few decades, Annecians remain true to tradition and many of their festivals have been going for centuries. Visit in mid-October and you'll see the Retour des Alpages (the returning of the cows from the mountains), when cattle parade through town and there's even more cheese than usual to be consumed.

Be aware that Annecy town gets extremely crowded during the school holidays and other public holidays in France. While it may be convenient to base yourself in town, with all of the restaurants and amenities on your doorstep, if you're looking for a tranquil paddleboarding experience it's better to skip the town's main lido and launch from one of the other towns on the lake; I've recommended starting from Doussard, at the southern end – it's much quieter and particularly good if you fancy paddleboard yoga classes. The lake, at just over 27km², has a plethora of lidos, slipways and launch spots, so feel free to choose the most convenient starting place for you. There are no islands on Lake Annecy, and it's much longer than it is wide. Paddling widthways across the lake is very doable, as in most places it is only 3km or so across but, at almost 15km long, you'll need some energy if you want to cross it there and back lengthways. The easiest place to cross the lake widthways is between Duingt and Talloires, which is the shortest crossing at just under 2km.

PADDLE THIS WAY

Doussard has the double advantage of being one of the quietest parts of the lake and one of the most sheltered, making it a perfect spot to launch your paddle; you can launch from the slipway at Skiwake74 (/// needier.verging.repeats). The village is on the edge of the Bauges Regional Park, so the hills rise steeply behind the lake, and along the banks, reed beds and trees mask little campsites.

The village of Talloires (/// finalists.intersect.chimes) is 9km north of Doussard. Known for being *un peu bobo* (rather fancy), it's nonetheless a more manageable size than Annecy town, and tends to get fewer crowds. There's a large, leafy lido

(Angon Beach) and a small harbour with pontoons, so it's easy to moor up your paddle and explore the village on foot.

Roughly 8km further north by water from Talloires' Angon Beach is the lido beach at Menthon-Saint-Bernard (/// monsoons.conspicuous.wriggled). A gorgeous town, it has plenty of hiking trails that lead straight up into the surrounding mountains, and the turreted Château de Menthon is rumoured to have been the inspiration for the Disney castle. The foundation stones of the castle were laid in the 10th century, and after that it was been added to like an elaborate Lego structure, with construction finally finishing 900 years later. The lido has summer diving platforms, plenty of sunbathing spots and easy slipways to alight with your paddle.

↑ Paddleboarders take to the water year-round (Jonathan Bal/S)

ESSENTIALS

GETTING THERE Direct trains run from Paris to Annecy. The nearest international airport is just across the Swiss border, in Geneva, and from here the bus takes approximately 1½ hours to Annecy town. Regular direct buses run between Annecy town and Doussard, taking half an hour. There's on-site parking at the watersports club in Doussard.

HIRE & LESSONS Skiwake74 (⚲ skiwake74.com) hires paddleboards and kayaks in Doussard on the southern side of the lake, and works with **Au Bout du Lac Yoga** (⚲ auboutdulacyoga.com ☉ Apr–Oct) which runs paddleboard yoga sessions. There are few environments more peaceful for your sun salutation than floating in the middle of Lake Annecy.

WHEN TO GO Early April to late October is when the watersports hire centres are open, but to maximise good weather and avoid the crowds, visit in May, June or September. Or, if you're feeling bold, go in January to watch (or participate in) the Glagla Race. Where else could you ski and paddleboard on the same day?

Pedalos, kayaks and SUPS are all available for hire during the summer (Marcello Celli/DT)

WHERE TO STAY & EAT Hôtel les Trésoms (⌖ lestresoms.com) is absolutely magnificent and just a short walk from Annecy town, with panoramic views over the lake and easy access to the water, so you can paddle right from your base; there's also a Michelin-starred restaurant. Right by Doussard at the quieter end of the lake is **Eurocamp La Ravoire** (⌖ eurocamp.fr), again with spectacular views and indoor and outdoor swimming pools. Their entertainment schedule is busy and keeps the whole family occupied.

Fret not, the dining options in town and around the lake aren't all Michelin starred. If your budget is more sparkling wine than champagne, there are two truly excellent restaurants on the banks of the lake: **La Cuillère à Omble** (⌖ lacuillereaomble.fr]) is good for fresh fish caught in the lake itself, and **Chez Ma Cousine** (⌖ chezmacousine.fr) does slap-up salads. Both are at the southern end. Avoid the tourist traps along Le Thiou in Annecy town.

TITBITS Strap on your hiking boots, there's just as much fun to be had off the water here. Mont Veyrier makes for a good day hike, taking between 5 and 7 hours depending on fitness. It's well marked and easy to follow, and climbs considerably in elevation for both views and a pleasing workout. Semnoz, the closest ski station to Annecy, becomes a hiker's paradise in summer, and has a year-round toboggan run.

34 NATURE'S PLAYGROUND

LIMESTONE INLETS BETWEEN CASSIS & MARSEILLE CREATE A WATER-BASED ADVENTURE PLAYGROUND.

WHERE	Cassis, Provence-Alpes-Côte d'Azur
STATS	17km return 🏊④ 🚣③
START/FINISH	CSLN, Grande Mer Beach, 13260 Cassis
	(/// accumulation.implies.overseer)

Thunderous rocky pillars soar more than 500m above the sea in this spectacular stretch of southern France, a landscape formed 120 million years ago from limestone. Now a 26km-long national park stretching between Marseille and Cassis, it has to be seen to be believed – a series of 26 rocky inlets, known as *calanques*, are an adventure playground for hikers, climbers and, most importantly, paddleboarders and kayakers. The first part of the paddle – the 3km from Cassis before you reach your first calanque – is the least interesting, but saying this does it a disservice, because it's still a notch up from most paddling routes you'll do. It's just that what's to come is nothing short of mind-blowing. From here, the scenery becomes a playground of precipitous, pockmarked rocks that mask inlets with water so varying in shades of blue and green it looks like elaborately cut stained glass.

The first time that I came here was on foot, following the GR51 between Toulon and Marseille. I hit the first stretch of calanques as the sun was rising and jumped into the crystalline water before enjoying a picnic breakfast on the beach. I was captivated, but I couldn't help feeling that the magic of this place lay offshore, and would be even better explored from a paddleboard. I wasn't wrong. Many of the calanques are easier to access by water, and along the limestone cliffs are a plethora of caves and sea arches, creating a natural, rocky obstacle course.

Exploring all of the calanques would be a round trip of over 50km – and, as camping is forbidden here, would make for an intensive day trip. This 17km route gives you plenty of variety and visits some of the most beautiful inlets. You'll paddle into caves and weave in and out of the rocks, contrasting between glassy flat water within the calanques and the more challenging bumps and waves of the sea, where there's nothing to break the passage of waves between here and Algeria.

Pack plenty of water – if you do make it to one of the few restaurants in the calanques (not included on this suggested route), you'll find that water is a more expensive commodity than beer here. Tides aren't an issue on the Mediterranean, but be aware of the winds, of which Le Mistral is the strongest, and most often experienced during the winter and early spring. You shouldn't attempt to paddle when the weather is bad, but be aware that any offshore winds can be dangerous. After Calanque d'en Vau in particular, the route is exposed, so keep an eye on clouds, and note – if the wind feels as though it's picking up, cut your paddle short. Be aware that once you reach the calanques there is no mobile reception.

Kayaks and paddleboards are both fine on this route, but since it is a sea paddle, take a long, rigid fin to aid movement if you're paddleboarding.

← These limestone cliffs of the calanques are largely formed from sea shells and fish bones (SS)

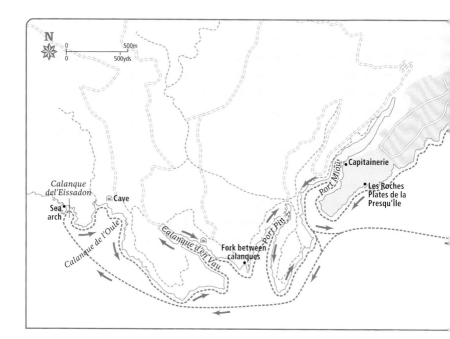

PADDLE THIS WAY

Launch from the beach by CSLN Cassis kayak hire (Grand Mer Beach (/// accumulation.implies.overseer). It's a nice beach, sandy and good for swimming, but where you're going is better. Facing the sea, paddle to your right (going past the bulk of Cassis town and the port). Hugging the shoreline is best regardless of the wind, because you'll see more, be more protected and you'll avoid a lot of the boat traffic. In season there are lots of tour boats passing, and some of them will make you feel very small aboard a paddle. They also create quite a bit of wash, which can easily unbalance even a seasoned paddler.

After passing the port and Cassis's lighthouse at the end of the pier, it's a 3km paddle alongside sand-coloured rocks adorned with the odd building or restaurant, and probably a whole host of sunbathers, before you reach Les Roches Plates de la Presqu'Île (/// crumbling.behalf.vicinity). This slightly sloping rocky ledge, is a particularly popular spot for sunbathers, often nude.

After Les Roches Plates de la Presqu'Île, keep paddling for a couple of hundred metres and follow the headland that curves to your right. Your first calanque, Port Miou, is 1,400m long and over 200m deep, and is a working harbour, with so many gleaming white yachts that it looks as though a flock of birds has settled on the water. You're not allowed to go past the Capitainerie (harbour master's office /// downs.defying.brochure) on a paddleboard, but from here you can still see the docked yachts, and you'll have your first experience of paddling down a limestone

inlet framed with craggy rock pillars and scrubby pines – dreamy.

Turn around at the Capitainerie to leave Port Miou the way you came, but this time, as you exit, head right, following the coastline. The next two calanques are only a kilometre away, in the shadow of immense limestone cliffs, and you'll pass the wide entrance that forks to access them (/// wishing.assessed.constituent), but push on and visit them at the end. The coast curves slightly to your right, and a kilometre later you'll pass the wide entrance to Calanque de l'Oule. Keep paddling and explore this on the way back, too; you're heading instead for a curious sea arch on the edge of Calanque de l'Eissadon (/// radar. cheers.equips), just 500m further on. You can paddle right through the sea arch, which is just big enough for two paddleboards fused together to pass through.

Turn around to head back the way you came, now with the coast on your left. From Calanque de l'Eissadon it's only half a kilometre to reach the start of Calanque de l'Oule. It's time to go caving. Look for the largest entrance you see in the rock face (/// keeper.turndown.mincing) – there are several small caves in the cliff that don't really go anywhere. The entrance is still deceptively small, but once inside, it opens out into a big cavern. You can hide out here, pretending you're a smuggler with a booty of rum, as you watch the passing tour boats and kayaks.

Back outside, keep paddling in the direction of Cassis, hugging the cliffs. You might see climbers when you look up as this is an extremely popular spot for cliff climbing.

Once you get to a triangular headland, 2km later, you've got a choice of two calanques. These are the ones you bypassed on the outbound journey. Since you're going to do them both, start with the one closest to you, Calanque d'en Vau, which involves a paddle of around 800m from the triangular headland to reach the beach.

En Vau (/// relax.uranium.zeroing) is widely thought to be the prettiest calanque. It's gorgeous, a soft-sand beach framed between towering limestone cliffs, where the mill-pond-still water becomes marbled in appearance with the varying depths.

Thanks to its good looks, it gets incredibly busy. There's a shallow cave on the right-hand side as you approach the calanque. As you're approaching En Vau by water, if the beach is too crowded, you can smugly moor up your paddle on the rocks further off the coast, many of which are flat and perfect for sunbathing, and enjoy the views in peace.

Exit Calanque d'en Vau and, heading in the direction of Cassis, turn immediately down the narrow water channel to your left, again around 800m long. This is Port Pin (/// systemic.bonfire.blasts), my favourite of the calanques. The limestone cliffs are a little lower here, allowing more sunlight in, but what I particularly like are all the scrubby trees around the rocks and beach, which make it feel extra wild. It tends to be marginally less crowded than En Vau (although still busy in season, as all the calanques accessible on foot are). A line of buoys stops the tour boats from going right up to the beach, but you're allowed to bypass these in your kayak or paddle, and there's plenty of rock sunbathing spots if you want to get out. One thing that makes this calanque feel particularly private is that the inlet twists and turns a lot, so you can't see the open sea straight away once you paddle away from the beach.

↑ The calanques are one of the prettiest places to paddle in the country (Matt Tilghman/S)

Turn around and paddle out to sea to leave Port Pin. As you exit the calanque, turn left, back towards Cassis, and paddle past the entrance of Port Miou, just over a kilometre after leaving Port Pin. Shortly after, rounding the rocky headland, you'll see Cassis open up in front of you; be sure to admire the absolutely enormous cliff face at the other side of the bay (which was behind you on the way out). This is Cap Canaille (/// solidifying.modest.quirks), and at 394m high it makes the calanques look small. Rust-coloured, with boulders that look like rubble at the bottom, it's formed of three types of rock: limestone, sandstone and puddingstone. Make a beeline for it, a 3km open-water paddle across the bay. If you're feeling really energetic or you're in Cassis for several days, there's spectacular paddling around here too, otherwise, turn towards the shore to have Cap Canaille on your right-hand side.

Keeping Cap Canaille on your right, hug the coast and paddle back towards Cassis, passing two sandy beaches on the way. The first, l'Arène (/// highly. overgrowth.mirage), a kilometre after Cap Canaille, is a delightful spot for a swim, with soft golden sand and far fewer crowds than on Cassis's beaches. After passing the two beaches, it's a further kilometre in the same direction to reach Grande Mer Beach, where you started from.

↑ On a kayak or a SUP you can get to calanques inaccessible by road (Patchanokk/S)

ESSENTIALS

GETTING THERE Marseille, a 40-minute (34km) drive from Cassis, has high-speed train connections to Paris and a major international airport. Buses and trains regularly connect to Cassis.

Parking in Cassis is some of the most expensive in the country and can easily set you back €25 a day. Bear this in mind when choosing your accommodation – some hotels have deals/on-site parking that are significantly cheaper than the public car parks in town.

HIRE & LESSONS CSLN Cassis (⌗ cassis-kayak.com) hires kayaks and paddleboards, as well as organising guided visits of the calanques. The staff are extremely knowledgeable about local places of interest, and this is one of the few watersports centres in France that stays open all year round.

WHEN TO GO Cassis gets rammed during the summer holidays: avoid July and August and travel in shoulder season, or even during the winter months. In winter, you may just have the calanques to yourself, but you run the risk of encountering the Mistral, the famous aforementioned winds which whip the sea here into a frenzy.

WHERE TO STAY & EAT While the **Best Western Cassis** (⌗ bestwestern. co.uk) won't win any awards for character, it's a great place to stay. An hour's complimentary use of the spa is included in your visit, the rooms are spacious, airy and comfortable, and the communal areas are excellent. It's only a couple of minutes' walk to the main beach and your paddle launch point.

A Table (7 rue Dr Séverin Icard; ✆ 04 42 73 27 51) has delicious vegetarian platters and plenty of meat and seafood dishes too.

Even the supermarket prices are inflated in Cassis so, if you're on a tight budget, consider stocking up before you arrive or shop at the biweekly local market (☉ morning Wed & Sat).

TITBITS Marseille has long been a city which gets a bad rap, but it's one of the most up-and-coming places in the country, and it's well worth tacking on a few days here to your trip. Excellent world cuisine, street art and parties that go on all night long give it a real buzz. The Cathédrale La Major, an enormous basilica on the seafront, looks a bit like a pinstriped version of a Russian Orthodox cathedral.

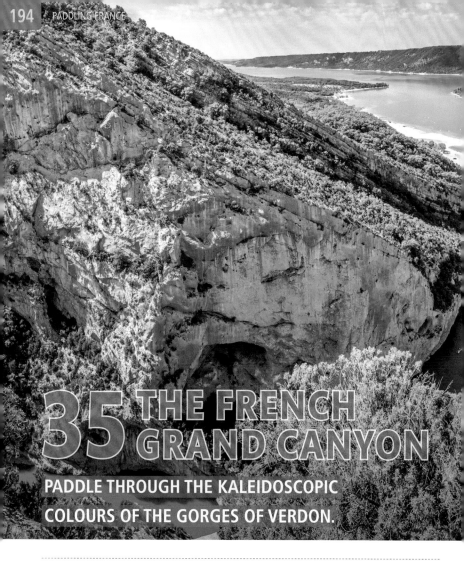

35 THE FRENCH GRAND CANYON

PADDLE THROUGH THE KALEIDOSCOPIC COLOURS OF THE GORGES OF VERDON.

WHERE	Lake Sainte-Croix, Verdon, Provence-Alpes-Côte d'Azur
STATS	Route 1: 7km round trip 🧍②🛶①; Route 2: 9km return 🧍④🛶③
START/FINISH	Route 1: Galetas Beach, Lake Sainte-Croix, 83630 Aiguines (/// confiscated.stirrup.slights); Route 2: Base Yannick, 04500 Montagnac – Monpezat (/// skewers.unsafe.dozen)

The Verdon gorges – often referred to as the 'Grand Canyon of Europe' – are the result of millions of years of erosion by the Verdon River. The water here glows a bright turquoise, particularly on a sunny day, an effect caused by the reflecting sunlight on the limestone sediment in the water. In the middle of the gorges, an enormous lake, Saint-Croix, spills out across the rocky landscape like a splodge of turquoise paint.

↑ The canyon is up to 700m deep in places (milosk50/S)

From either end, the river winds a skinny, meandering course through immense gorges, creating a paddling route that goes through prehistoric landscapes, boxed in by rocks that look like holey lumps of cheese.

This is a double-paddle bonanza, but it wasn't planned this way. When I arrived at the Verdon gorges, I had one paddling route in mind – a fairly short route along the main canyon by Moustiers-Sainte-Marie from Lake Sainte-Croix. It was gorgeous, peppered with caves, and the intermittent sunlight shining through the cliffs created a myriad of colours on the water. Alas, owing particularly to low water levels when I visited in spring 2023, it wasn't possible to get as far up the canyon as you once could. The views were still spectacular though, with the limestone rocks sprinkled with an impossible number of caves and holes, and swallows darting in and out of them. The water was every bit

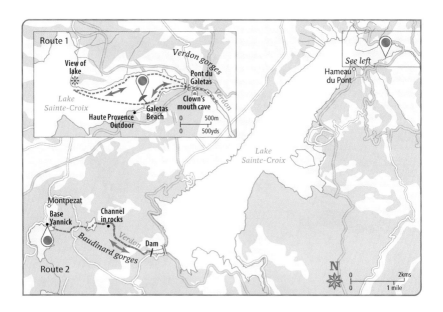

as turquoise as photos had suggested, and the walls of the gorge towered hundreds of metres above me.

After my paddle, I heard about a second paddling route on the western end of the lake that also went through limestone gorges, although these weren't nearly so high. With strength still in my limbs, I took to the road and drove for half an hour across a limestone plateau full of lavender fields to reach the start point at Montpezat. This second route was mind blowing, the water a deep navy rather than turquoise, with small caves at water level to be explored, and little mossy waterfalls dribbling down into the river. *Et voilà*, that's why you have two routes here that you simply have to test.

You can use a kayak or a paddleboard for either but, if using a paddleboard I recommend taking local advice or doing your research on the water levels in advance of paddling the first route. If water levels are low, you risk cutting your paddle short by using a fin, which will run aground more quickly. If you're a novice paddler, opt for the first route as the second is better for intermediate and advanced paddlers – or tackle the second route in a kayak to make it easier.

I'd recommend beginning the first paddle as early in the day as you can, as the gorges get extremely busy with pedalos and kayaks alike soon after 09.00.

At the end of the second route is a dam. The energy company that controls it regularly alternates between feeding water into Lake Sainte-Croix and draining it. As a result, you won't know until leaving the lake and arriving on this stretch of the Verdon whether the dam will be pulling you towards the lake and pushing you away from it. The pull (or push, depending on the direction) increases in intensity the closer you get to the dam. If you're really lucky, you might find the dam pulls you all the way down the river, changes direction and then spits you back to the lake again. If you're really unlucky, you could find the opposite, which means a stiff, upstream paddle and then paddling upstream again for the return. Allow extra time in case this happens.

PADDLE THIS WAY

ROUTE 1 The launch point, Galetas Beach (/// confiscated.stirrup.slights), is a long stretch of shingle just west of Hameau du Pont. Turn right and follow the lakeshore for a kilometre until you reach a bridge, Pont du Galetas (/// nuisance. elevators.dovetail). Pass under the bridge and you'll immediately be travelling into the gorge. Paddling here is easy, and well sheltered from the elements. Less than a kilometre after the bridge, look out for a vast cave above you on your right-hand side (/// commercially.aspiring.thinkers). It looks a little like a clown's mouth, and you'll see little birds darting in and out of it.

Carry on upriver as far as the river will allow you, gliding over water so blue that it would put a chlorine-filled swimming pool to shame. For me, it was approximately 3km into the gorge (/// stumpy.traffic.numeracy) that the kayak ran aground and I was forced to retreat. Retrace your steps and pass under Pont du Galetas once again, but instead of turning left and returning to your start point, cross to the other side of the lake, directly in front of you. Keep the bank on your right-hand side, and paddle towards the centre of the lake until you reach a rounded headland (/// dunked.kooky.caseworker). Paddle 100m or so to your

↑ Anna kayaking the Verdon River (Rhona Kappler)

right and, as soon as you emerge around the headland, you'll get a panoramic view of most of Lake Sainte-Croix. From here, cut back diagonally across the lake to your left to return to where you started from.

ROUTE 2 Although this route is becoming better known, you're likely to experience far fewer crowds than on the first route. The whole paddle goes along the Verdon River, but it doesn't quite feel like a river as it's punctuated by several lakes – from the air it looks a little like a snake that has swallowed several rats.

Launch from a little beach hidden in the woods below Base Yannick (/// skewers. unsafe.dozen) at the foot of the village of Montpezat, on the banks of the Verdon. Paddle to your left, around a small headland that blocked your view as you launched – the landscape instantly starts opening up. There's a small bay (/// jeopardy.causes. streaks) to your left, often with boats at mooring, but cut straight across it to reach the mouth of the next section of river directly in front of you. Here you enter into a low 2km-long gorge, passing under a road bridge 100m before emerging into a

ESSENTIALS

GETTING THERE The Verdon gorges may look remote, but they're actually very accessible from much of southeastern France, although having a car is extremely useful. The gorges are pretty much equidistant between Nice and Marseille (150km) – both of which have good train and plane connections – with the drive taking around 2½ hours. There's also a direct bus from Marseille to Moustiers-Sainte-Marie (3 hours).

There is ample parking at the launch point for route 1; for route 2, you can park at Base Yannick, where the paddle starts.

HIRE & LESSONS The most convenient hire centre for the first route is **Haute Provence Outdoor** (⊘ haute-provence-outdoor.com ⊙ Apr–Oct), which hires paddleboards and kayaks. For the second, **Base Yannick** (⊘ canoe-verdon.fr ⊙ Apr–Oct) is right at the starting point and rents canoes and kayaks (no paddleboards) and also organises guided outings.

WHEN TO GO Water levels vary year to year; as the water was already extremely low in April, when I did the first route, I'd recommend coming early in the season rather than in the height of summer. April to June is the best time to go.

WHERE TO STAY & EAT There's lots of accommodation in the chocolate-box village of Moustiers-Sainte-Marie, which is just 10km north of the starting point of the first route. This village has been voted one of the prettiest places in France several times, and is convenient if you're relying on public transport, but prices are often at a premium.

small lake (/// supressed.frankly.teeters). From a satellite photo it's star-shaped but when you're in the water it looks round. Make as straight a line as you can to cut straight across it, aiming for a channel in the rocks (/// fastens.roughing.cynically). Paddle into this channel and keep going in a straight line, as the Baudinard gorges get progressively higher around you. At the end of the next section of river is the dam (/// cements.zigs.aspirations). It's impossible to tell in advance whether the dam will be pulling water towards it or pushing it away, so be mindful of this as you paddle and be aware that, if you're unlucky, you might have the water current against you in both directions, which makes for a pretty sporty paddle.

It's 2.5km from the lake to the dam. Along the way are trickling waterfalls tumbling down the cliffs, and mossy, rocky overhangs masking small caves. The water here, rather than being turquoise, is more of a deep navy, and it feels like being in a watery forest. Just before reaching the dam, a line of yellow buoys and a rather flimsy fence stops you from going any further. Turn around here and paddle back the way you came.

Les Jardins de l'Ermitage (⊘ jardinsdelermitage.com) is closer still to the first route, just a 4km drive south, and is within easy walking distance from the lakeshore. It's great for travellers arriving by car (there's very little in the way of public transport). Rooms, if a little gaudy, are spacious with plenty of outdoor seating. The gardens are full of flowers in spring and summer and, after dark, the gardens and ponds come alive with the sound of croaking frogs.

Kako Bistrot (⊘ kakobistrot.com) in Moustiers-Sainte-Marie looks like a retro hairdresser, but it's actually a quirky wine bar. Food is limited to charcuterie-heavy planches but the wine list is excellent, and it's one of the places that stays open latest in this village.

La Cantine (rue de la Bourgade, Moustiers-Sainte-Marie ✆ 04 92 77 46 64) doesn't have a fancy-looking menu, but they somehow manage to turn a humble burger into a work of art. Vegetarians are spoilt for choice, too.

Since Moustiers-Sainte-Marie is very popular with day-trippers, many restaurants either shut up shop entirely mid-week or close very early in the evenings. Check opening hours before you go.

TITBITS On the hill above Moustiers-Sainte-Marie is a 12th-century chapel that appears to cling to the cliff face; there are 262 steps to walk up to it. Look out for a golden star suspended on a chain between the chapel and the rock face just across from it. There are several legends behind why this star is here, one of which says that, much like in *Romeo and Juliet*, two young lovers from warring families took their lives here because they weren't allowed to love each other.

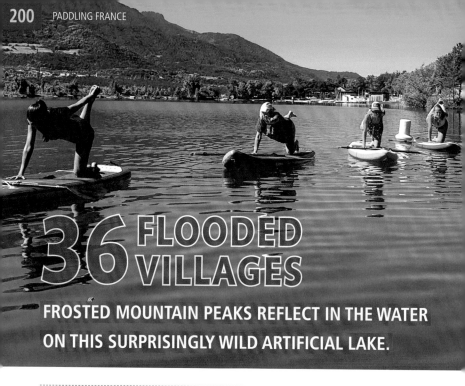

36 FLOODED VILLAGES

FROSTED MOUNTAIN PEAKS REFLECT IN THE WATER ON THIS SURPRISINGLY WILD ARTIFICIAL LAKE.

WHERE	Lake Serre-Ponçon, southern Alps (Provence-Alpes-Côte d'Azur)
STATS	Free paddle 🏄 ② 🛶 ①
START/FINISH	Les Hyvans, 3530 D403, 05230 Chorges
	/// embarrassed.penning.delved

Encircled by the mountains of Écrins National Park, the highest point of which rises to over 4,000m, Lake Serre-Ponçon is nothing if not scenic. In summer, the surrounding mountains are green and tree covered, and the royal-blue lake looks like a jewel among them. In winter, the contrast between the bright blue and the blinding white snow of the mountains is dazzling. When I paddled here in mid-April the mountains had more than a dusting of snow still clinging to the peaks, which reflected magically in the water. Paddling so early in the season, I had the vast lake to myself.

An artificial lake, 28km² Lake Serre-Ponçon was created primarily to control flooding from the Durance River, which was damaging agricultural land, but also to generate hydroelectricity by harnessing the river's power. The project began in the 1950s and was completed the following decade, with two villages razed and flooded to allow for the lake's construction. It's hard to believe, however, that the lake is artificial; its banks are so wild, peppered with creeks and woodland and tumbling little waterfalls, and it seems harmoniously at one with its mountain backdrop.

The biggest giveaway that the lake wasn't naturally formed, however, is a chapel on an island in the water. Saint-Michel is the only surviving building of one of the flooded

↑ Lake Serre-Ponçon is great for paddlers and kayakers of all abilities (@serreponçonaloha)

villages, as the land it stands on was higher than the village around it. It's strange to see the traditional church spire, like you'd see throughout the Alps amid fields and villages, on a tiny patch of earth surrounded by water. Rather than looking apocalyptic, however, it looks peaceful and idyllic.

The lake's size means there are many paddling adventures that you can enjoy here, so I've picked out a few of my favourite spots and left this as a free paddle. In fine weather it's extremely easy to paddleboard or kayak around Serre-Ponçon, but be aware that the weather can change quickly in the mountains, even if the lake itself only sits at an altitude of 780m. Most of the lake is deep (up to 90m at the deepest point), so you can use a fairly long, rigid fin if paddling, and there are lots of slipways and lidos to launch from around along the shore.

The paddleboard club at Serre-Ponçon, Aloha SUP (/// midriff.feud.soulless), is exceptional, so if you're looking for route inspiration I highly recommend going out on one of their tours. They organise sunset and sunrise paddles, and also multi-day paddle and camping trips around the lake. Owner Jérôme is just about the most enthusiastic guide you can find.

PADDLE THIS WAY

There are many launch points around the lake, but I recommend setting off from Les Hyvans holiday camp (/// embarrassed.penning.delved) which has a gentle slope down to the water's edge making things nice and easy. Of all the beauty spots on the lake, the Saint-Michel Chapel (/// hairstylist.antlers.reforming) is the most

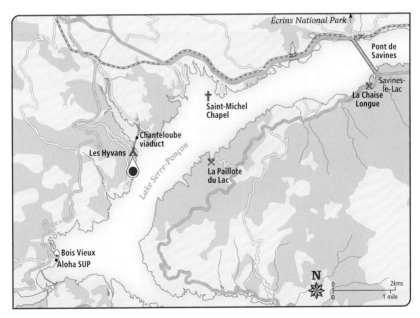

famous, a little church on an island halfway along the lake, closer to the northern shore. The origins of the chapel actually predate the lake by some 900 years: the original was built on a hill in this spot during the 12th century. The present building is more recent, dating from either the end of the 17th or beginning of the 18th century (records are unclear) after the original was destroyed in 1692 by the army of Victor Amadeus II, a Duke of Savoy. The chapel wasn't meant to survive the lake's construction, but was high enough to remain above the rising water. In winter, and sometimes in early spring, when the water level is low, you can often walk out to the chapel from the northern shore; the rest of the year, you can paddle to it. Unfortunately, since it has been vandalised several times in the last few years, it is no longer possible to go inside.

Other particular points of interest are the 1958 Pont de Savines (/// difficulties. brusque.cooled), 5km east of Saint-Michel Chapel, a 45m-high bridge that is almost a kilometre in length; you can zigzag through its various arches. Predating Pont de Savines by 50 years is Chanteloube viaduct (/// bonanza.cliffs.destination), which spans a creek on the northern shore, just west of Saint-Michel Chapel and which once had a railway line crossing it. Chanteloube's viaduct has curved arches, whereas Pont de Savines, are square and box-like. The creek spilling out behind the viaduct is one of the prettiest, and wildest looking around the lake perimeter.

The hanging oak of Bois Vieux (/// subscribed.slurping.cartoony) at the lake's far western side, is another beautiful spot. A wild creek with an oak tree that seems to be sprouting out of the water, this is a lovely place to go swimming because the creek can only be accessed by water so it's never crowded.

↑ This church is all that remains of a flooded village (Francoisroux/DT)

ESSENTIALS

GETTING THERE Wherever you're coming from, it's not a quick journey to get to Serre-Ponçon, but the travel time is worth it. The closest place of any size is Gap, which has decent train connections from Valence and Grenoble. There's an **Avis** car hire outlet at the station (⊘ avis.fr). Chorges train station (also with direct links to Valence) is even closer to the lake (5km away), but there are no car-hire outlets here, so you'll need to rely on public transport or taxis. Marseille's airport is a two-hour drive away, and the airports of Turin and Nice are both approximately 3½ hours by road.

HIRE & LESSONS Aloha SUP (⊘ serre-poncon-aloha.fr ⊙ May–Sep) was one of the first paddleboarding clubs in the country. They run lessons and coaching classes to improve your technique, as well as sunset picnic paddles, SUP yoga and straightforward paddleboard rental too.

WHEN TO GO May to September is the best time to paddle Serre-Ponçon, as the water levels are at their highest and the temperatures warmest. If you're not afraid of the cold you can come at any time of year but, contrary to most paddling sites in France, the lake is at its lowest during the winter, as water is drained out of it. This means that the banks often have a large stretch of sludge-like mud before you reach the water, and the island of the Saint-Michel Chapel is left high and dry. The bonus is that the mountains around you still have a good dusting of snow, but after dragging your paddleboard up and down the muddy bank both you and the board will be in need of a good scrub.

WHERE TO STAY & EAT Les Hvyans (⊘ vacances.probtp.com), on the northwestern shore, 8km south of Chorges, couldn't be more perfectly located, with a jetty that juts out into the lake. Service is friendly and the rooms closest to the lake are spacious with excellent views. Dining is canteen-style with plenty of options and there's a lively entertainment schedule.

You're not short of lakeside dining options at Serre-Ponçon, but be aware that they almost exclusively open in season. **La Paillote du Lac** (⊘ paillotedulac.com) and **La Chaise Longue** (⊘ lachaiselongue-savines.business.site), both on the southern shore, are two of the best, both with epic views and plenty of al-fresco seating.

TITBITS The steep walk to Lake Saint-Apollinaire, perched at an altitude of 1,452m, is one of the prettiest hikes you can do in the area. The scenery makes wild swimming idyllic and it feels reminiscent of a Canadian wilderness. Drive up to the car park at Réallon ski station, 10km from Picoune on the northern shore, from where an 8km loop walk takes you to the lake.

37 LIFESTYLES OF THE RICH & FAMOUS

EXPLORE THE HIDDEN CAVES OF CAP D'ANTIBES, UNDER THE GARDENS OF BILLIONAIRES' MANSIONS.

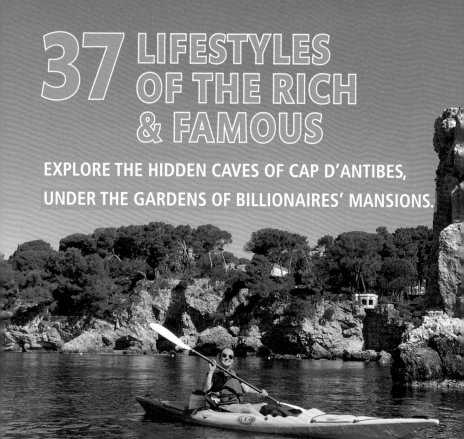

WHERE	Cap d'Antibes, Provence-Alpes-Côte d'Azur
STATS	7km round trip 🛶 ③ 🏄 ②
START/FINISH	Port du Crouton, 171 boulevard Maréchal Juin, 06160 Antibes
	/// percentages.ravished.puffy

As a decidedly un-fancy person, I wasn't sure I'd like Antibes, with its famous Bay of Billionaires. I'm pleased to say I was completely wrong: move over Monaco and Saint-Tropez, Antibes is the glitz of the Mediterranean done well, in a curiously unshowy way that feels lived in (albeit many of the residents are very moneyed, but not all of them).

This is an area rich not only in terms of its residents, but in landscape too. These views are worth millions of euros, but with your kayak or paddleboard, you get them for free. The Mediterranean Sea is crystal clear, and agave, olive and aloe trees all spring from the scrubby rock that surrounds the town. There's plenty of fish to be found too, with species

↑ Anna kayaking around the Cap d'Antibes (Blue Drop)

such as John Dory, octopus and squid; look out for the catch of the day on restaurant menus after your paddle.

Divers, it's worth exploring below the surface as well as above it. Under the water, below the small striped lighthouse La Pierre Formigue in the middle of the bay, is an abandoned film set, used for *The Mermaid and Child* in the 1960s. The film was never aired, but the model town constructed for filming is still there, complete with a church, hairdresser and grocer. Easy Dive Juan les Pins (⊘ easydive.fr) organises dives for both beginners and qualified divers.

You can paddle this route using a paddleboard or a kayak, but bear in mind that, as it's a sea paddle, a kayak will be significantly easier on choppy days; use a long, rigid fin if you plan to go by paddleboard. From the superyachts of Port du Crouton marina, the scenery gets rapidly more rural as you paddle out around Cap d'Antibes and, while you'll see several mansions and luxury hotels as you go, many of them are at least partly obscured by foliage to ensure the privacy of their residents.

PADDLE THIS WAY

Launch from Port du Crouton (/// percentages.ravished.puffy), between Juan Les Pins and Cap d'Antibes; there's a shallow beach between the two piers that makes for a good launch point.

Head straight out to sea, sticking close to Cap d'Antibes, the big headland to your left, drawing a diagonal as you go. After 1.5km, you'll pass the five-star Hôtel du Cap-Eden-Roc (/// dustbin.toddlers.coupon) on your left, one of the most famous hotels in the world. It has been a hotel to the stars for a very long time. In the 1930s, Wallis Simpson and the Duke of Windsor were regulars, and other famous guests have included F Scott Fitzgerald, Ernest Hemingway, Marlene Dietrich and Elizabeth Taylor. You can't paddle right up to the hotel or you'll get a flea in your ear pretty quickly, but the outdoor pool and decking are on full display so, if

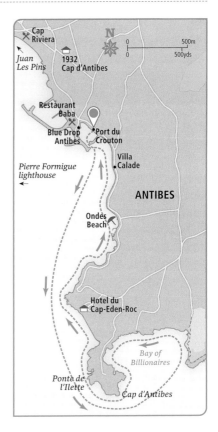

you've got good eyesight, it's certainly not out of the question that you could spot a celebrity.

Continuing to hug the headland, round Ponte de l'Ilette to your left, looking out for the lighthouse (/// scissors.carting.reappeared). A squat, white cylindrical tower just 13m high, it's fringed by Scots pines and palm trees. Once you come around this little headland, you've reached the Bay of Billionaires (/// hearths. misprint.binding). Houses here are said to cost up to €200 million, and, while I'd imagine the *caves à vin* (wine cellars) are pretty impressive in all of these homes, you can do your own cellar exploration in the natural caves in the bay (without being able to see into the real cellars of course). They're quite literally under the front gardens of these homes, and you can paddle in and out of them freely. It's the next best thing to conning Sotheby's into thinking you've got a multi-million budget and need to look around the houses. One of the deepest is at (/// guests.hairball.deposits) and there are also a few inlets to the right where you can moor up your paddle and go for a swim.

From here, retrace your paddle past Pointe de l'Ilette and Hôtel du Cap-Eden-Roc again, but this time make for the des Ondes Beach (/// cushions.

↑ Many of the richest people in France live on the Cap d'Antibes (AerialDronePics/S)

unread.compositions) a couple of hundred metres after the hotel. It's open to the public, with shallow, safe waters for swimming and shrubbery masking it from the road. At the far end of des Ondes Beach is a curious, cylindrical stone building with a window jutting out into the sea. It's an old changing cabin, and you can alight and explore it if you wish. Continue to retrace your route back to the port; be sure to look out for Villa Calade (/// shivered.grilled.houseboat), a pale pink Art Deco building surrounded by palm trees, which is currently a private residence.

ESSENTIALS

GETTING THERE Antibes is easy to reach from Nice (which has an international airport) or Cannes, sitting almost exactly halfway between the two, and connected to both by regular buses and trains. If arriving by car, in season, note that parking is difficult and expensive, but the rest of the year on-road parking is generally easy to find.

HIRE & LESSONS Youthful and full of enthusiasm, the team at **Blue Drop Antibes** (blue-drop.fr) rents kayaks and paddleboards for autonomous outings, and offer excellent guided visits where they share their insider knowledge of the area.

WHEN TO GO Peak season is during the summer holidays in July and August, but visiting in spring or autumn can be a delight here. Temperatures are more comfortable and there are far fewer crowds, but most hotels and restaurants are still open.

WHERE TO STAY & EAT A stay at **1932 Cap d'Antibes** (all.accor.com) feels like stepping back in time. The rooftop restaurant and pool are a delight, with views over the entire bay.

If you get hungry while on the water, opt for either **Cap Riviera** (cap-riviera.fr) or **Restaurant Baba** (capdantibes-beachhotel.com), both of which are convenient stopping points on your route. Cap Riviera has plenty of seafood, and the price point is reasonable given the location. Restaurant Baba belongs to the Cap d'Antibes Beach Hotel, and the real winner here is the cocktail bar, where you can enjoy your mojito with your toes in the sand. Away from the water, opt for the rooftop restaurant at **1932 Cap d'Antibes** hotel (accor.com), which serves tapas with a panoramic view of the coast. Advance reservations recommended.

TITBITS Out to sea, between Cannes and Cap d'Antibes, is a curious island monastery, the Abbaye de Lérins. Dating from the 11th century, it's still the home of Cistercian monks who cultivate vines and produce their own wine on the island. You can visit on a boat trip from Cannes.

38 RIVIERA GARDENS

PADDLE PAST CANDY-COLOURED HOUSES & CLIFFTOP GARDENS ALONG THE FRENCH-ITALIAN BORDER.

WHERE	Menton, Provence-Alpes-Côte d'Azur
STATS	9km return 🏃 🛶 ②
START/FINISH	Centre Nautique de la Ville de Menton, 6 promenade de la Mer, 06500 Menton /// gracing.boxful.sunniest

The Riviera town of Menton has a curious little microclimate. People here must have one of the most enviable lifestyles in the world. A guide at the watersports club told me how even in February (when Menton's famous lemon festival takes place), locals will head up to the Alpes-Maritimes to ski in the morning (the closest ski stations are only an hour or so away) and then come back and swim in the mild waters of the Mediterranean in the evening, skis propped along the beach wall.

The town centre is only 7km from the border between France and Italy, and the mountains rise up to create a natural frontier (now cemented by border control, although since paddlers pass this by sea it's not something you have to worry about). Menton is

↑ Menton's candy-coloured buildings (Antoine Jallat)

in perpetual summer hues, and even on the greyest day, the pink, orange and terracotta buildings of the higgledy-piggledy town sprawling up the hill behind the beaches are impossibly vibrant. As you cross the border into Italy, the sunset shades of Menton's buildings give way to a vast garden, and the riot of colour that ensues comes from the abundance of flowers and shrubs. It's a place that seems perennially in bloom.

Menton, a frontier town, has changed hands numerous times in history. It was held by the Duke of Savoy, then the Republic of Genoa. It was an exclave of the Principality of Monaco until 1860, when it became French, from which point it has been luring tourists and artists alike.

I first came here as a teenager, visiting family friends who lived in the town. We'd walk into Italy to visit Hanbury Garden, a clifftop garden with a cactus-filled drop down to the Mediterranean. Our friends (who were artists) would paint, while my sister, their daughters and I would sketch (in my case, badly). For me, Menton and the gardens were colour. Returning to the area as an adult, I wondered if it would be anything like I remembered. Would those brighter than bright colours have faded? Would the wonder of it be diminished after all my travels around France?

The answer was not at all. I recreated the journey we used to make to the garden, but this time, instead of walking into Italy, I retraced the route by paddleboard.

This paddle starts from one of Menton's main beaches, framed by a palm-lined boulevard. It's incredibly sheltered, making it perfect for first-time paddlers, but be aware that as you approach the Hanbury Garden you're more exposed to the elements should the winds pick up. It's safest to stick as close to the coast as possible, where the hills will protect you from the worst of the winds.

PADDLE THIS WAY

Start from the beach in front of the Centre Nautique de la Ville de Menton (/// gracing.boxful.sunniest) and paddle out to sea between two piers. Once the piers are behind you, turn to admire Menton from the sea: the water jade and turquoise in colour, and climbing up the hill behind, the buildings of Menton's old town in oranges, yellows, reds and pinks, like tiles in a pottery workshop.

Turning back around to put Menton behind you, turn left and paddle past Menton Garavan Port (/// scrapers.unserved.buzzword), a sheltered harbour for pleasure boats. You can probably already see border control (/// keypads.clinging.hills) on land ahead of you: little more than a few arches on the road separating France from Italy. It's 2km from the beach you started from, keeping the shore close on your left-hand side.

Ciao, you're now in Italia! The cliff climbs dramatically just after the border, and all the warm, pinkish colours of Menton are suddenly replaced by vibrant greens; the border to mark the barrier between the two countries may be understated, but nature has its own way of demarcating France and Italy.

Another 2.5km following the coast takes you to below the Hanbury Garden (/// snacked.sleeps.gagging). Founded in 1867 by an English businessman, Thomas Hanbury, the UNESCO World Heritage Site gardens sit on the clifftop, 103m above you. The 18ha contain plants from all around the world, including agaves, aloes, succulents, palms and olive trees. It's possible to walk all the way up to them from the sea, following a steeply climbing path that passes through a eucalyptus forest, bamboo and rose gardens. You can moor your paddle at the beach in front of Caffè dei Giardini Hanbury (/// shirt.purport.unstated).

Paddle back the way you came, with the coast on your right-hand side and Menton laid out before you. Keep your eyes on the top of the hill at the highest point in Menton town as you return. Just before the old town, on the crown of

ESSENTIALS

GETTING THERE Menton is a half-hour (30km) drive or train journey from Nice, along a winding coastal road that has a deserved reputation as one of the most scenic in the country. It's a route that is extremely popular with cyclists, so take care going around the bends, accidents happen here frequently. Nice's airport has flights to several different UK cities, and the city has TGV and sleeper-train services from Paris. Car hire is available from both Nice's airport and train station.

HIRE & LESSONS The **Centre Nautique de la Ville de Menton** (⌀ voile-menton.fr), where this paddle starts, hires kayaks and rigid paddleboards so stable that you could pogo stick your way to Italy without falling off them.

WHEN TO GO Even in the winter, Menton is spectacular and much warmer than the rest of the country. Come in February for La Fête du Citron, or at the start of the summer season (April/May), when the Mediterranean sun is already warming the flame-hued buildings of the old town but the heat hasn't yet become oppressive. The summer holidays see the most crowds.

the hill, is an opulent Catholic cemetery, and some of the gilded domes of family tombs are visible from the water. Disembark at the beach in front of the Centre Nautique de la Ville de Menton, where you began your paddle.

WHERE TO STAY & EAT Hotel Lemon (⌂ hotel-lemon.fr) has gorgeous, spacious rooms that seem far superior to both their price point and star rating. It's a short walk from the seaside promenade, which makes parking a little easier.

La Loca tapas restaurant (◻ lalocamenton) serves cocktails that will knock your socks off and has an extensive wine list as well as an ever-changing tapas menu. They're open exclusively in the evening, every day except Monday. Check their events schedule, which includes DJ nights, themed parties and even exhibitions. For a light lunch, smoothies or a hit of caffeine, head to **Edwige Coffee** (◻). The staff are extremely friendly and there's plenty of choice for vegetarians and vegans.

TITBITS Unlike most places on the Côte d'Azur, Menton's biggest annual event is in February when the town celebrates its lemon festival, La Fête du Citron. Giant sculptures are made out of oranges and lemons, there are carnival parades and live music. Some of the statues reach up to 10m tall and use some 15 tonnes of fruit. The story goes that Eve, not content with an apple, pocketed a lemon in her fig leaf as she left the Garden of Eden and waited to plant it until she arrived in a paradise that resembled the garden she had left behind. That paradise was Menton.

↑ The views from the Hanbury Garden are spectacular (Bernd Zillich/S)

39 BETWEEN CLIFFS & CAVES

PADDLE INTO CAVES THAT OPEN UP INTO THE SKY, PAST PRECIPITOUS CLIFFS & AROUND UNINHABITED ISLANDS STRETCHING OUT TOWARDS ITALY – SOUTHERN CORSICA IS MOTHER NATURE AT HER MOST DRAMATIC.

WHERE　　　　Bonifacio, Corsica
STATS　　　　14km return 🏄 ④ 🛶 ③
START/FINISH　The pontoon at Piantarella Beach, 20169 Bonifacio
　　　　　　　　/// birdseed.infest.whiten

In Corsica's wildly dramatic southern peninsula, cliffs that tower over 100m high plunge into the sea with the steepness of a drop slide, crowned with buildings so close to the edge they look as though they could topple over. The clifftop town of Bonifacio was my reason for visiting this part of the island, but on the approach I discovered a wild coastline of caves, islands inhabited solely by birds and some of the most perfect white-sand beaches I'd ever seen.

This route was never meant to be included in this book, but when I arrived in Bonifacio, lured by the history (the town dates from the 9th century) and the views stretching all the way across to Sardinia, I heard about a cave – Saint Antoine Cave. A scalped cave with an almost perfectly round hole in its roof, a cave which you could paddle right into, and I knew I had to test it out.

Reader: this is a paddle of kings, queens and emperors. If Ajaccio-born Napoléon Bonaparte had been a paddleboarder, this would have been the route he would have chosen. If the Dukes of Genoa, who built many of the tower fortifications around the island, hadn't been so engaged in defending Corsica from invaders, I'm fairly sure they'd have grabbed their kayaks and explored Saint Antoine Cave. Put simply, this route is unmissable.

Bonifacio is the nearest town to the start point, and the best place to base yourself. Corsica gets extremely busy during the summer, particularly with holidaymakers from mainland France, but, luckily, the island is so full of beautiful beaches that even at

↑ On a calm day, the water is crystal clear at Piantarella (SS)

this time of year a short walk (or even better, a paddle) will get you to a completely isolated spot.

The start of this paddle, from the pontoon on the idyllic little beach of Piantarella, is the most sheltered part of the route, the worst of the elements blocked by a sprinkling of granite islands spread between the Lavezzi Islands and Corsica. Once you come out of the bay, you're in open water and the sea can get extremely choppy (Corsica's weather is very changeable). Duck in and out of caves and around gnarled, weather-beaten cliffs as you make your way to the showstopper: Saint Antoine Cave with its natural skylight. You can do this route by kayak or paddleboard, but I'd recommend it for experienced paddleboarders only, not least because it's pretty long.

PADDLE THIS WAY

Launch from the pontoon (/// birdseed.infest.whiten) at Piantarella Beach, a sheltered, sandy bay hemmed in by tiny granite islands. Turn right to paddle

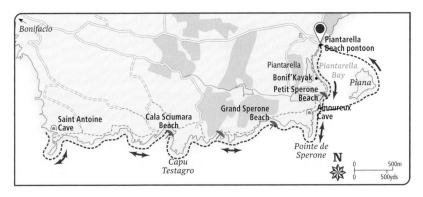

across the bay. It's a paddle of roughly 500m to reach the western end of the beach. From here, keeping the coast close by, look for the little headland on your right and round it. The beach that you reach just after the headland, Petit Sperone (/// saluting.filtration.fleeced), is a crescent moon of white sand, completely surrounded by scrubby trees and gently sloping rocks. Just after the beach is a cave, Amoureux Cave ('Lovers' Cave' /// reckoning.translators.backbone) which you can paddle into. At low tide there's a little beach inside, and the cave roof is so flat it could have been drawn with a ruler.

Continue paddling to round Pointe de Sperone (/// summoning.cottons. willingness), 500m further along, a long, skinny headland that juts out into the sea. A further 500m takes you to the next small yellow-sand beach, Grand Sperone (/// increments.bickered.producing), which is a lovely place for a swim. You'll find a tiny, unnamed beach that avoids any crowds 1.5km further on; just under a kilometre on from this little beach is the next headland, Capu Testagro (/// submerging.concept.staffers). A craggy peninsula, it looks as though it has weathered many a storm. Follow the coast around the corner, revealing Cala Sciumara Beach (/// banner.quells.asleep), which is only accessible by water or via little dirt tracks, and has clear waters and is the perfect place for picnicking.

Keep paddling from Cala Sciumara Beach, with the coast on your right, as the cliffs get higher and higher next to you. Some 500m further is a short, stubby headland with fragmented rocks splintering into the water. After another 1.5km, the cliffs become a sort of pale, golden colour, and the rocks nearest to the sea flatten out, rather than dropping vertiginously into the ocean. Another 500m has you facing a golden rocky headland, where the rock furthest out to sea is separated from land by a narrow strip of water. Paddle around this and hug the coast to arrive at Saint Antoine Cave (/// conductor.blackens.unplayable). It's a geological marvel, a cave only accessible by sea (or perhaps sky if you're a good climber, but I can't vouch for this). The sliver of sand at the back of the cave is bathed again and again by the ebb and flow of the waves, and the sunlight pours like a spotlight through the almost perfect circle in the cave roof. You can paddle right into the cave, but if the seas are rough this can be dangerous. If you're unfortunate with the weather, there's a hiking trail (page 217) that goes from Bonifacio all the way to the top of the cave.

After the grotto, paddle back the way you came. When you get to Pointe de Sperone, don't turn left into Piantarella Bay; instead, loop around the outside of the island directly in front, Île Piana (/// lifter.inclines.complaining), which is the closest island of the Lavezzi archipelago that occupies the narrow strait between Corsica and Sardinia. It's forbidden to alight here as it's an important breeding ground for shearwaters, and the island positively swarms with birds all year round. From here, the paddle back to Piantarella's pontoon is just shy of a kilometre.

↑ A bird's-eye view of Pointe de Sperone (SS)

ESSENTIALS

GETTING THERE Corsica Ferries (⌖ corsica-ferries.fr) run services from three ports on the mainland: Marseille, Toulon and Nice. Ajaccio, the island's capital, is the main port, but Porto-Vecchio is much closer for this route. Ajaccio airport has flights to the UK and is a 2½-hour (130km) drive from Bonifacio; Porto-Vecchio is just half an hour (30km) but has fewer ferry services. There's car hire available from both Ajaccio and Porto-Vecchio towns. Seasonal direct flights run between London airports and Figari Airport (a 25km drive from Piantarella with car hire available). No public transport runs to Piantarella and the pontoon, but buses run between Porto-Vecchio and Bonifacio (30 minutes), from where you can also hire a car.

HIRE & LESSONS Bonif'Kayak (⌖ bonifacio-kayak.com ☉ Apr–Oct) has an outlet right on the beach where this route starts and rents kayaks and paddleboards as well as running SUP yoga classes. It's worth calling or emailing in advance as they're not always on site. Please note opening and closing dates are often flexible in Corsica, and many businesses, including watersports rentals, often choose last minute to push back their summer opening. If visiting in April or October, call before arriving in Corsica to make sure they're definitely open.

WHEN TO GO Corsica is highly seasonal; June and September are the best months to visit, avoiding the crowds and accommodation premiums of peak summer. If

visiting between October and March you'll find that there's very little open. The weather can be unpredictable too, not just on the coast, but also in the mountains (where snow isn't unheard of even in June and September).

WHERE TO STAY & EAT
Hôtel A Madonetta (⌖ amadonetta.com) is very well located, just steps from Bonifacio's port. The exterior is rather austere looking, but inside the rooms are light, airy and spacious.

There's no shortage of good dining options. **Restaurant l'An Faim** (✆ 04 95 73 09 10 ⬛ LAN-FAIM) serves typical Corsican specialities, which means plenty of *brochiu* (a soft, Corsican cheese). **Mama Gina** (⬛ Mama-Gina) is an excellent pizzeria that serves food late. Both are in Bonifacio's old town.

TITBITS
Take trainers or hiking boots; Corsica's coastline is just the tip of the iceberg. As well as the famous, two-week GR20 that traverses the spine of the Corsican mountains, there are three *mare à mare* (coast to coast) hiking trails. The closest one to Bonifacio links Porto-Vecchio to Propriano, a distance of 83km.

A fantastic half-day hike east along the coast from Bonifacio takes you to the top of Saint Antoine Cave. Leaving Bonifacio, follow the signs to Sentier du Pertusato and take the footpath that runs largely along the clifftop for 6km, past old World War II bunkers. The path descends steeply to give you a view right down into Grotte de Saint Antoine through the circular hole in the roof.

↓ The Lavezzi Islands pepper the stretch of water between Corsica and Sardinia (SS)

40 ISLAND IDYLL

PADDLE AROUND BOULDERS ERODED INTO PERFECT SPHERES THAT DOT THE WHITE SANDS OF A BAY THAT LOOKS AS THOUGH IT BELONGS IN THE INDIAN OCEAN.

WHERE	Palombaggia, Corsica
STATS	Free paddle 🏄 🛶 ①
START/FINISH	Palm Beach, route de Palombaggia, 20137 Porto-Vecchio
	/// shimmers.refs.internally

A crescent of sheltered sand, as white as a Hollywood smile, hidden among the hills of southern Corsica, regularly tops lists as the prettiest beach in France. The steep and bumpy dirt road down from the hills reveals the kind of beach that would crown a travel agent's window display. Crystalline waters, strewn with smooth, semi-submerged boulders – the kind I've only seen in photos of the Seychelles – and a smattering of granite islands that protect the beach and frame either end, spilling out from the coast as though someone had upended a child's tub of marbles – this beach lives up to the hype.

For a long time, this beach was Corsica's best-kept secret – having been a malaria hotspot as recently as the 1940s, few people ventured here. When the disease was finally eradicated, hippies and wild campers began to discover the pristine sands and, for a good three decades, the beach must have seemed like a desert-island paradise. Water, electricity and telephone lines arrived here in the 1970s, and with them the beginning of the tourism industry. Palombaggia's legendary beauty has meant that tourism numbers

↑ Palombaggia is often thought to be France's prettiest beach (Eva Bocek/A)

have increased to the point where the summer holidays (July and August) can get very busy indeed. Visit a little out of season (April to June or September/October), however, and you'll get a sense of what the mid-20th-century hippies must have experienced. Several beach bars and restaurants now line the shore, but they've been tastefully built to blend almost seamlessly with the surroundings and, although holiday houses and hotels are visible up in the hills, these too are subtle smudges on the landscape rather than offensive, seaside tower blocks. Paddle offshore and turn around to look at the landscape, and you'll see that it still looks wild.

Paddling here is easy, and it's more sheltered than most of the coast, even on a windy day. As always when undertaking a sea paddle, be aware of offshore winds that can quickly drag you out to sea. You can use a paddleboard or a kayak, and the only slight annoyance to be aware of is the possibility of snagging your fin on one of the boulders in the water. The ones closest to shore are clearly visible, as they stick out of the water, but 50m or so from the beach, some scattered granite rocks sit below the water. That being said, the water is so clear you can spot them easily.

PADDLE THIS WAY

Start anywhere on the beach (/// shimmers.refs.internally); the water is extremely shallow for quite a stretch.

I recommend paddling out to sea for a couple of hundred metres. Once you've paddled out, turn to face the beach; the white, boulder-strewn sand looks like something from a travel brochure, set against a rather savage and mountainous backdrop. The hill directly up from Palm Beach Restaurant (/// surfs.centrally. fixture) has a few buildings, most of which are holiday homes, and some carefully camouflaged hotels, masked by pine and juniper trees.

Two of the most scenic spots lie at opposite ends of the beach. At the western end lie the semi-submerged boulders (/// simulates.hillsides.akin) that are so reminiscent of the Seychelles. The water laps gently around them as you paddle, and it's so shallow and clear here that it looks like you're paddling on blown glass. At the eastern end of the beach are clusters of rust-coloured rocks that frame a small, unnamed beach (/// slithery.grounded.plaster) adjacent to Palombaggia, which has a beach restaurant (I PINI) and a beach bar-restaurant (La Pailotte). The food at La Pailotte is much better quality.

If you're not content with just a bay paddle, I recommend paddling west to go past a series of small granite islands that splinter from the shore.

Two much larger granite islands are visible straight in front of you from Palombaggia Beach: Île Pietricaggiosa (/// welds.binging.drills) and Île Piana

ESSENTIALS

GETTING THERE Corsica Ferries (⚓ corsica-ferries.fr) runs direct services from Nice to Porto-Vecchio, which is just 20 minutes (11km) by road from Palombaggia. There's also a seasonal bus that goes between Porto-Vecchio and Palombaggia (45 minutes). Seasonal direct flights run between London airports and Figari Airport (27km drive from Palombaggia with car hire available).

HIRE & LESSONS Camp'in Pirellu (⚓ pirellu-rsv.com ☺ May–Sep) hires stand up paddleboards and is based just behind Palombaggia Beach.

WHEN TO GO April to October is the best time to visit Corsica – between November and March virtually all hospitality is closed, and winter storms are often violent. Avoid the summer holidays if you can; although Palombaggia isn't the easiest place to access, it has become very well known and can get very full in July and August.

WHERE TO STAY & EAT It's all about the view here, so **Palom'bolla** (⚓ palombolla.com), with wigwam bubbles (transparent domes with wooden slats and

(/// bleeped.undertaken.backfired). The latter is low, not much above sea level, and humped – it looks a bit like a sleeping sea monster. Though both islands look really close to the shore, they're actually a 2km paddle out to sea, and since they're so rocky it's difficult to beach your paddle here, although you can paddle around them.

a tent-like covering that can be pulled over the bubbles) that open up to a panorama of the sea and sky, is really special. In Porto-Vecchio you can sleep on a sailing boat with **St Loca Voile** (⌂ stlocavoile.com). Whether you're at port or at sea is a question of personal preference and dependent on the weather and season. It's fantastic value, but check the house rules on their website in advance and be aware that this is true sailor living – there's no shower on board, so you'll need to shower at port.

There are many fantastic restaurants and beach clubs on the beach, but my favourite is **Palm Beach**, (◼ Palm Beach Palombaggia), which has friendly service and delightfully fresh salads. All of the seating is either outdoor or semi-outdoor, it's right on the beach, and it's a great place to park up for your paddle.

TITBITS If you're inspired to dive after seeing how clear the water is, there's a dive club at the easternmost end of the beach. **Kalliste Plongée** (⌂ lekalliste-plongee.corsica ☉ May–Sep Mon–Sat) organises dives directly from Palombaggia Beach, as well as around the Îles Cerbicale a short distance offshore (including Île Pietricaggiosa and Île Piana mentioned opposite). They also offer underwater 'scooter' trips, where snorkellers hold a motor that looks a little like a buoyancy float, which propels them through the water.

↑ An aerial view of Palombaggia on a calm day (dronepicr, CC BY 2.0)

FRENCH PADDLING VOCABULARY & GLOSSARY

It seems to be a common misconception among the French that their English is *terrible*. In fact, in the cities at least, it's not hard to find someone who speaks at least some English. In rural France, particularly in areas that see less foreign footfall, speaking a little French goes a long way and will make your trip much more enjoyable. Deepl.com is a good, free to use translation platform for written French. The DuoLingo app is a great way to brush up school French and gain confidence in conversation. The French expect a degree of formality often not employed in English. Remember to use *vous* (the formal version of 'you') when addressing anyone you don't know, people in a professional capacity or anyone older than you. *Tu* is reserved for your friends, or children. If you're not sure which to use, err on the side of caution, use *vous* and take cues from the person you're talking to. If in doubt, you can always ask *est-ce que je peux vous tutoyer?* (*Can I be less formal with you?*)

Below is a list of paddling-specific vocabulary to get you started. *Pagayez fort, les rivières, lacs et océans de l'Hexagone vous attendent.* (Paddle strong, France's rivers, lakes and oceans are waiting for you.)

PADDLING VOCABULARY

beach	*plage*	rain	*pluie*
boat	*bateau*	raincoat	*imperméable*
buoy	*bouée*	rapids	*rapides*
canoe	*canoë*	river	*rivière/fleuve*
cliff	*falaise*	rocks	*rochers*
current	*courant*	sand	*sable*
dam	*barrage*	sea	*mer*
ferry	*ferry*	storm	*orage*
island	*île*	stream	*ruisseau*
kayak	*kayak*	sun hat	*chapeau de soleil*
lake	*lac*	suncream	*crème solaire*
life jacket	*gilet de sauvetage*	swimming	*maillot de bain*
lifeguard	*sauveteur*	costume/shorts	
lock	*écluse*	tide	*marée*
paddle	*pagaie*	towel	*serviette*
paddleboard	*planche de paddle*	wetsuit	*combinaison*
pump	*pompe*	wind	*vent*

GLOSSARY

auberge	inn
bastide	a fortified medieval new town founded in the Middle Ages. Usually rectangular, with streets laid out in a grid and a porticoed central square.
cabane	wooden hut, often with a bar or restaurant
castrum	a rectangular Roman army camp, which often grew into a permanent settlement; it was often used as a village that grew up around a seigneur's castle
cardo	a north–south street in a Roman castrum
causse	limestone plateau
cave	cellar
chai	wine or spirit storehouse
château	mansion, manor house, palace, wine estate. A strictly military castle is a *château forte*.
chemin	path
clocher-mur	the west front of a church that rises high above the roofline for its entire width to make a bell tower – a common feature in Romanesque churches in southwest France
cloître	cloister
col	mountain pass
commune	in the Middle Ages, the government of a free town or city; today the smallest unit of local government, encompassing a town or village
cornière	an arched portico surrounding the main square of a bastide
couvent	convent or monastery
decumanus	east–west street in a Roman castrum
église	church
gare (routière)	station (bus station)
gave	river (specific to the Pyrenees)
gîte	shelter (or holiday home); *gîte d'étape* basic shelter for walkers
gouffre	karstic chasm or sinkhole
grotte	cave
halle	covered market
hôtel	originally the town residence of the nobility, by the 18th century the word became used for any large residence or public building; a *hôtel de ville* is a town hall.
lauze	heavy flat black stone used for tiling often steep roofs (specific to southwestern France)
lavoir	communal washbasin, usually covered with a roof

lieu-dit	a place name, often a small hamlet
mairie	town hall
marché	market
mas	(from the Latin *mansio*) a large farmhouse, or manor or hamlet (specific to southwestern France)
modillion	a sculpted corbel projecting from the cornice of a church
woppidum	pre-Roman fortified settlement, usually on a height
orry	small dry-stone building with a corbelled dome. Many were built as shepherd's huts, others as refuges for villagers in plague times. Also known as *bories, gariotes, caselles* or *cabannes.*
parlement	a juridical body, with members appointed by the king; by the late Ancien Régime, *parlements* exercised a great deal of influence over political affairs
pays	a region or country
plan d'eau	artificial lake
pont	bridge
randonnée	walk; *Grande Randonnée* (GR) a major hiking trail
retable	a carved and/or painted altarpiece, usually consisting of a number of scenes
routiers	English mercenaries in the Hundred Years' War
sauveterre	a village or town founded under a guarantee against violence in wartime, agreed to by the Church and local barons; their boundaries are often marked by crosses on all the roads leading to them
tour	tower
trumeau	the column between the twin doors of a church portal, often carved with reliefs
tympanum	semi-circular panel over a church door, often the occasion for the most ambitious ensembles of medieval sculpture
vieille ville	historic centre

INDEX

INDEX OF ADVERTISERS

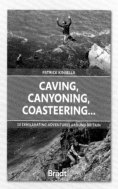

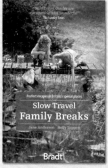

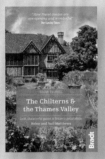

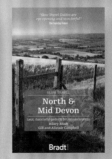

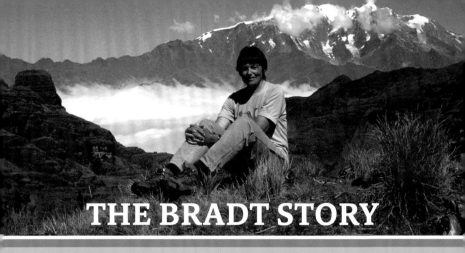

THE BRADT STORY

In the beginning
It all began in 1974 on an Amazon river barge. During an 18-month trip through South America, two adventurous young backpackers – Hilary Bradt and her then husband, George – decided to write about the hiking trails they had discovered through the Andes. *Backpacking Along Ancient Ways in Peru and Bolivia* included the very first descriptions of the Inca Trail. It was the start of a colourful journey to becoming one of the best-loved travel publishers in the world; you can read the full story on our website (**bradtguides. com/ourstory**).

Getting there first
Hilary quickly gained a reputation for being a true travel pioneer, and in the 1980s she started to focus on guides to places overlooked by other publishers. The Bradt Guides list became a roll call of guidebook 'firsts'. We published the first guide to Madagascar, followed by Mauritius, Czechoslovakia and Vietnam. The 1990s saw the beginning of our extensive coverage of Africa: Tanzania, Uganda, South Africa, and Eritrea. Later, post-conflict guides became a feature: Rwanda, Mozambique, Angola, and Sierra Leone, as well as the first standalone guides to the Baltic States following the fall of the Iron Curtain, and the first post-war guides to Bosnia, Kosovo and Albania.

Comprehensive – and with a conscience
Today, we are the world's largest independently owned travel publisher, with more than 200 titles. However, our ethos remains unchanged. Hilary is still keenly involved, and **we still get there first**: two-thirds of Bradt guides have no direct competition.

But we don't just get there first. Our guides are also known for being **more comprehensive** than any other series. We avoid templates and tick-lists. Each guide is a one-of-a-kind expression of an expert author's interests, knowledge and enthusiasm for telling it how it really is.

And a commitment to wildlife, conservation and respect for local communities has always been at the heart of our books. Bradt Guides was **championing sustainable travel** before any other guidebook publisher. We even have a series dedicated to Slow Travel in the UK, award-winning books that explore the country with a passion and depth you'll find nowhere else.

Thank you!
We can only do what we do because of the support of readers like you – people who value less-obvious experiences, less-visited places and a more thoughtful approach to travel. Those who, like us, take travel seriously.

Bradt GUIDES

TRAVEL TAKEN SERIOUSLY